The Visual
and Spatial
Structure of
Landscapes

The MIT Press   *Cambridge, Massachusetts*   *London, England*

The Visual
and Spatial
Structure of
Landscapes

TADAHIKO HIGUCHI
Translated by Charles S. Terry

First MIT Press paperback edition, 1988

We wish to acknowledge with gratitude a grant
from The Japan Foundation to help with production costs of this book.

This book was set in Sabon by Graphic Composition, Inc. and printed and bound by Halliday Litho-
graph in the United States of America.

Library of Congress Cataloging in Publication Data

Higuchi, Tadahiko, 1944–
    The visual and spatial structure of landscapes.

    Translation of: Keikan no kōzō.
    Bibliography: p.
    Includes index.
    1. Landforms—Japan.   2. Landscape assess-
ment—Japan.
    I. Title.
GB438.J3H5313   1983   915.2'02   82–20819
ISBN 0-262-08120-2 (hardcover)
        0-262-58094-2 (paperback)

SOURCES AND CREDITS
PHOTOGRAPHS
Mizushima Takashi: 2.16, 3.14, 4.19, 4.23, 5.4,
5.10, 5.11, 5.14, 5.15, 5.26, 8.2, 8.4, 8.7, 8.8, 10.4,
10.7, 10.9, 10.10, 11.5, 12.3, 12.7, 14.1, 14.4;
Kyodo Tsushinsha: 3.10, 4.7, 4.21, 5.5, 5.21, 12.6;
National Parks Association of Japan: 2.4 (Inoue
Masahiro), 4.10 (Wazaki Mitsuo), 5.25 (Kazama
Yoshio); Sato Hironori: 4.22; Ueda Motohisa: 14.3;
Superstudio: *c.* 1970, 5.6; Shogakkan (Zenrin-ji):
5.28; Shibundo (Kyoo Gokoku-ji): 9.1; Shibundo
(Kankikō-ji): 9.7; Yamatokeikokusha: 12.2; Shi-
bundo (Engaku-ji): 12.9; Shibundo (Nezu Museum
of Art): 11.4; Shibundo (Dannō Hōrin-ji): 11.6;
Shibundo (Atami Museum of Art): 13.5; Harvard
University Press: 14.6. Photographs other than these
were taken by the author.

ILLUSTRATIONS
The Architectural Press: 3.8, 3.15, 3.16; Whitney
Publications: 4.4; Architectural Book Publishing
Company: 4.15; Riverside Press: 5.1, 5.7, 5.8; *Architectural Review*: 13.7. The following maps, originally made to scales of 20,000:1 to 25,000:1, were
reprinted in smaller scale with the permission of the
National Geography Section of the Ministry of
Construction: 4.3, 4.8, 8.1, 8.3, 8.6, 9.2, 9.4, 10.1,
10.3, 10.5, 10.6, 10.8, 11.1, 11.3, 12.4, 12.8, 13.1,
13.3, 14.2.

I
_____

*Visual
Structure of
Landscapes*

Contents

II

*Spatial
Structure of
Landscapes*

Foreword

In this book I have made an attempt to clarify the visual structure of landscapes. Visual structure in this instance was taken to mean the appearance of a given scene from a freely chosen point of observation; the indexes are concerned with the visibility or visual perception of landscapes. Since these indexes had to do with vision in general, they should be applicable to visual environments other than landscapes.

I do not attempt to deal with problems relating to form or composition, such as proportion, symmetry, or harmony. These remain for future consideration. The discussion of indexes touches on the sequential development of landscapes as the point of observation shifts, but the subject needs to be examined separately in the light of the findings presented here. Aside from these matters left for future consideration, the indexes introduced here should go a long way toward clarifying the basic visual characteristics of landscapes.

Seven classic types of Japanese landscape are abstracted from actual surveys and from documentary evidence, and an attempt is made to explain the significance of these types as well as to describe their spatial structures and the spatial elements of which they are composed. The conceptual schemes of Kevin Lynch and Christian Norberg-Schulz bear on certain compositional elements that determine the spatial structure of these landscape types. No doubt this analysis is possible because we are dealing with Japan which is rich in landscape beauty and variety. Our task in the future, however, will be to take these compositional elements into consideration in drawing up plans for land utilization and development, to devise optimal ways of using the intrinsic elements of landscapes to protect and preserve their identity.

To date all too little research has been done on spaces that are lived in or experienced—spaces that have been formed, ordered, and fulfilled by human habitation. One can only agree with O. F. Bollnow, who wrote:

It is surprising that in the development of philosophy and psychology over the past few decades, we have had a detailed exposition of experienced time, but almost nothing dealing with experienced space. There have, to be sure, been studies of spatial structures (visual space, audible space, and so on), as well as of the cognitive space that is constructed from these, but we have no amplification taking us into the real or total space as it is lived in and experienced. (*Neue Geborgenheit*, p. 171)

This unexplained hiatus is the treatise of Bollnow's seminal work, which along with my examination of experienced space, has as its only supports the work of Lynch and Norberg-Schulz. Another future consideration will be to amplify the findings obtained here with respect to the seven classic spaces through applications to more concrete lived-in spaces.

Associated with the question of space as a support for man's existence is the idea of landscape space as home, or homeland, aptly signified by the German term *Heimat*. The image of home, or homeland, in Japan today is laden with existentialist connotations and with the eminently contemporary question of alienation, loss of homeland. In considering the basic question of visibility or invisibility, I was led to questions of modern man's very existence. I do not, however, end with a tidy conclusion, about the universality of specific individual problems but rather suggest newer, broader fields for consideration.

For designers—engineers, architects, urban planners, and gardeners—who are charged with implanting physical installations in a setting, it is basic and essential to grasp the nature of that setting as a visible spectacle and to understand its spatial structure. Yamaoka Yoshinori asked, "How can men talk to each other on land that has lost its spirit?" We

must learn to exercise sensibility toward the terrains we deal with and to make sure that we do not destroy their spirit. Indeed, we will not arrive at truly beautiful visual surroundings until designers have learned to consider the natural terrain, the city, various architectural elements, and other visual factors as composing an integrated whole. If this work is of use to designers wishing to adopt this approach, it will have served its purpose.

This book evolved from my doctoral dissertation, *Keikan no kōzō ni kansuru kisoteki kenkyū* ("Basic Research on the Structure of Landscapes"), which was published in Japanese. I am grateful for the support and assistance of many teachers, colleagues, and friends. My thanks are due, first of all, to Professor Yasojima Yoshinosuke, my research counselor, who acted as my mentor and guide from the very inception of the project. I am also deeply indebted to Professor Ashihara Yoshinobu, Professor Suzuki Tadayoshi, and Assistant Professor Nakamura Yoshio for their innumerable criticisms and suggestions. Cooperating with me on the research that went into the chapters on depth and angles of depression were Shinohara Osamu and Satō Hironori. Valuable advice came also from Assistant Professor Shioda Satoshi and from Yamaoka Yoshinori.

Professor Kevin Lynch assisted me not only by speaking of my work to his colleagues in America and Europe but by introducing me to The MIT Press. Without his help and that of Professors Ashihara and Hoshino Ikumi, publication in English would not have been possible. Nor would I have had the courage to pursue the possibility of an English version had it not been for the kind urging of Professor Philip Thiel.

For preparing the English text, I am grateful to Charles S. Terry, who undertook not merely to render into English what I had written but to make the numerous allusions and quotations comprehensible to readers lacking a deep knowledge of Japanese history and culture. I should like also to express thanks to Mizushima Takashi who provided many of the photographs, to Nagase Katsumi and Nishaya Naoka who drew a large number of the illustrations, to my secretary, Sato Yoshiko, and to Miyazaki Shinobu of Gihōdō Shuppan who published the Japanese edition.

Finally, I wish to acknowledge with deep thanks the research grant provided by the Kajima Foundation to cover the cost of translation.

I

*Visual
Structure of
Landscapes*

1

Indexes of
Visual
Structure

Thanks to modern economic growth and the development of transportation facilities, the people of Japan are better able today than ever before to indulge their propensity for going places and seeing things. The population density of our cities having reached a critical point, urban inhabitants feel a stronger and stronger urge to flee from their cramped everyday surroundings and find havens where, if only briefly, they can enjoy the smell of the earth, feel the embrace of nature, revel in scenic beauties that traffic-clogged streets and high-rise apartment buildings deny them.

Sightseeing is not new to Japan. In prehistoric times the ancestors of the modern Japanese made an annual event of going to the nearby mountains at the beginning of spring and worshiping mountain deities hitherto cut off from them by the winter's snow. Local and national rulers made ritual journeys to the hills to survey their domains. In later centuries, after cities had developed, outings to view the cherry blossoms in spring or the crimson maple leaves in autumn became national pastimes. Even religious pilgrimages to famous temples and shrines became in many ways a form of group recreation, sufficiently secular in character to cause the appearance of a whole category of towns whose principal incomes derived from the premodern equivalent of tourism. Today travel has become the foundation of a burgeoning leisure industry. Resorts of one kind or another have sprung up, and are springing up, all over the country, even in places not blessed, as the resorts of a few decades back were, by the presence of some celebrated natural or historical attraction.

Natural beauty has a natural appeal to mankind. Confucius said, "The wise man loves the rivers and lakes; the benevolent man loves the mountains." For the Japanese poet Matsuo Bashō (1644–1694), "he who would live elegantly is a friend of the four seasons in their natural state." The neo-Confucian scholar Fujiwara Seika (1561–1619) declared, "The person who is fond of natural scenery creates the opportunity for discovering the Way." Somewhat more specifically, Shiga Shigetaka (1863–1927) wrote: "There is nothing like a mountain peak for converting, elevating, and sanctifying human nature." From this it is clear that the beauty of nature has, since ancient times, had many different meanings to many different observers. Yet the quotations given seem to bear out Hegel's assertion: "Natural beauty can justify its name only in its relationship to that which is spiritual."[1]

In comparison with Bashō, who traveled about the Japanese countryside as a mendicant priest, or with the white-robed pilgrims who made their way to Kumano's land of the dead, the modern traveler has an easy time of it. That, however, in no way alters the fact that to return to nature and drink in its beauties is a restorative and inspirational experience for human beings in general. In the words of Nakai Masakazu (1900–1952), a well-known art critic, "To come into contact with nature, to suddenly see oneself as one ought to be and understand what one must hold onto, to become aware of what is truly important, healthy, and valuable to oneself— this is a tremendous happening. It signifies one's discovery of what there is in oneself that must be guarded to the death."[2] Whether all the contemporary sightseers who travel in droves to Japan's famous scenic spots are as deeply moved as Nakai is debatable, but in any case their urge to go is not in itself cause for lament.

Consciously or unconsciously, we all distinguish between various types of views, and it is instructive to consider the conscious or unconscious criteria we employ. When we speak of a bird's-eye view, the view from the top or the view from below, we are drawing a distinction with respect to the point at which the observer is situated. When we talk of a long-range view, or a middle- or short-range view, the criterion is the distance of the object from the observer. When we distinguish between the main object in sight and the background, we are usually thinking not so much of distance as of the visual structure of the prospect. And when we mention vistas or panoramas, we are drawing a contrast on the basis of breadth or scope.

These common distinctions offer valuable hints as to how we should proceed with a scientific analysis of views in general, and landscapes in particular, for they tell us, in effect, the features that are meaningful to the ordinary eye.

Uehara Keiji, in his important work on Japanese landscapes, attempted to analyze the nature of a view in terms of the following five elements: (1) viewpoint, (2) range of vision, (3) direction, (4) principal feature, and (5) distance.[3] Adopting a somewhat different approach, R. B. Litton, Jr., of the University of California proposed six analytical factors: (1) distance, (2) observer position, (3) form, (4) spatial definition, (5) light, and (6) sequence.[4]

Uehara's five elements are without doubt basic, and Litton's contribution is valuable because he added not only the concept of sequence—the transformation that takes place when the point of view shifts—but also the idea of a projecting form against a receding spatial definition.

A more thoroughgoing examination of the visual structure of landscapes was provided by the nineteenth-century German architect and urban planner Hans Märtens, who held to the principle that the total aesthetic impression is related to the range and distance that a normal human eye can encompass. Märtens's ideas with respect to distance and angle of elevation have become standard in the field of urban design.[5]

Having reviewed various earlier theories, we have arrived at the following eight criteria or indexes for determining the visual structure of landscapes:

1. Visibility or invisibility. This concerns the fundamental question of what can be seen and what cannot be seen from a given viewpoint.

2. Distance. This has to do with the changes that take place in the appearance of an object as the distance between the observer and the object varies.

3. Angle of incidence. When a landscape is conceived of as a concatenation of surfaces, the angle at which the line of vision strikes each surface determines to a large degree what can be seen of it. This index evaluates the comparative visibility of the various surfaces in a given landscape.

4. Depth of invisibility. This gauges the degree of invisiblity in terms of the depth of the unseen section with respect to the line of vision.

5. Angle of depression. This clarifies the viewer's sense of position as he looks at a scene from above.

6. Angle of elevation. This indicates the nature of the upward view and the limits of visible space.

7. Depth. This clarifies the degree of three-dimensionality of the landscape as it unfolds before the viewer.

8. Light. The appearance of a landscape changes drastically in accordance with the manner in which the light strikes it. This index has to do with the transformations that take place as the position of the source of light moves from front to side to back.

Although these eight criteria were postulated for the purpose of analyzing natural landscapes, they would presumably be applicable in the study of any view or prospect.

The object of our study is the landscape as a background for buildings or livable environments. The topography of Japan, which lacks deserts or savannas, is by the same token rich in variety. When we who live in this country conjure up images of the place where we and our ancestors sprang from, these images are almost certain to contain mountains and streams. These natural features are an integral part of the environment in which most Japanese live or once lived. And mountains, streams or rivers, forests, lakes compose the settings that Japanese associate with Japan, in the broad sense.

In general, a natural setting may be regarded as the totality of the visual relationships between a point of view and the objects viewed. When natural elements of the settings are considered in research, the research falls in the category of the so-called "science of relationships," but there is a danger that the study can be expanded indefinitely, which is what happened in the past in geographic research.[6]

The study of visual environments does indeed cover a very large range. Even if the area is limited to particular types of natural landscapes, and if we concentrate on what Hegel spoke of as the relationship of natural beauty to "that which is spiritual," we find a number of possible approaches. In attempting to analyze the Japanese view of nature, for example, Tsuda Sōkichi (1873–1961), Watsuji Tetsurō (1889–1960), Ienaga Saburō (1913–   ), Kamei Katsuichirō (1907–66), Karaki Junzō (1904–1980), and other scholars have considered it primarily in terms of the history of ideas and spiritual beliefs.[7] The landscape was interesting to these men for the spiritual or emotional effect it produced on the viewer, and the objects of their study were, for the most part, books, poems, paintings, or other works of art—creative expressions inspired by the natural environment.

Another important school of thought has delved into Japanese traditions from the ethnological viewpoint and discussed the Japanese terrain in terms of the part it has played in the actual lives of the Japanese people. This approach is to be found in the numerous works of Yanagita Kunio and Origuchi Shinobu (1887–1953), to name only the two most prominent writers in this field. Among the ethnologists, the objects under consideration were not artistic or literary creations but local customs, religious traditions, and the like, which reflect the influence of topographical surroundings on everyday existence. For those of us who see landscapes as belonging properly to our normal environment, the work of Yanagita, Origuchi, and their colleagues is particularly interesting.

In the field of geography we have what is known as the landscape approach, which, having been originated by Otto Schlüter, became for a time the mainstream of geographic studies. Schlüter and his followers restricted the object of their research to that landscape (*Landschaft*) which is the visible form assumed by the world's surface and then attempted to clarify the relationship between nature and man (or society). Attention was focused on specific sites, and an effort was then made to discover the causal relationships between these regions and the societies that had grown up within them.

By way of contrast to these various approaches, we adopt the attitude of the landscape planner or designer, who is in a position to manipulate the natural environment. In considering the relationship between natural beauty and the human frame of mind, or the interconnections between the landscape and the point of view, we are concerned primarily with the external factors. We are dealing, in other words, not so much with psychological effects as with the tangible features of what is seen. The indexes proposed are intended to aid the designer in determining the function of these features, particularly those topographical elements that form the background or foundation of the landscape, and to examine their visual and spatial structure with relation to a development plan. We cannot completely ignore the human element, but the aspect of it that interests us most is the nature of man's visual perception of his surroundings.

Historically, certain physical features tended to cause shifts in human attitudes toward landscapes; we concentrate on this phenomenon rather than on what psychological factors caused certain landscapes to be regarded as remarkable or unique.

As subjects for study we have chosen areas or sites that have long been valued for their scenic appeal. In analyzing the reasons why they have been valued, we employ indexes and concepts that would be meaningful to persons who manipulate environments to explain why certain landscapes have been treasured and are meaningful in a technical sense.

Camillo Sitte, in the preface to his classic study of the European plaza, said the following of his methodology: "I thought it would be proper to study the plazas, roads, and urban structures of the past and discover what it was that made them beautiful. My reason was that if we could find out why they were beautiful, we could apply the same principles to our own cities with similar results."[8]

Principles and indexes that are of objective value to planners and designers often derive from an author's subjective perception of what is beautiful. Perhaps beauty is too nebulous or too profound to be grasped by scientific methods. Landscapes constitute a particular form of beauty and are without doubt both nebulous and profound, but certainly it is not totally impossible to treat them as objects of scientific observation and research. Engineers make scientific analyses of soil, water, and concrete to determine the methods they will employ. In a similar fashion we must ask ourselves what the basic elements in landscapes are and attempt to ascertain their visual and spatial characteristics before we attempt to design environments that are fundamentally physical in character.

2

Visibility
of Landscape
Structure

The very definition of the word "landscape," as given in the *Oxford English Dictionary*, is "a view or prospect of natural inland scenery, such as can be taken in at a glance from one point of view."

We are interested not in how well something can be seen or how striking it is to the eye but simply in whether it can be seen at all. Broadly speaking, four methods are useful for studying visibility and invisibility: direct observation, construction of a replica, analysis by means of aerial photography, and construction of a digital terrain model that can be analyzed by computer. The last two methods call for explanation.

The Aerial Photography Method

Information about the visibility and invisibility of topographical features can easily be obtained by using a pair of stereographic aerial photographs and a stereoscope. The basic technique involves a series of manual operations tracing lines of observation between a point P fixed on the photographs as the observer's position and a point Q selected as the object being viewed. The points are connected by straight lines so that, when the photographs are viewed through the stereoscope, the line PQ is seen in its proper position in space. Since this line represents the line of vision, if it is interrupted by a mountain or some other salient feature, point Q is not visible from point P. By varying the position of point Q, it is possible to determine which areas in the photograph are visible from point P and which are not. Then, by plotting the contours of the visible areas (for example, the ridges of mountains) on a coordinate graph centered on P, a perspective drawing of the view can be prepared. (See figures 2.1, 2.2) There is no need to prepare a model from topographical charts since the actual terrain is visible in the viewer. The areas of visibility, along with other types of information, can

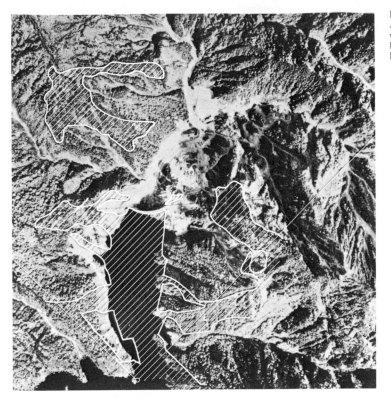

Figure 2.1
Areas of visibility and invisibility (vicinity of Lake Kurobe, Toyama Prefecture)

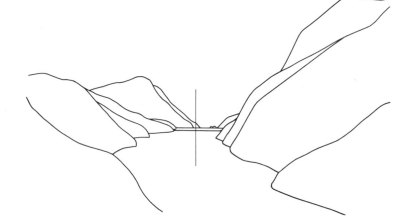

Figure 2.2
Perspective made in accordance with the areas of visibility and invisibility in figure 2.1, as determined by the aerial photograph method

7 *Visibility of Landscape Structure*

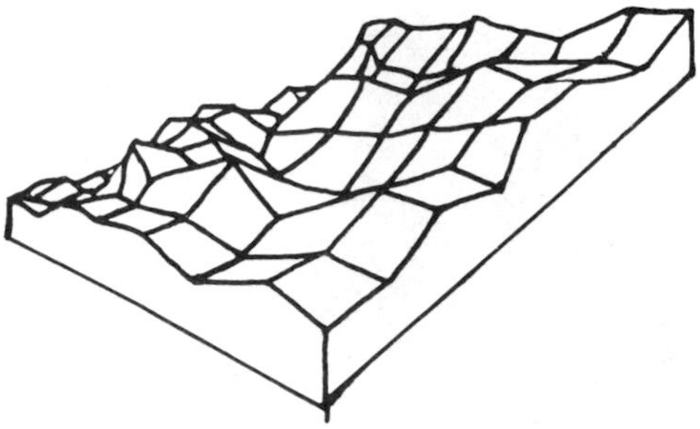

Figure 2.3
Terrain model

easily be seen from the photographs, giving the designer a clear account of the most important elements in a landscape.

The author devised this method in cooperation with Nakamura Yoshio, and it has proved to be effective, but there remains room for technical improvements in the process of drafting.[1]

The Digital Terrain Model

The digital terrain model was first used as a means of determining visibility by the Urban Design Institute of Tokyo University in preparing a tourist development plan for the Bandai-Inawashiro region of northeast Japan. The method proved to be a good one for obtaining an understanding of the terrain, and with certain improvements it has come into wide use today.

In principle visibility and invisibility are ascertained by a computer-generated graphic analysis of whether or not lines in space connecting the observer's position with any given object are interrupted by some obstacle. The degree to which the computer model faithfully reproduces the actual terrain depends on the source from which the data were taken. Data may be taken from a contour map or an aerial photograph, but each has an important disadvantage. The contour maps do not indicate the height of the flora growing on the land, and the aerial photograph requires the use of a photogrammetric drafting instrument.

Data for topographical points may be derived for the points of intersection on a square or rectangular grid (figure 2.3), for random points chosen to represent the main features of the terrain (mountaintops or high and low points along the ridge of a mountain range), or for points along the contour lines at various heights. When a contour map is used, the last method is, of course, easy, and it is possible to use a digitizer in conjunction with it. In calculating the visibility and invisibility, however, the grid system is the simplest.

Whichever method is used, the accuracy of the model is governed by the density of the points of reference. As a general rule, if the scale of the map is 1:1,000, the points on the grid should be spaced at intervals of from ten to twenty meters; for a scale of 1:5,000, twenty to twenty-five meters; and for a scale of 1:10,000, fifty to a hundred meters.

The method employed to interpolate the values for the areas enclosed by the points of reference depends on the density of these points. For example, when a grid is used, the analyst must decide what curve best approximates the actual shape of the land enclosed by any four reference points. Current studies of the digital terrain model as a device for ascertaining visibility have centered on means of achieving maximum accuracy. To a great extent the degree of accuracy required depends on the purpose of the survey. If the area involved is quite large, there is usually not as much need for accuracy in sections far removed from the observer's position as in sections close by. Thus it is possible to have one standard of accuracy for nearby areas and another for distant areas.[2]

The great advantage of using the digital terrain model is that, once it has been prepared, it can be used as the basis for computerized calculations of other values involved in the visual structure of the landscape. This method is extremely convenient in the planning stage and in confirming the results of on-the-spot surveys.

DISTANCE

Are we concerned with a bamboo grove outside the window or a stand of windblown cypress trees on a nearby hill or a hazy range of mountains in the distance? The manner in which the view unfolds depends on how far it extends, and the quality or texture of the object viewed varies with its distance from the observer. The problem is to find a standard or

index that indicates the effect of longer or shorter distances.

The appearance of any object, be it mountain, building, or human being, changes with its distance from the point of view (see figure 2.4). If we start from the bottom of a tree-covered slope and gradually move away from it, it will undergo a continuous change in aspect. Beyond a certain distance we discover that the change is not merely in size but in sharpness and hue. It is difficult, however, to determine just where the visual transformation took place. We can retrace our steps and repeat the process, but this is likely only to add to our confusion.

At what point does the slope begin to look qualitatively different? And what is the significance of this alteration? These are difficult questions but basic for setting up an index of distance. Fortunately, the problem has attracted the attention of a number of previous writers, whose ideas and methods can profitably be reviewed at this stage.

Previous Research

Choosing human scale as a standard for determining the distance of urban elements, Märtens worked out a mathematical relationship between the size of the object (a human being) at different distances and the angle formed by the rays from the observer's eye and the outlines of the object.[3] He also studied the psycho-optical effects of this angle.

Märtens's criterion for measuring architectural space was based on the distance at which a person's face can be identified, which he related to the width of the nasal bone, the smallest part of the face that must be seen in order for identity to be established. It is known from physiological optics that the maximum interval is about twenty-one to twenty-five meters (seventy to eighty feet), at which distance the nasal bone occupies an angle of 1 minute in our field of vision. As

Figure 2.4
Changing appearance as
distance varies (Rikuchu
National Maritime Park,
Iwate Prefecture)

Hans Blumenfeld has noted, Märtens is to be credited with the first important scientific definition of the human scale of distance in urban spaces, and the only one made before the mid-twentieth century.[4]

Edward Hall, discussing social environment in *The Hidden Dimension* offered an interesting analysis of the distances people maintain between one another.[5] Like Märtens, Hall adopted a human scale, but in this case the maximum interval considered is not more than twelve meters (roughly forty feet). In arriving at his conclusion, he relied not only on sight but on the action of other senses as well. However, in his concern with such factors as the size of the field of vision and the segment of the angle of vision occupied by the object perceived, Hall resembles Märtens.

In contrast, Ashihara Yoshinobu takes architecture, rather than the human form, as the standard for measuring urban spaces, which he analyzes in terms of the changes in appearance resulting from differences in distance.[6] Takahashi Takashi also examines objects other than human beings in terms of the distances from which they are discernible, though in the end he resembles Märtens in laying emphasis on the angle of vision.[7]

Most of the research on the subject has been confined to urban landscapes that are no more than 1,600 meters (about one mile) from the viewer's eye.[8] Natural landscapes, however, often extend from the window sill to mountains so distant that they take on a purple hue. (A fairly common expression used in Chinese and Japanese to describe a beautiful natural setting means literally "purple mountains, clear waters.") When the degree of atmospheric haziness becomes a factor, discernibility is often a question not so much of angle of vision as of the contrast between an object and its background. In Japan weather stations all over the country record visibility thrice daily, at 9 A.M., 3 P.M., and 10 P.M.

Data are given for an object occupying a vertical angle of 0.5 degree and a horizontal angle of 5 degrees in the range of vision.[9] The effect of climatic conditions on the view is predictable from the results.

Nakamura Teiichi and Ishiwara Shūji have carried out an interesting experiment in which they observed the discernibility of treed and treeless areas at a fixed time each day for a full year and then compared these results with visibility data prepared by the weather bureau.[10] Their method differed from that of Märtens in that they were attempting to show that the ability to perceive the object depended not on the angle of vision but on the degree of contrast between the object and its background.

A common feature of all the methods in the literature cited is that the observations and experience entailed confirm the assertion made at the beginning of this section that, as the distance from the object increases, a gradual (quantitative) change in the appearance of the object becomes a qualitative change. In each case, in order to explain the nature of the qualitative change and the basis for it, the observers set up an object to be taken as a standard and then considered its appearance in terms of physiological optics—the range of vision and the angular segment occupied by the object, or the degree of light contrast between the object and its surroundings. We make use of the methods adopted by previous researchers in establishing a distance index for landscapes.

A Standard for Landscape Distances

In his analysis of distance in urban landscapes, Blumenfeld spoke of three classes: the intimate human scale, the normal human scale, and the public human scale; Hall, on the other hand, recognized four: intimate distance, personal distance, social distance, and public distance. We will consider a more traditional division of distance into foreground, middle ground, and background. These categories are founded on the theory of space in painting and photography where they serve an important compositional purpose in the creation of three-dimensionality on flat surfaces.[11] To eliminate compositional nuances and confine our attention to sheer distance, we shall speak of short-distance views, middle-distance views, and long-distance views.

Märtens chose the human form as the standard object for his observations, and Ashihara Yoshinobu selected architecture. What should be taken as a standard for landscapes? To pose this question is to ask what the basic element in a landscape is. In the case of Japan, if not elsewhere as well, the answer must certainly be trees and forests. With its abundant rainfall and temperate climate Japan is well wooded and has large sections of forests; in fact, as Kira Tatsuo observed, "unless the hand of man interferes with natural processes, everything eventually turns into forests."[12]

Common sense and everyday experience confirm that trees generally form a prominent element in the landscapes we see and admire. It seems appropriate therefore to use trees as standards for classifying distances and how they affect the appearance of what we see.

The relationship of trees to the short-, middle-, and long-distance views can be described as follows:[13]

1. In a short-distance view trees are recognizable as individual units from any point of observation (figure 2.5). The leaves, trunks, and branches are discernible as belonging to particular trees, and people are able to relate the size of each tree to their own height. In other words, the trees are near enough to be sensed as separate trees.

In landscapes the relationship between wind and trees is an element of considerable importance. We are dealing with a short-distance view when we are able to hear the wind blowing through woods or see the branches waving and the leaves fluttering:

The sound of the wind,
Ruffling the leaves of bamboo
Outside my window—
A dream flitting swiftly by
In a momentary nap.
—Shikishi Naishinnō (d. 1201)[14]

In the dead of night,
The moon drops behind the peak
Outside my window,
And I hear a stormy wind
Wheeze through the dark cypress grove.
—Eifukumon-in (1271–1342)[15]

Living in a land of many small valleys bordered or surrounded by mountains, the people of Japan have developed a special sense of closeness to nature. The short-distance view of landscape was of enormous importance to Japanese poets of the past who perceived seasonal and other changes as an intimate part of their daily lives.[16]

2. In a middle-distance view the outline of the treetops is visible but not the details of individual trees (figure 2.6) At this range the trees are too distant to be sensed as units, although they form the texture of the visible surface; trees or clumps of trees of different varieties are perceived as spots within the texture. Also sense impressions other than vision cease to play a part. One does not feel but merely views, and the variations in the shape of the terrain become important compositional elements. We see the forest rather than the trees. In general a middle-distance area is the principal part of the landscape; or, to put it differently, a middle-distance view, in which juxtaposition of topographical patterns gives a strong sense of depth, is what we usually think of when we say landscape. In the middle-distance range mist and haze begin to influence the general appearance of the view, causing subtle changes in lighting and perspective.

Figure 2.5
Short-distance view, in
which each tree is visible

Figure 2.6
Middle-distance view, in
which the trees become
textural units

Figure 2.7
Long-distance view, in
which not even the varia-
tions in texture can be seen

3. In a long-distance view the contours of the treetops cannot be perceived; the eye can observe only major topographical features such as valleys or crests or clustery distributions of plant life (figure 2.7). Because of the influence of atmospheric perspective, the texture is uniform, and colors are visible only as lighter or darker parts of an overall blur. The color of the mountains is weaker than that of the sky and may serve to emphasize the features of a middle-distance view.

The most salient aspect of a long-distance view is the outline of mountains against the sky. Succession in the long-distance range can be determined only by observing the fashion in which the component forms overlap; consequently there is little sense of depth. The long-distance view usually functions as a backdrop.

In connection with the short- and middle-distance views, if the trees stand on sloping ground, we see trees above trees above trees on up to the top (figure 2.8), and, if the ground is flat, we see only the trees standing in the frontal row (figure 2.9). Strictly speaking, we are concerned with the visible parts of the trees, but experience has shown that it makes little difference if we take the actual height of the treetops as being equivalent to the visible height.

What then is the quantitative value that separates a short- from a middle-distance view? Observations indicate that the maximum distance for a short-distance view is one at which the horizontal angle of steady gaze at a particular tree is about 1 degree (figure 2.10). This distance is approximately sixty times the size of the object. As a general rule the size of the trees growing on Japanese mountains is about six meters for broad-leaf trees, about three meters for acicular crypto-merias, and about four meters for pines.[17] In cases where the trees are mostly broad-leaf trees, the point at which a short-distance view changes to a middle-distance view is about 360 meters from the object; in the case of acic-

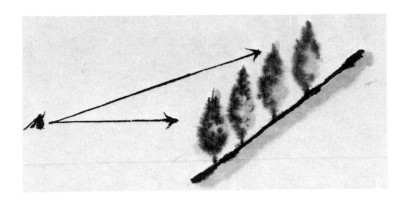

Figure 2.8
Appearance of trees on
sloping terrain

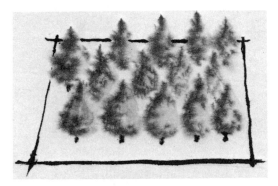

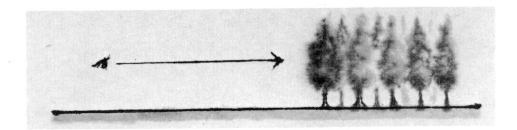

Figure 2.9
Appearance of trees on a
flat terrain

15 *Visibility of Landscape Structure*

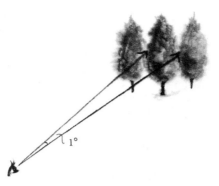

Figure 2.10
Minimum horizontal angle
for a short-distance view

1°

3′

Figure 2.11
Minimum horizontal angle
for a middle-distance view

	Very clear	Clear	Cloudy	Drizzle	Intermittent rain (light)	Light rain
Noon	45 km	40 km	30 km	10 km	15 km	10 km
Morning/Evening	20 km	15 km	10 km	5 km	8 km	8 km

Intermit-tent rain	Steady rain	Intermittent snow (light)	Light snow	Intermittent snow (ordinary)	Ordinary snow	Fog
8 km	6 km	15 km	7 km	4 km	2 km	0.6 km
4 km	3 km	7 km	4 km	2 km	1 km	0.3 km

Figure 2.12
Weather and visibility
(from *Kishōgaku
handobukku*)

ular trees the point varies between 180 and 140 meters from the object.

Since a middle-distance view is transformed into a long-distance view at the point where it becomes impossible to distinguish the outlines of individual trees or sense the texture of the whole, one might suppose that this point would fall at a distance from which the individual treetop occupied a horizontal segment of 1 minute in the range of vision, as was the case with the nasal bone in Märtens's research. Observations carried out by the author and Satō Hironori, however, show that the outlines of treetops become indiscernible when the angle is less than about 3 minutes (figure 2.11). In this connection it might be noted that, according to Takahashi Takashi, 3 minutes is the minimal angle of vision at which a person can immediately identify a black design on a white background.[18]

Since there remains a need to test this finding on a large number of observers, the 3 minute angle is adopted here only provisionally. If this is indeed the correct measure, the distance we are seeking is about 1,100 times the size of the treetops, or 6.6 kilometers in the case of broad-leaf trees and 3.3 to 4.4 kilometers in the case of acicular trees.

Atmospheric Factors

The distance indexes described here are based on the assumption that the object is viewed in clear weather, when atmospheric perspective is not a factor. When, however, the landscape involves distances of several kilometers or several tens of kilometers, atmospheric conditions must be taken into consideration.

As indicated in figure 2.12, even on very clear days visibility in the morning and evening is less than half what it is at midday. Visibility is reduced even more drastically under rainy or snowy conditions. It is difficult to generalize on this subject beyond remarking that visibility decreases rapidly as the humidity rises above 70 percent and that particular regions are apt to vary appreciably one from another.

In figure 2.13 appear the data collected in Nara and Kyoto by the weather bureau, which recorded visibility figures in the two locations at 3:00 P.M. every day during 1954. The two areas in question are both plains, and they are adjacent to each other. Yet from the microclimatological viewpoint they are quite different. They illustrate the difficulty of drawing the sorts of generalizations given in figure 2.13 and emphasize the need for examining the special regional conditions throughout Japan. Nevertheless, the information provided by the weather bureau helps us determine the limits within which landscapes in various regions are visible under differing atmospheric conditions. The specific effects of weather conditions on the distance indexes given for middle- and long-distance views have yet to be studied.

Distances in Some Prehistorical and Historical Settings

In the prehistoric Jōmon period, which began some ten thousand years ago and lasted for about eight thousand years, Japan was largely covered with laurisylvan forests, the trees usually glossy-leafed evergreens of the beech family.[19] Although the Jōmon culture is often said to have been based on hunting and gathering, farming in some form existed from the middle of the Jōmon period onward. In the late stages there was fairly extensive cultivation of nuts and rootstock. During this semiagricultural age the spaces in which people lived were not separated from nature but enclosed within it, deeply shaded by the laurisylvan growth, abounding in land leeches, and festooned with fat hanging vines. The development of rice cultivation, which began around 300 B.C. and rapidly spread throughout the inhabited parts of the country, meant the

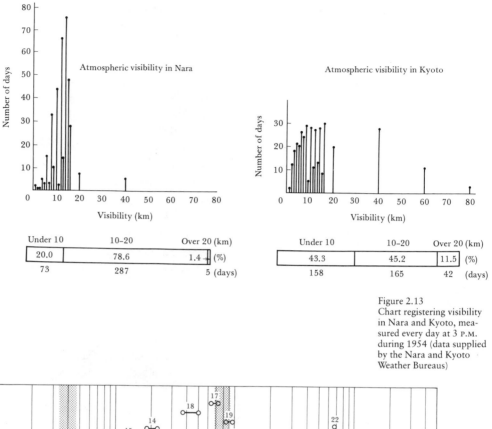

Atmospheric visibility in Nara

Under 10	10–20	Over 20 (km)
20.0	78.6	1.4 (%)
73	287	5 (days)

Atmospheric visibility in Kyoto

Under 10	10–20	Over 20 (km)
43.3	45.2	11.5 (%)
158	165	42 (days)

Figure 2.13
Chart registering visibility in Nara and Kyoto, measured every day at 3 P.M. during 1954 (data supplied by the Nara and Kyoto Weather Bureaus)

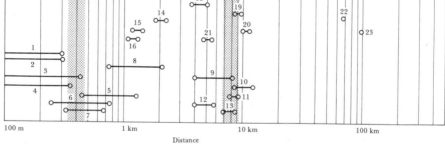

Distance

Figure 2.14
Distance ranges of various mountains forming principal objects in landscapes (place from which viewed appears in parentheses)

Borderline ranges separating short-distance range from middle-distance range and middle-distance range from long-distance range when treetops measure 6 to 8 meters

1 Middle Sembon at Mount Yoshino (between teahouse and Mount Tōbi)
2 Lower Sembon at Mount Yoshino (the Empress's Retreat)
3 Mountain in Sekisui-in Garden (Sekisui-in)
4 Mountain in Jōjū-in Garden (Jōjū-in)
5 Mount Arashi (Tenryū-ji)
6 Mount Kinugasa (Golden Pavilion)
7 Mount Buttoku (Byōdō-in)
8 Mount Miwa (entrance to Omiwa Shrine)
9 Sakurajima (Sengen-en)
10 Eastern mountains of Nara (Jikō-in)
11 Mount Hiei (Shōden-ji)
12 Mount Hiei (Entsū-ji)
13 Mount Hiei (Daitoku-ji)
14 Mount Unebi (site of Fujiwara Palace)
15 Mount Miminashi (site of Fujiwara Palace)
16 Mount Kagu (site of Fujiwara (palace)
17 Mount Arashi (site of Heian Palace)
18 Mount Otowa (site of Heian Palace)
19 Mount Hiei (site of Heian Palace)
20 Mount Ikoma (site of Heijō Palace)
21 Mount Kasuga (site of Heijō Palace)
22 Mount Tsukuba (Edo)
23 Mount Fuji (Edo)

18   *Visual Structure of Landscapes*

clearing of forests to create open fields, but, since a plentiful supply of water was needed for the growing rice, the places chosen for habitation were usually damp valleys where the pleasant gurgling of mountain streams could be heard. No doubt the typical farming community in the early days of rice cultivation was situated in an area such as that described in the *Izumo fudoki*, a gazetteer of the Izumo area in western Honshu, probably compiled in the early eighth century:

The reason why [this place] is called Nita is that the great deity Ōnamochi-no-mikoto, who governs all under heaven, said of it, "This land is neither large nor tiny. Upstream the branches of the trees mingle together; downstream the roots and stalks of reeds cover the ground. This is a damp, humid [*nita-shiki*] little district." Therefore it is called Nita.[20]

This description fits the Mikumari Shrine type of landscape, discussed in chapter 10, which is a small basin near the point where a stream exits from the mountains. From the lowlands in such places, the mountains usually form a short-distance, or at most a middle-distance, view, and one supposes that the ancient inhabitants not only heard the wind blowing through the trees on the slopes but also felt intimately involved with the seasonal changes taking place there. It was a long time before people moved down to the larger plains, thus removing themselves from their source of firewood as well as from the places where the spirits of their dead ancestors had always lived.[21]

The most ancient Japanese imperial palaces were in *yamato* ("mountain-interval-places"), little valleys or meadows between or at the feet of mountains. Such sites were either identical with or similar to those of the earliest agricultural communities. The following two poems from the *Kojiki* ("Record of Ancient Matters," Japan's earliest history), attributed

to the consort of the mythical Emperor Jimmu, testify to an early sense of oneness with nature:[22]

Clouds are rising
From the Sai River;
On Unebi Mountain
The leaves of the trees are rustling;
The wind is about to blow.

On Unebi Mountain
During the day the clouds shift restlessly;
Now it is night,
And as if to warn that the wind is about to blow,
The leaves of the trees are rustling.[23]

From the late prehistoric through the early historic periods, when the imperial palaces were at the foot of Mount Katsuragi or Mount Miwa or in the small mountain-encircled plain at Asuka (modern Nara Prefecture), the surrounding landscape was of the short-distance type, possibly verging on the middle-distance type. Only in the late seventh century, when a Chinese-style imperial city was constructed at Fujiwara (also in Nara Prefecture), did the early Japanese advance out into the broader flatlands (figure 2.14). Even then the three mountains on the north, east, and west were only from one to two kilometers from the palace, at which range the texture and spots formed by the treetops began to matter more than the details of the individual trees. Nara, which became the capital in 710, and Heiankyō (modern Kyoto), which succeeded it in 794, were farther from the mountains, but even so Mount Kasuga was only five kilometers from Nara, and Mount Otowa only four to five kilometers from Heian. In either case the farthest visible mountains were no more than about ten kilometers removed.

Throughout the eight hundred years during which Heian remained the undisputed center

Figure 2.15
View from the Sekisui-in at
the Kōzan-ji (Kyoto)

of Japanese civilization, the chief bearers of culture remained accustomed to short- and middle-distance landscapes. After the beginning of the seventeenth century, when the cultural pivot began to shift to the Tokugawa shogun's capital in Edo (modern Tokyo), it became necessary for people to develop a new attitude toward nature, for the most impressive mountains visible from this new city were Mount Fuji, a hundred kilometers to the west, and Mount Tsukuba, seventy kilometers to the northeast.

In Japan there are a number of historical gardens designed chiefly to take advantage of a mountainous landscape in the offing. It is worthwhile at this point to examine the distances involved in some of the more representative of these.

At the gardens of the Sekisui-in at the Kō-zan-ji (figure 2.15) and the Jōjū-in at the Ki-yomizu-dera, the mountain constituting the principal element in the landscape is in the short-distance range and appears to be an integral part of the garden design.[24] Looking out over the Jōjū-in garden, for example, when the wind sweeps over the hill one can see the fluttering of the leaves on the trees at the most distant point, which is about four hundred meters from the customary point of observation.

By way of contrast, to judge from the size of the treetops, Mount Buttoku as seen from the garden of the Byōdō-in in Uji, Mount Kinugasa as seen from the garden of the Golden Pavilion in Kyoto (figure 2.16), and Mount Arashi as seen from the garden of the Tenryū-ji in Kyoto are on the borderline between a short- and middle-distance range. The vertical angle of vision occupied by the individual treetops when gazed at steadily is about 1 degree, and the contrasts in texture formed by variations in the types of trees are both lovely and lively. This is an important point in fixing the place from which to view a mountain. A

Figure 2.16
Mount Kinugasa seen from
the Kinkaku-ji (Kyoto)

good illustration is the view of Mount Arashi from Togetsu Bridge (figure 2.17).

In the Edo period (1600–1868) many famous gardens were designed to take advantage of a distant mountain view, which was known as a "borrowed landscape" (*shakkei*). Such was the case with the gardens of the Entsū-ji, the Shōden-ji, and the Daitoku-ji, all of which looked toward Mount Hiei, northeast of Kyoto (figure 2.18); the garden of the Jikō-in, which faced the mountains east of Nara; and the Sengen Garden in Kagoshima, whose view was toward the volcanic island Sakurajima. In these instances the borrowed landscape is from four to ten kilometers away, which is to say either in the middle-distance range or on the borderline between the middle- and long-distance ranges. At this distance the atmospheric perspective caused by climatic effects exerts a delicate influence; only when the visibility is fairly low do the distant mountains begin to appear hazy and purplish.

Fujiwara Seika, who visited Edo in 1594 to lecture to Tokugawa Ieyasu (1542–1616), included Mount Fuji and Mount Tsukuba among the four greatest sights in the Kantō region. Later the two mountains were used countless times as subjects in prints by Andō Hiroshige (1797–1858) and Katsushika Hokusai (1760–1849). Matsudaira Sadanobu (1758–1829), councilor of state to the shogunate in the late eighteenth century, took the unusual step of having a window installed in the middle of a *tokonoma* (alcove for decorations) in his teahouse so that he could look out at Mount Fuji, and many other daimyo, including Lord Tokugawa Mitsutomo of Owari, Lord Ichihashi of Shimōsa, and Lord Tokugawa Harutomi of Kii, are recorded to have built pavilions or teahouses with a view of the celebrated peak.

The obsession with Mount Fuji, and to a lesser extent Mount Tsukuba, in the Edo period must certainly have resulted from Edo's being situated on a large plain, far removed from the nearest mountains. At the same time it indicated a willingness to accept a very distant mountain as the principal view for a house or garden. This is a great change from the attitude of earlier times. These faraway mountains had no visible texture; there was no way of knowing whether or not the wind was blowing through the trees on them, or indeed whether or not there were any trees on them for the wind to blow through. The color of the mountains revealed nothing of nature's ever-changing hues. Mount Fuji, Mount Tsukuba, and other mountains visible from Edo were, in fact, flat surfaces whose most outstanding feature was the outline they formed against the sky.

The new attitude toward mountains may have had something to do with what Karaki Junzō has called the "urban provinciality" (*kuruwa-sei*) of the Edo period. "After the beginning of the Edo period," Karaki writes, "sympathy or a sense of oneness with nature disappeared from the surface: no more did people watch the progress of the seasons, the flying cherry blossoms, the falling leaves, the floating clouds, the flowing streams, and feel within their hearts the flying cherry blossoms, the falling leaves, the floating clouds, the flowing streams. No longer did these sights inspire them to compose poems." Instead, he continues, "natural phenomena and the sights of the changing seasons became ornamental accessories to life," [25] not essentially different from the decorative pictures of birds, flowers, or scenery that people hung inside their houses to remind them of the beauties of nature. Whether one accepts this view or not, it is certain that the Japanese of the Edo period acquired a new taste for the distant "borrowed landscape."

Figure 2.17
Mount Arashi and Togetsu
Bridge (Kyoto)

Figure 2.18
Mount Hiei as a borrowed
landscape, seen from inside
the garden at the Entsū-ji
(Kyoto)

3

Visual
Perception of
Planes

ANGLE OF INCIDENCE

Thus far, landscapes have been discussed in terms of ground features and transformations in the appearance of trees as the distance from the point of observation increases or decreases. Landscapes can also be analyzed in a more abstract fashion, as consisting of a variety of intersecting planes (figure 3.1). In this case the appearance of the scene is equivalent to the total visual effect of the individual planes, which depends largely on the angle between the individual planes and the line of vision. This angle of incidence, as it is called, is an important index to the ease with which any given surface can be seen.

ANGLE OF INCIDENCE AND EASE OF VISION

A landscape composed of water surfaces and land surfaces stretches out before our eyes. What sort of geometrical planes can be abstracted from it? J. J. Gibson, well-known for his research on depth perception, came to the conclusion that our visual environment is composed ultimately of two kinds of planes (figure 3.2), which he called frontal and longitudinal surfaces.[1]

To obtain the angle of incidence with relation to a frontal surface, we will accept Ernö Goldfinger's and Ashihara Yoshinobu's figure of 60 degrees for the angle encompassed by our vertical range of vision.[2] The angle of incidence θ for this plane is 90 degrees minus the angle of depression or elevation. As shown in figure 3.3, at the center of the plane, O, the angle is 90 degrees. As the point of incidence approaches the extremities of the field of vision, Y and Y', the angle decreases to 60 degrees, which is still ample.

The situation is, of course, different with longitudinal surfaces. In this case $\theta =$ the angle of depression. As indicated in figure 3.4, this angle decreases as the point of incidence moves from A to D, toward the center of the field of vision. At the center the value is 0

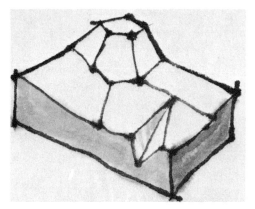

Figure 3.1
Landscape seen as com-
posed of surfaces

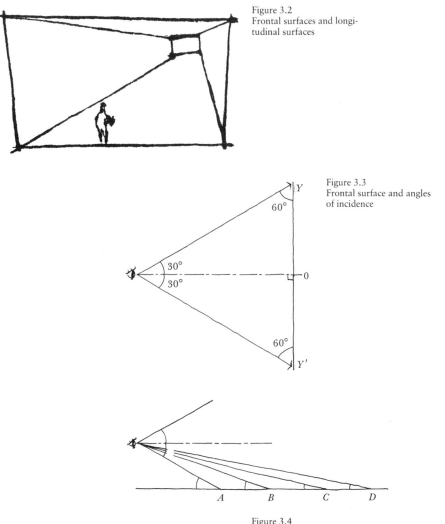

Figure 3.2
Frontal surfaces and longitudinal surfaces

Figure 3.3
Frontal surface and angles
of incidence

Figure 3.4
Longitudinal surface and
angles of incidence

degrees when it is some infinite distance from the eye. Conversely, the angle increases as the point of incidence approaches the eye, the limit being 30 degrees at the nearest point in the field of vision.

Figure 3.5 demonstrates how a plane becomes larger and easier to see as the angle of incidence increases, the progression being from I to III as the angle grows larger. The angle of incidence for the frontal plane is always larger than for longitudinal surfaces; thus the frontal surface is easier to see.

To increase the visibility of a horizontal plane below the eye, such as the surface of a lake, the ocean, or a flat terrain in a landscape, the point of view can be raised so as to increase the angle of incidence (figure 3.6). This necessarily has the effect of increasing the distance encompassed by the field of vision (figure 3.7).

It remains to adopt a standard surface and attempt to determine at what angle of incidence it becomes difficult to see the surface, and particularly at what point it ceases to be sensed as frontal and becomes instead longitudinal.

In physiological optics clear vision is possible within a vertical angle of vision of 3 degrees and a horizontal angle of vision of 12 degrees. It may well be possible to adopt a standard surface fitting these requirements and, by using the method indicated in figure 3.7, to measure the angles of incidence that allow for ease of vision. Such values, however, have not yet been proved to have much meaning in the case of landscapes. It therefore seems more practical to examine several actual examples and try to arrive empirically at the desired qualitative definition.

Mount Arashi

Concerning Mount Arashi, west of Kyoto, Yoshida Tōgo (1868–1918), an expert on historical geography, wrote, "Skirted on the north by the Ōi River, it is a place that is praised in the spring for its cherry blossoms and in the fall for its colorful leaves. It rises majestically from the white sand, green moss, and clear water below, like a wall of luxuriant verdure a thousand feet high."[3]

From Saga Meadow on the other side of the river Mount Arashi does indeed resemble a great wall. The angle incidence is so large that the mountainside has the appearance of a frontal surface. This is true whether it is seen from Togetsu Bridge or Kameyama Park, or in the past the Tenryū-ji.

It is said that the Emperor Kameyama (r. 1259–1274) planted the cherry trees here, having brought the seedlings from Mount Yoshino in Yamato province (Nara Prefecture). Later Ashikaga Takauji (1305–1358) is thought to have planted more cherry trees from Yoshino, as well as maple trees from Tatsuta. The following comment appears in another source:

To this place called Mount Arashi, [they] transferred seeds [sic] of cherry blossoms from Yoshino and, taking seedlings of maples from Yoshida, . . . transplanted a thousand so as to take care of the spring and the fall. The mountain is like yellow tie-dyed fabric; it is as though embroidered brocade had been spread on the ground.[4]

Though this description is not completely clear, the likening of the texture of the mountain to a dyed or embroidered fabric is a strikingly appropriate image. The effect results from the fact that the mountain forms a large surface with a high angle of incidence.

At one point the *Masukagami* ("Mirror of Increase") says, "The Tonase Waterfall looked just as though it were inside the palace walls."[5] The Tonase Waterfall was on Mount Arashi, and the sentence may be construed to mean that the mountain was a borrowed landscape, that appeared to be a part of the palace garden. By the distance standards set in

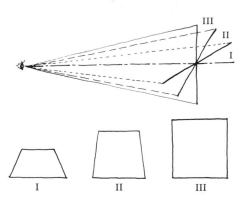

Figure 3.5
Visibility of a plane in relationship to its slope

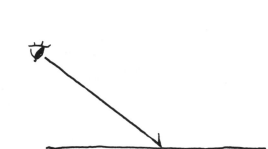

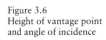

Figure 3.6
Height of vantage point
and angle of incidence

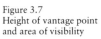

Figure 3.7
Height of vantage point
and area of visibility

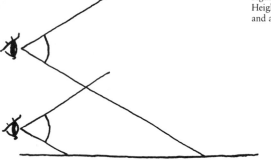

chapter 2, Mount Arashi was close enough to yield this visual effect. At the same time its angle of elevation (see chapter 4) when seen from the opposite side of the river is large enough to make it look more or less like a vertical barrier, so that the total appearance is that of a little world unto itself, stretching out to fill the field of vision. The Emperor Kameyama and Ashikaga Takauji picked a splendid place to plant their cherry trees and maples.

The slope of Mount Arashi is about 35 degrees. The angle of incidence is therefore 35 degrees at ground level. Since the angle of elevation at the summit is 20 degrees, the angle of incidence at this point is 15 degrees.

Mount Yoshino

Situated southwest of the city of Nara, Mount Yoshino is renowned for the beauty of its cherry blossoms. It is said that the following poem by Ki no Tsurayuki (c. 868–945 or 946) was the first to be composed on this subject:

Lines Sent to a Person in Yamato
Since I have not climbed
The Mountains of Yoshino,
I can do nothing
But listen to others talk
Of the cherry blossoms there.[6]

In the same tenth-century anthology in which this poem appears, there is another poem on the Yoshino cherry blossoms by Tsurayuki's cousin Ki no Tomonori (?–907).[7] It would seem therefore that the cherry blossoms had gained quite a reputation by Tsurayuki's day, and probably their fame dated back to much earlier times, for the *Man'yōshū* contains the following poem attributed to the Emperor Temmu (r. 672–686):

Good people of old
Looked oft at Mount Yoshino

And said that it was good.
Good people of our time,
Take a good look
At the good mountain of Yoshino!
Good people,
Take a good look![8]

The point that interests us here is that the beauty of the Yoshino cherry flowers is no doubt connected with the angles of incidence of the slopes on which they grow, as viewed from the usual observation points.

Three famous spots for looking at the cherry blossoms of Yoshino are Lower Sembon, Middle Sembon, and Upper Sembon. Sembon means literally "a thousand trees," but in this case it may be interpreted simply as a multitude. Lower Sembon is in the neighborhood of a slope known as "Seven Curve Hill," while Upper Sembon is on "Ninety-Nine Turn Hill." As suggested by these names, the slopes in question are very steep and present a wide angle of incidence to the viewer. Witness the fact that one of the special sights at Upper Sembon is a cascadelike stand of trees known as the "waterfall of cherry blossoms." No doubt the cherry trees in this area, like those on Mount Arashi, were planted by someone who understood how spectacular the blossoms would look on a steep slope with a large angle of incidence.

It is worth noting that the sharply curving roads leading up the slopes play an important part in the total view, for, unlike straight roads, a curving road through the mountains offers a succession of large and continually changing frontal views. As one climbs up the slopes at Yoshino, one's eye is met by a series of near-vertical planes, the texture of which is formed by the blossoming cherry trees on either side of the road. In the field of urban design this effect is spoken of as a folding screen (figure 3.8) or deformation.[9] It can be explained very clearly by reference to the successive angles of incidence.

A further point in Mount Yoshino's favor is that from the paths of ascent at Lower Sembon and, especially, Upper Sembon, one can look down across the cherry trees toward the valley below. Slopes of this sort make for a richly varied landscape. The best vantage point at Lower Sembon is one favored by the Empress Dowager Shōken (1850–1914) and hence known as the Empress Dowager's Retreat. Because of a slight curve in the ridge of the mountain, the slope of Lower Sembon is directly across a valley from here. The whole blossom-covered surface is taken in within a visual field ranging between an angle of elevation of 0.5 degree and an angle of depression of 30 degrees. Since the angle of slope here is about 30 degrees, the angle of incidence varies from 29.5 to 60 degrees, which is very large. Moreover the distance is at most 300 meters from the Empress Dowager's Retreat, so that each treetop is distinct down to its finer details.

Mount Yoshino proper is a horseback-shaped ridge carved out by the Saso and Seko Rivers, with Saso Valley on one side and Onsen ("Hot Springs") Valley on the other. Middle Sembon (figure 3.9) is the vicinity surrounding Onsen Valley. Here, too, there are steep slopes covered with cherry trees. The ridge of Mount Yoshino is parallel to another ridge on the other side of the valley, close to the top of which stands a temple called Nyoirin-ji; the slopes of the two mountains consequently face each other. Gorōbei Teahouse is near the top of a promontory projecting into the valley between the two. The three large surfaces to be viewed here present large angles of incidence and are covered with cherry trees.

The slope of the mountain on which the Nyoirin-ji is situated is 30 degrees or more. From Gorōbei Teahouse, the pagoda of the temple has an angle of elevation of 7 degrees, but no cherry trees are planted about the 3 degree line. As a result the angle of incidence

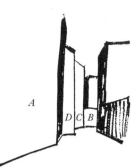

Figure 3.8
Facades appearing as large surfaces with large angles of incidence along a curving road (from Ivor de Wolfe)

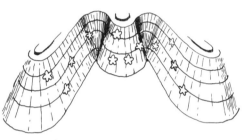

Figure 3.9
Middle Sembon

of this slope is 27 degrees or more. As in the case of Lower Sembon seen from the Empress Dowager's Retreat, the view is a short-distance one, having a depth of no more than 300 meters.

Mount Daimonji in Kyoto

Each year, on the night of August 16, a great bonfire in the shape of the Chinese character *dai* 大 , meaning "large," is lit on the side of one of the mountains to the east of the city of Kyoto. The event, which is said to have originated during the time of Toyotomi Hideyoshi (1536–1598), is a part of the annual Bon festival, a Buddhist celebration honoring the dead.

The great burning character, which can be seen from anywhere in the city, stretches from a point 280 to 350 meters above sea level. The slope of the mountain is no less than 32 degrees. It is doubtful that another site could be found in the general vicinity that is so clearly visible from the city and at the same time is near to a gently sloping area where preparations for such a gigantic bonfire can be made.

Residents of Kyoto say that the best place from which to view the flaming character is at the Kamo River on the east side of the city. From the Great Kamo Bridge the central part of the character has an angle of elevation of about 5 degrees, so that the angle of incidence is about 27 degrees (figure 3.10).

Green-Hedge Mountains

Since ancient times the expression, "green-hedge mountains lying layer upon layer," *tatanazuku aogaki* in Japanese, has been used epithetically in poems praising the country's beauty. An example is found in a famous poem attributed to the mythical hero Yamato Takeru no Mikoto:

Yamato is
The most excellent part of the land;
The mountains are green hedges
Lying layer upon layer.
Nestled among the mountains,
How beautiful Yamato is![10]

The space in question is a plain from any point on which the slopes of the surrounding mountains can be seen. To the agricultural communities of prehistoric times, the appearance of budding green leaves on the slopes signaled an end to the confinement of winter and the beginning of a new farming season. *Tatanazuku aogaki* is said to have contained an element of fetishism.[11]

The religion of the primitive Japanese was determined to a large extent by the terrain on which they lived. In a valley surrounded by green mountains, the people must at all times have been able to see, not far away, steep slopes with high angles of incidence.

Mount Arashi, Mount Yoshino, and Mount Daimonji have slopes of more than 30 degrees, and the angles of incidence are in the same general range. The Japanese Office of Economic Planning classifies inclines of 15 degrees or more as steep slopes. Slopes of more than 15 degrees but less than 35 degrees are regarded as quasi cliffs, and those of more than 35 degrees are classed as cliffs.[12] The mountains chosen here therefore would be considered quasi cliffs verging on cliffs.

A slope of less than 15 degrees appears more horizontal than vertical and performs the function of adding depth to the view; inclines of more than 15 degrees begin to function as vertical planes, and those of more than 30 degrees might for all practical purposes be considered as vertical. Since the appearance of the slope depends on the point from which it is viewed, the angle of incidence cannot be discussed in terms of the angle of slope alone. Still it offers an indication as to the visibility of inclining surfaces.

Figure 3.10
The burning character on
Mount Daimonji (Kyoto)

DEPTH OF INVISIBILITY

When a section of a landscape is invisible, the reason is either that it is too far away to be seen under current atmospheric conditions or that it is hidden by some other object. In measuring the depth of invisibility, we are concerned with the latter case, in which it becomes pertinent to know the size of the area blocked off and the depth to which it sinks below the line of vision.

Invisibility Resulting from Blockage

The degree of invisibility of an area can be indicated by the height of vertical lines dropped from the line of vision, as seen in figure 3.11. In this drawing D_A, D_B, and D_C represent the depth of invisibility of the points A, B, and C, respectively. In general this depth is related more closely to the distance of the barrier to the eye than to the size of the barrier. In figure 3.12, for example, it can be seen that an object of height H situated a certain distance from the eye produces the same depth of invisibility as an object of height $10H$ at ten times that distance from the eye. The nearer the obstacle is to the eye, the greater it is likely to affect the invisibility index. A small object very close to the point of observation can hide a very large area. This is particularly important in landscapes. The relationship is a simple proportion, but the effect on the view is very large.

Furthermore, when the obstacle is very close to the eye, slight differences in its height can cause enormous changes in the depth of invisibility beyond it. In figure 3.13 the depth of visibility caused by a wall of height A is much larger than that caused by a wall of height B, and that caused by a wall of height B is much larger than that caused by a wall of height C, although AB is equal to BC.

Kevin Lynch, having observed that cutting off the height of the obstacle at eye level causes the viewer to experience a feeling of vagueness and uncertainty, advises that walls ought to be either higher or lower than eye level.[13] One can interpret this as being a result of differences in the depth of invisibility. In any case, in designing landscapes, differences in this factor take on a special importance. The particular effect can be observed in a number of examples.

Design Techniques in Connection with Depth of Invisibility

The garden of the Shōden-ji in Kyoto is famous for its use of Mount Hiei as a borrowed landscape. As can be seen in figure 3.14, the earthen wall, about two meters tall, combines with the trees just outside it to cut off the view of everything between the garden and the mountain, which is about seven kilometers away. This effect was made possible because the Shōden-ji is situated on a slight eminence. A similar landscape is to be observed at the garden of the Entsū-ji, also in Kyoto. In this case there arise questions concerning the horizontal depth of the view, which will be touched on again in chapter 5.

Two techniques mentioned by Sylvia Crowe, though based on theoretical rather than real examples, can be explained and evaluated with reference to the depth of invisibility index. The first is diagramed in figure 3.15, where a sand dune eighteen meters high is seen to block off from view a cooling tower forty-five meters high and a factory thirty meters high. By measuring the depth of invisibility of the landscape when viewed by a person standing on the beach, it is possible to determine how high a building can be constructed inland without disturbing the view from the beach. The depth of invisibility can thus be used as a deciding factor when the aim is to protect a given landscape from unsightly structures. As shown in figure 3.16, it is possible to hide a group of large steel towers from view by making use of nearby trees.[14]

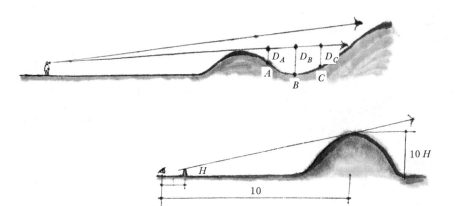

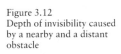

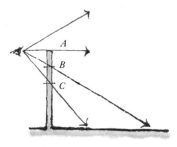

Figure 3.12
Depth of invisibility caused
by a nearby and a distant
obstacle

Figure 3.13
Varying depths of invisibility caused by walls of different height

Figure 3.14
The garden at the Shōden-ji, with Mount Hiei in the background (Kyoto)

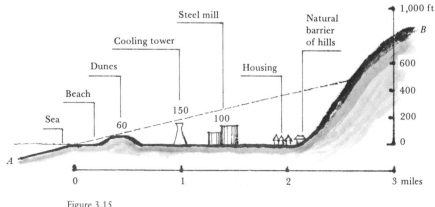

Figure 3.15
Depth of invisibility caused by a sand dune (from Sylvia Crowe)

Figure 3.17, taken from Gordon Cullen's studies on townscapes, demonstrates that, by lowering the level of a road, it is possible to hide electric power lines from view by placing them only a slight distance away from a highway.[15] As we make wider and denser use of the land, increasingly more problems arise in harmonizing development projects with the landscape. Environmental problems arising from a juxtaposition of an industrial plant with a scenic spot can often be solved by using the depth of invisibility index effectively.

Yet it must be stressed that depth of invisibility is only one of the many indexes that must be taken into consideration in the ecological protection of landscapes. Visibility or invisibility is not the only criterion for deciding whether a particular project damages the setting in which it is placed. In Hiraizumi, Miyagi Prefecture, the back side of a mountain was mercilessly cut away on the excuse that it could not be seen from the Mōetsu-ji, a famous temple site in the area; similarly, near Kamakura, which is bordered on three sides by mountains, the mountainsides not visible from the city itself were covered by a plethora of new housing. Elevated highways are permitted to cut through mountain settings when they are not actually visible from residential areas or lookout points. Developments of this sort harm the ecology in ways that have nothing to do with visibility.

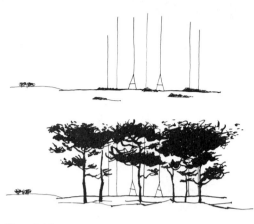

Figure 3.16
Trees hiding a group of steel towers (from Sylvia Crowe)

Figure 3.17
Careful landscaping suggested by Gordon Cullen

4

Space-Position Relationships

In general, places that are thought to afford good views are hills, mountains, or structures from which it is possible to look down on the surroundings. That views from above are popular in Japan is amply evident from the fact that on almost any mountain or hill that offers such a prospect there is an observatory platform of some sort. Looking downward, one's range of vision is large, and the view is panoramic. Because of the elevation the distance to the horizon is relatively great, and the relationships linking the physical elements of the landscape—mountains, rivers, plains, lakes, or the ocean—are clearly visible. It is often interesting to match the features of the visible terrain with a map of the region. Frequently the details are obscured, but one has the pleasure of being able to take in everything at once.

The basic nature of this landscape can be clarified by using an index called the angle of depression, which is the angle between the horizontal and the ray entering the eye from the object being viewed. Test studies carried out at Tokyo Tower, which has observation stations 150 and 250 meters above ground level, show an interesting relationship between the angle of depression and the ease with which certain objects can be seen.

Results of Experiment

From Tokyo Tower the landscape in any direction looked different from the upper platform than from the lower. This was only to be expected because the area visible from the higher platform is larger than that visible from the lower platform and consequently more stable in appearance. Of course, the principal element as seen from the higher point is farther away than as seen from the lower point.

Particularly interesting was the change in the appearance of Tokyo Bay. From the 150 meter level (figure 4.1) the surface of the

Figure 4.1
Tokyo Bay seen from the
150 meter observatory
platform at Tokyo Tower

Figure 4.2
Tokyo Bay seen from the
250 meter observatory
platform at Tokyo Tower

water looked flat, because of the relatively low angle of incidence. Ships laying in the harbor appeared to be more or less piled on top of one another. The sight of the bay and ships lacked visual stability and did not give the impression of spreading out panoramically at one's feet. At the 250 meter level (figure 4.2) the scene was very different. Although the bay was now too far away to be imagined as being "at one's feet," it occupied a more stable position in one's range of vision. The depth of vision was increased, as well as the angle of incidence presented by the surface of the water. Ships did not appear to be so closely stacked.

The whole of Tokyo is visible from the tower. Views in other directions were not so intrinsically interesting as that of the bay, but certain objects and sectors seemed particularly stable and easy to see at both the upper and lower levels.

When a hand level was used to measure the angles of depression of objects seen from the two platforms, these angles were found to be between 8 and 10 degrees. Applying this 8-to-10 degree range to the view toward the bay, from the 150 meter platform the view stretched from the bay to the townscape almost directly in front of the tower, and from the 250 meter platform it just barely reached the surface of the water ("just barely" is enough to explain the effects observed), for the bay was now in the easy-to-see range, as shown in figure 4.3.

Henry Dreyfuss, in his analysis of human factors in design, has come to the conclusion that the normal line of vision of a human being, when standing, is about 10 degrees below the horizontal and, when seated, is about 15 degrees below the hotizontal (figure 4.4). Dreyfuss considers the most suitable range for display to be from horizontal to 30 degrees below horizontal. These findings seem to confirm that an angle of depression of 8 to 10

degrees is indeed optimum for viewing landscapes from above, and not necessarily only for looking at a flat scene from Tokyo Tower. A depression of 10 degrees, it would appear, is based on a special feature of normal human vision; and a display range of 0 to 30 degrees indicates that people have a natural tendency to look down rather than up.

Landscapes viewable from above have a special appeal because they give the viewer the impression that he holds the landscape in his own hands, so to speak. If we accept Dreyfuss's observations, this phenomenon would result not only from the fact that an elevated viewpoint means a relatively large angle of incidence from a flat surface below but also that the natural line of vision can extend farther from the eye without encountering an obstruction.

By way of testing Dreyfuss's 10 and the 8-to-10 degree angles observed at Tokyo Tower, a random sampling of twenty-seven persons visiting the tower was conducted. The range at which these informants found the view to be easiest to see varied between 5 and 15 degrees, but the average was 9.4 ± 1.5 degrees, which agrees with the earlier findings.

Because the range included at an angle of depression of about 10 degrees is easy to see, in a view looked down on from above, the central object of attention tends to be lying in a range with a 10 degree angle of depression. When the angle of depression reaches 30 degrees, which is the limit of Dreyfuss's display range, it is at the bottom of the normal human visual range of 60 degrees and may be considered the lower boundary of a landscape viewed from above (figure 4.5).

Analysis of Ports and Lakes

A port presents a flat surface. In order to view it effectively, it is necessary to ascend to a height corresponding to a sufficiently large angle of incidence. When the natural terrain includes no hill high enough for this purpose,

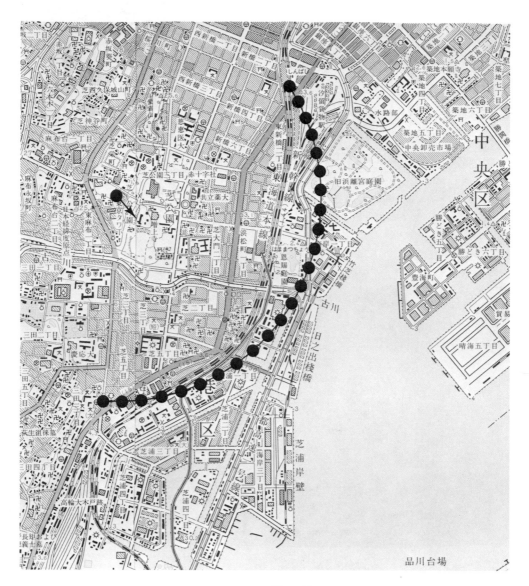

Figure 4.3
Map showing that the dot-
ted line representing a 10
degree angle of depression
from the 250 meter obser-
vatory platform at Tokyo
Tower reaches within a
very short distance of Tokyo Bay

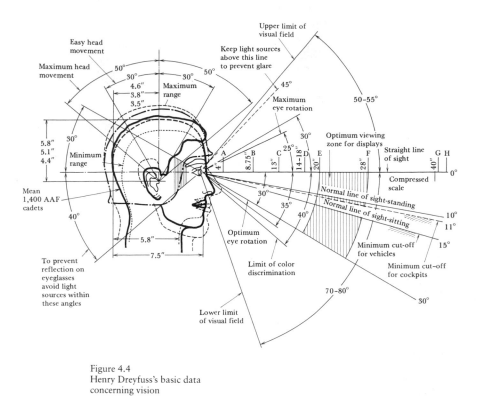

Figure 4.4
Henry Dreyfuss's basic data
concerning vision

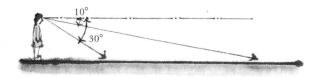

Figure 4.5
Angles of depression

it often happens in Japan that people build a marine tower or similar structure to serve as an observation platform.

After the experiments at Tokyo Tower, Shinohara Osamu carried out similar tests at the port cities of Mombetsu, Kushiro, Hakodate, Kamaishi, Yokohama, Kobe, Hakata, and Nagasaki.[2] His conclusion was, "The question of whether there is a feeling of tension with the port depends on whether the surface of the water lies within a line having an angle of depression of 10 degrees." Here, the expression "feeling of tension with the port" means a sense of visual oneness with the body of water in the harbor, or the feeling that the port is spread out at one's feet. When the water surface is farther away than the line representing a 10 degree angle of depression, the port appears to be "there," rather than "here." Two examples come readily to mind, one at Yokohama and one at Hakodate.

At a park in Yokohama looking down on the harbor (figure 4.6), the 10 degree line is obstructed by a series of warehouses and does not reach the surface of the water. Because of a series of reclamation projects in the bay, the viewer has no sense of visual unity with the water.

In the case of Hakodate the whole city and harbor are visible from the top of Mount Hakodate, and the view from here at night is one of the most splendid in the whole of Japan (figure 4.7). As can be seen from figure 4.8, the mountain slopes down sharply toward the city, providing a large unobstructed range of vision. The line representing a 10 degree angle of depression embraces the city and the harbor, and the visual structure is therefore such that the whole view spreads out at one's feet.

The situation with lakes is similar to that with ports. Being flat surfaces, they are best seen from nearby hills or mountains. Satō Hironori, having analyzed eight typical Japanese lakes, came to the following conclusions:

1. To maintain the visual relationship between the surface of the lake and the point where the viewer stands, it is necessary for the angle of depression to be 10 degrees.

2. When the lake extends beyond a point where the angle of depression is 2 degrees, the surface seems large, and the more distant parts of it lose clarity.

3. When the nearer part of a lake has an angle of depression of more than 30 degrees, the surface seems nearly directly below the viewer and may even cause him to have a fear of falling.[3]

Figure 4.9 shows the range of angles of depression for the eight lakes when they are viewed from representative vantage points. In only two cases, Lake Kussharo as viewed from Biboro Pass and Lake Akan as viewed from Semboku Pass, is the waterline farther away than a point corresponding to a 10 degree angle of depression. All others can be viewed at a depression angle of more than 10 degrees (figure 4.10). This confirms that lakes ought to be viewed from points where the nearer shore has a depression angle of 10 degrees or more.

Angle of Depression and Sense of Visual Nearness

The angle of depression largely determines whether the viewer senses an object to be near or far. As we have seen, an angle of 10 degrees marks the point at which a landscape, port, or lake begins to seem close by and constitutes the center of the view. The composition of the visual field laying between 10 and 30 degrees, the lower limit of vision, in fact, is larger than the portion laying beyond 10 degrees (figure 4.11). Yet people sense the area beyond 10 degrees to occupy most of their visual range, presumably influenced by the subconscious knowledge that this more distant area is, in an absolute sense, the larger.

With an angle of 10 degrees and an eye level of 1.5 meters, the line of vision of a person walking on a flat surface is 8.6 meters

Figure 4.6
The port of Yokohama seen
from Minato no Mieru
Oka Park (Kanagawa
Prefecture)

Figure 4.7
Night View of Hakodate
(Hokkaido)

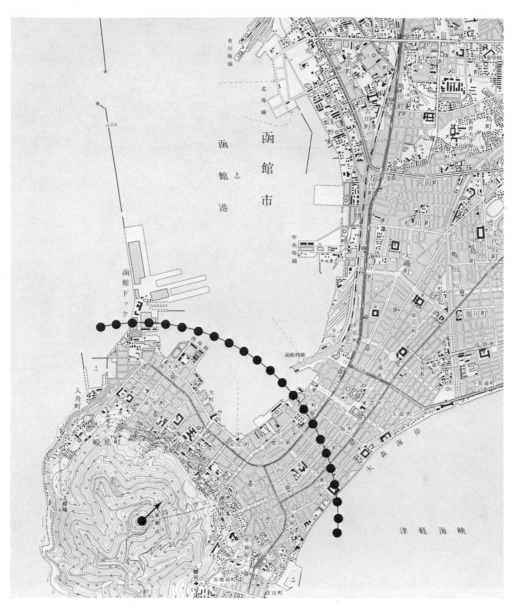

Figure 4.8
Map showing that the dotted line representing 10 degree angle of depression from the top of Mount Hakodate cuts across the town and harbor

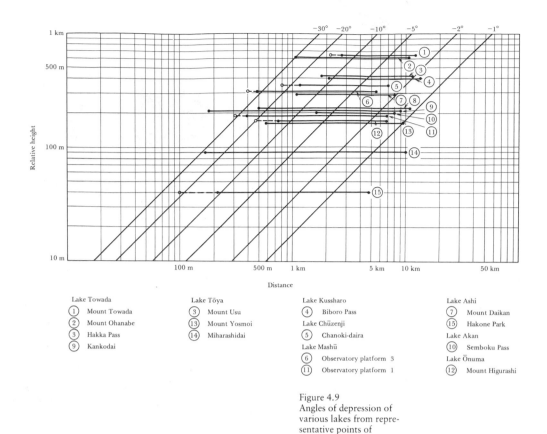

Figure 4.9
Angles of depression of
various lakes from repre-
sentative points of
observation

Lake Towada
① Mount Towada
② Mount Ohanabe
③ Hakka Pass
⑨ Kankodai

Lake Tōya
③ Mount Usu
⑬ Mount Yosmoi
⑭ Miharashidai

Lake Kussharo
④ Biboro Pass
Lake Chūzenji
⑤ Chanoki-daira
Lake Mashū
⑥ Observatory platform 3
⑪ Observatory platform 1

Lake Ashi
⑦ Mount Daikan
⑮ Hakone Park
Lake Akan
⑩ Semboku Pass
Lake Ōnuma
⑫ Mount Higurashi

long, and the point at which the line of vision strikes the surface is 8.5 meters in front of him. This, according to Dreyfuss, is the ordinary line of vision for human beings. As the eye level is raised, the distance between the viewer and the object increases. For example, at a height of 150 meters (the lower observatory platform of Tokyo Tower), the line of vision extends a distance of about 870 meters. The normal line of vision is much freer than on the ground, and the viewer experiences a sense of openness.

Gordon Cullen, in speaking of the concepts of "here" and "there," suggests that the borderline between them lies not at a point equidistant from the viewer and the horizon but at a point corresponding to an angle of depression half that of the horizon (figure 4.12, top).[4] The equiangular concept, however, seems somewhat arbitrary. As we have seen, when the waterline lies within the 10 degree range, we have a sense of oneness with the body of water or, in other words, feel it to be "here" rather than "there." The line of demarcation appears to be the locus of the point having a depression angle of 10 degrees rather than that corresponding to Cullen's equiangular theory (figure 4.12, bottom).

In determining the lower boundary of a landscape viewed from above, several factors must be taken into consideration: the 30 degree angle considered to be the limit of perfect color vision, the 44 degree angle representing the outer limits of vision when the gaze is steady, the 30 degree angle thought by Dreyfuss to be the lower limit of the display range, the 30 degree angle in which the head can be moved up or down without strain, and the 30 degree angle classed by Dreyfuss as the most suitable range for movement of the eyes.

The lower limit of the view is clearly different from the lower limit of the field of vision, for the former encompasses that which can be seen by moving both the head and the eyes whereas the latter includes only that which

Figure 4.10
Lake Mashū seen from Observatory 3 (Akan National Park, Hokkaido)

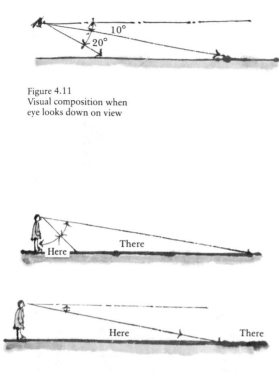

Figure 4.11
Visual composition when
eye looks down on view

Figure 4.12
Angle of depression and
concepts of "here" and
"there"

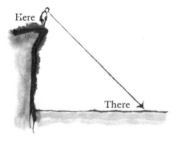

Figure 4.13
Limit of angle of depres-
sion and vertical sense of
"here" and "there"

can be seen when the eye gazes straight ahead. Our observations indicate that, even if the head is moved, people do not look fixedly at an object closer than the normal lower limit of the field of vision.

On level ground, when the eye is at a height of 1.5 meters, the range of vision corresponding to a depression angle of from 30 to 40 degrees is from 1.2 to 1.7 times the eye level height, or from 1.8 meters to 2.5 meters from the feet. Unless the viewer is standing on a cliff, this range is sensed as being immediately in front of him. When the point of view is elevated, the 30-to-40 degree range seems directly below, and the distinction between "here" and "there" becomes a matter of vertical distance (figure 4.13). Depending on the height of the viewpoint, this distinction can cause the viewer to shrink back for fear of falling.

ANGLE OF ELEVATION

A downward view is free and open whereas an upward view is limited and apt to be closed because the process of looking up at an object tends to limit the mobility of the human body and to cut off the line of vision at a point above the horizontal. With the most stable line of vision for the average person being about 10 to 15 degrees below the horizontal, it follows that the very process of looking up involves a certain amount of stress. Presumably this is why the term "look up to" connotes the idea of paying respect or reverence. "Looking up to" someone or something requires a visual effort.

Märtens's Rule

Märtens's discussion of the part played by the angle of elevation in viewing buildings and monuments called into question Sitte's analysis of the piazza.[5] He theorized that "to view the exterior of a work of art with ease, one must stand at a point where one's natural range of vision (which is to say, Augen Kegel's visual elliptical cone) encompasses the whole object while at the same time permitting one to discern individual parts of the object as details."[6] In short, Märtens took the objective position that the total aesthetic effect of a given object is related to the special characteristics of the human eye's range of vision and to the human being's visual powers. He defined the range of vision (the elliptical cone) in terms of an angle of elevation, an angle of depression, and lateral angles to the right and left: "The angle of elevation alone is the standard that determines whether a piece of architecture makes a good total first impression on us or not." Märtens considered that "the height of a building was more important than its width in determining its visual effect."

Märtens did not deal with the angle of depression, perhaps because the buildings and monuments that constituted the vista of the city rose above the horizontal planes formed by streets and plazas (figure 4.14):

As the viewer draws closer to a building from a relatively distant point, the building gradually emerges from its background and begins to create a "purely pictorial" impression. It first begins to take on monumental characteristics when its angle of elevation reaches 18 degrees. When this angle increased to 27 degrees, the building fills the range of vision, and the eye sees the larger details. Eventually, when the viewer reaches a point where the angle is 45 degrees, he is at the best place for observing the comparatively small details (plant motifs, for example).[7]

Since from physiological optics the upper limit of the angle at which the building would come to occupy the whole field of vision is about 30 degrees, Märtens's theory is justified with respect to the angles of 27 degrees (obviously calculated from the fact that the distance from the viewer would be approximately double the height of the building) and 45 degrees, but the basis for the angle of 18 degrees is less clear. Perhaps it

Figure 4.14
Changes in the appearance of a building as the angle of depression varies

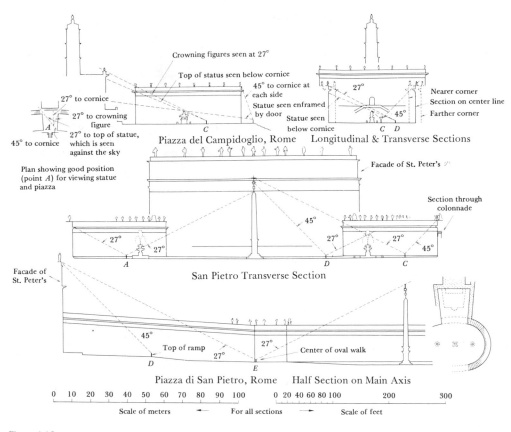

Crowning figures seen at 27°

Top of status seen below cornice

45° to cornice at each side

Statue seen enframed by door

Statue seen below cornice

27° to cornice

27° to crowning figure

27° to top of statue, which is seen against the sky

45° to cornice

Plan showing good position (point *A*) for viewing statue and piazza

Piazza del Campidoglio, Rome

Longitudinal & Transverse Sections

Nearer corner
Section on center line
Farther corner

Facade of St. Peter's

Section through colonnade

San Pietro Transverse Section

Facade of St. Peter's

Top of ramp

Center of oval walk

Piazza di San Pietro, Rome   Half Section on Main Axis

| 0 | 10 | 20 | 30 | 40 | 50 | 60 | 70 | 80 | 90 | 100 |

Scale of meters   For all sections

| 0 | 20 | 40 | 60 | 80 | 100 | | 200 | | 300 |

Scale of feet

Figure 4.15
Hegemann and Peets's
analysis of a Renaissance
piazza

represents the point at which the distance of the viewer from the building would be about three times the height of the building—an interval that presumably would be in accord with actual experience. In any case Märtens's acute observations have been accepted and supported by experiments of numerous planners and designers.

Is the Märtens's rule applicable to landscapes? Would it hold if mountains were the objects viewed, rather than buildings? These questions revolve about an enormous difference in spatial scale. Märtens was concerned with urban spaces and a human scale involving a visual range of 21 to 24 meters.[8] When Werner Hegemann and Elbert Peets applied Märtens's principle to an actual urban area, they were working with a Renaissance piazza (figure 4.15), which, as Camillo Sitte had pointed out, involved distances of no more than 135 meters.[9] Ashihara Yoshinobu called the object of his studies "exterior space in architecture."

Landscapes, however, stretch out over intervals ranging from several hundred meters to ten or more kilometers, and the mountains viewed vary in height from a few hundred meters to a few thousand. There is perhaps little reason to quarrel over the angles of 30 and 45 degrees, which are backed by optical theory, but smaller angles are another matter. Since Märtens's figure of 18 degrees appears to have been derived experimentally and lacks theoretical support, it seems appropriate to repeat the experiment by examining the angles of elevation of various mountains as seen from the gardens or other observation points from which they are normally viewed.

Analysis of Mountainous Landscapes

Although a view of a mountain involves an angle of elevation, not all views are of the same type. It is one thing if the mountain rises

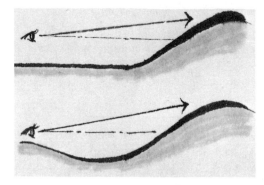

Figure 4.16
Two types of views of mountains

from a flat area on which the observer is standing but quite another if the observer is separated from the mountain by a valley or depression, in which case the addition of an angle of depression to the angle of elevation makes the mountain appear larger and more impressive (figure 4.16). For the sake of simplicity, as well as to facilitate comparison with Märtens's theory, the discussion here is confined to angles of elevation of mountains rising from flat surroundings. Some of the mountains chosen were consciously employed as borrowed landscapes by the designers of gardens; others simply happened to be visible from gardens designed before the concept of the borrowed landscape came into existence.

It was found that the mountains observed (figure 4.17) fell into the following three classes:

1. Mountains having an elevation angle of 20° or more:
Mount Daimonji (upper middle reaches, where the torches in the great burning character come together) seen from the Silver Pavilion at the Jishō-ji—31.5°,
Mount Shiun seen from the Ritsurin-en—22°
Mount Arashi seen from the Tenryū-ji (figure 4.18)—20° to 20.5°.

2. Mountains having elevation angles of between 5° and 15°:
Mount Buttoku seen from the Phoenix Hall of the Byōdō-in (figure 4.19)—10°,
Mount Asahi seen from the Phoenix Hall—8°,
Mount Otowa seen from the Shirakawa-in of the former Hosshō-ji—10°,
Higashiyama (the Eastern Mountains of Kyoto) seen from the Shirakawa-in—8°,
Mount Kasuga and Mount Hana seen from the Daijō-in in Nara—6.5° and 8°,
Mount Kinugasa seen from the Golden Pavilion at the Rokuon-ji—10°,
Jaya Peak seen from the site of the Shūrin-ji—12°,
Mount Hiei seen from the Entsū-ji—7.5°,
Mount of Lanterns and the mountain of the Kōdai-ji seen from the Jōjū-in at the Kiyomizu-dera in Kyoto—10° and 12°,
Mount Hiei and Mount Daimonji seen from

the Sanshi Suimei-dokoro—6° and 6.5°,
Middle peak of Sakurajima seen from the Sengen-en in Kagoshima—7.5°,
Mount Nosaka seen from the garden of the Shibata Residence—10°,
Mount Ibuki seen from the garden of the Daitsū-ji—5.5°,
Higashiyama seen from the Murin-an—10.5°,
Mount Daimonji seen from the Seifū-sō—7°,
Mount Wakakusa and Mount Kasuga seen from the Isui-en in Nara—9° and 9.5°.

3. Mountains having angles of elevation of less than 5°:
Mount Hiei seen from the Shōden-ji—4.5°,
Mount Takamado and Mount Shiro seen from the Jikō-in in Nara—2° and 2°,
Mount Sō seen from the Kōraku-en in Oka-yama—4°.

The great majority of these mountains have elevation angles in the range between 5 and 12 degrees. If the three mountains having elevation angles of more than 20 degrees and the two having elevation angles of 2 degrees are omitted, the average for the remaining twenty-two is 8.3 ± 1.1 degrees.

It is interesting to compare these figures with the angles of elevation of some of Japan's most celebrated peaks as seen from the observation points traditionally associated with them:

Mount Fuji from Tagonoura—9°,
Mount Fuji from Sengen Shrine—11.5°,
Mount Fuji from Lake Yamanaka (figure 4.20)—11°,
Mount Fuji from Oshinomura—11°,
Mount Fuji from Lake Kawaguchi—9°,
Mount Yōtei from Kuchan—10°,
Mount Iwaki from Hirosaki—6°,
Mount Iwate from Morioka—5.5°,
Mount Chōkai from Kisakata—10°,
Mount Chōkai from Fukura—8°,
Mount Bandai from Inawashiro—13°,
Mount Tsukuba from Makabe—8.5°,
Mount Nantai from Senjōgahara—12°,
Mount Asama from Miyota—10°,
Mount Haruna from Shibukawa—7°,
Mount Daisen from Ōkamiyama Shrine—7°,
Mount Ishizuchi from Komatsu—9.5°,
Sakurajima from Kagoshima—10°.

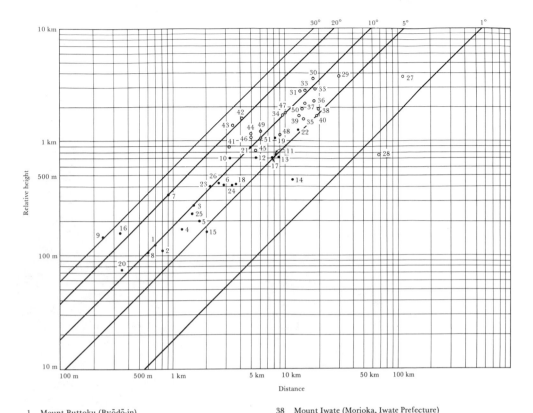

1 Mount Buttoku (Byōdō-in)
2 Mount Asahi (Byōdō-in)
3 Mount Otowa (Hosshō-ji, Kyoto)
4 Higashiyama (Hosshō-ji, Kyoto)
5 Mount Kasuga (Daijō-in, Nara)
6 Mount Hana (Daijō-in, Nara)
7 Mount Arashi (Tenryū-ji, Kyoto)
8 Mount Kinugasa (Golden Pavilion, Kyoto)
9 Mount Daimonji (Silver Pavilion, Kyoto)
10 Jaya Peak (old Shūrin-ji, Shiga Prefecture)
11 Mount Hiei (Daitoku-ji, Kyoto)
12 Mount Hiei (Entsū-ji, Kyoto)
13 Mount Hiei (Shōden-ji, Kyoto)
14 Mount Shiro (Jikō-in, Nara)
15 Mount Sō (Kōraku-en, Okayama Prefecture)
16 Mount Shiun (Ritsurin, Takamatsu)
17 Mount Hiei (Sanshi suimei-dokoro, Kyoto)
18 Mount Daimonji (Sanshi suimei-dokoro, Kyoto)
19 Sakurajima (Sengen-en, Kagoshima)
20 Mountain of the Kōdai-ji (Kiyomizu-dera, Kyoto)
21 Mount Nosaka (Mr. Shibata's garden, Fukui Prefecture)
22 Mount Ibuki (Garden of the Daitsū-ji, Shiga Prefecture)
23 Higashiyama (Murin-an, Kyoto)
24 Daimonji (Seifū-sō, Kyoto)
25 Mount Wakakusa (Isui-en, Nara)
26 Mount Kasuga (Isui-en, Nara)
27 Mount Fuji (Nihombashi, Tokyo)
28 Mount Tsukuba (Fukagawa, Tokyo)
29 Mount Fuji (Tagonoura, Shizuoka Prefecture)
30 Mount Fuji (Fujinomiya, Shizuoka Prefecture)
31 Mount Fuji (north side of Laka Yamanaka, Yamanashi Prefecture)
32 Mount Fuji (Oshinomura, Yamanashi Prefecture)
33 Mount Fuji (north side of Lake Kawagushi, Yamanashi Prefecture)
34 Mount Yōtei (Kuchan, Hokkaido)
35 Mount Iwaki (Hirosaki, Aomori Prefecture)
36 Mount Chōkai (Kisakata, Akita Prefecture)
37 Mount Chōkai (Fukura, Akita Prefecture)

38 Mount Iwate (Morioka, Iwate Prefecture)
39 Mount Daisen (Ōkamiyama Shrine, Shimane Prefecture)
40 Mount Daisen (Yonago, Shimáne Prefecture)
41 Mount Kaimon (Hirakiki Shrine, Kagoshima Prefecture)
42 West Hodaka Mountains (Kappabashi, Gifu Prefecture)
43 Front Hodaka Mountains (Kappabashi, Gifu Prefecture)
44 Mount Bandai (Inawashiro, Fukushima Prefecture)
45 Mount Tsukuba (Makabe, Ibaraki Prefecture)
46 Mount Nantai (Senjōgahara, Tochigi Prefecture)
47 Mount Asama (Miyota, Nagano Prefecture)
48 Mount Haruna (Shibukawa, Gumma Prefecture)
49 Mount Ibuki (Lake Mishima, Gifu Prefecture)
50 Mount Ishizuchi (Komatsu, Ehime Prefecture)
51 Sakurajima (Kagoshima)

Figure 4.17
Chart showing distribution
of angles of elevation for
various mountains as seen
from observation points associated with them (in parentheses following the
names of the mountains)

Figure 4.18
Mount Arashi seen from
the Tenryū-ji (Kyoto)

Figure 4.19
Mount Buttoku seen from
the Phoenix Hall of the
Byōdō-in (Kyoto)

Figure 4.20
Mount Fuji seen from Lake
Yamanaka (Yamanashi
Prefecture)

The average angle of elevation for these twenty examples is 9.1 ± 1.5 degrees. One would suppose that the visual incline would be steeper at these famous landmarks than when these mountains are viewed farther away, from gardens (or often from rooms facing on gardens), but actually there is very little difference. By way of contrast, where the angle of elevation is exceptionally large, as of the Hodaka Range seen from Kappa Bridge (21 to 22.5 degrees, figure 4.21) and Mount Nantai seen from the shore of Lake Chūzenji (17.5 degrees, figure 4.22), the mountains are not of the sort that are thought of as a part of the everyday scene in which people live and work but rather special sights that travelers from afar go to see. From the figures given, the angle of elevation of 8.7 ± 1.0 degrees, which is the average for mountains viewed from gardens and mountains viewed "in the rough," appears to be the norm and characteristic of Japanese landscapes as a whole.

When the elevation angle is in the range of 8 to 10 degrees, the mountain is valued because of its appearance as a mountain. In cases where the elevation angle is lower than 5 degrees, it functions more as a variation in the skyline. If the elevation angle is much higher than 15 degrees, the mountainside becomes a more important element than the mountain as an entity.

At the Golden Pavilion the view is expansive enough to cause a writer of earlier times to remark, "The appearance of the moutains is particularly attractive. To be away from the city and gaze upon the mountains in the distance is an indescribably happy experience."[10] On the other hand, at the Silver Pavilion, where the angle of elevation of the neighboring mountain is between 23 and 31.5 degrees, one has the feeling that one is confronting an immensely steep barrier.[11] There is no long-range view, and the space has an austere Zen quality, resembling that of the rock gardens at the Saihō-ji.

Figure 4.21
The Hodaka Range seen from Kappabashi in Kamikōchi (Chūbu Mountains National Park, Nagano Prefecture)

When one views Mount Shiun from the bridge that overlooks the Kikugetsu Pavilion and the South Pond, the mountain functions not as a mountain but as a wall setting off the landscape in front of it. The angle of elevation here is 22 degrees. In the past a similar situation must have existed at the Tenryū-ji where Mount Arashi, as viewed across Sōgen Pond from the garden of the priest's residence, was said to resemble an "embroidered brocade," a textured backdrop of sorts. This effect is lost today because the trees in the garden block off from view everything but the top of the mountain. The statement in the *Masukagami* ("Mirror of Increase") suggesting that a waterfall on Mount Arashi appeared to be a part of the garden reinforces the conjecture that the wall-like mountainside was the central feature from the gardener's vantage point. Mount Nantai as seen from the Tachiki Kannon Temple at Nikko (18 degrees) produces the same general effect, though in this case the fact that the mountain is free-standing lessens the viewer's sense of being closed in. In contrast, the Hodaka Range seen from Kappa Bridge seems overwhelming in its massiveness. From these examples it would appear that an angle of elevation in the range of 18 to 20 degrees does not, as Märtens suggests with regard to art objects, permit us "to see the work as part of the total scene" but rather has the effect of the 27 degree elevation angle that Märtens ascribes to architecture. Thus at 18 degrees, rather than 27 degrees, the mountain fills the range of vision, and the eye sees the larger, massive character of the slopes.[12]

When the angle of elevation is very low, the mountain can hardly become the subject of a painting unless it has a startling skyline. The Jikō-in temple in Nara, for example, is on an eminence overlooking the Yamato Plain. For the distant mountains (elevation angle of 2 degrees) to seem larger, to prevent the landscape from dispersing, the sky, which would normally occupy most of the visual field, is cut off by the use of long, low-hanging eaves on the building from which the scene is usually viewed (figure 4.23). That Mount Fuji and Mount Tsukuba, which when viewed from Edo (now Tokyo) have elevation angles of only 2 and 1 degrees, respectively, were difficult subjects for artists is evident from the numerous devices Hokusai and Hiroshige employed in their prints to make the mountains stand out. Though Fujiwara Seika (1561–1619) included the two peaks among the four great beauty spots of eastern Japan ("anyone who does not visit them has not lived," Seika decreed), they are so distant that they are frequently not visible from Tokyo, and, when they are, they occupy only a tiny portion of the skyline.

Under the circumstances the figure of 9 degrees suggests itself as the approximate angle of elevation for viewing mountains in general. This value is close to the 10-to-12 degree range that Märtens classed as *reinmalerisch*, or suited to the purposes of the painter. When the angle is less than 5 degrees, it becomes necessary to employ some special means of making the mountains function effectively as a distant view; when it is in the neighborhood of 20 degrees, the profile of the mountain is not indiscernible, but, unless it is particularly beautiful, its slopes are likely to attract more attention than its overall shape. It may be added that, in the course of making this study, it was noted that when the angle of elevation is less than 4 to 5 degrees, most people seem to take in the whole view of the mountain easily without moving their heads up and down.

Laboratory Tests

To test the conclusions suggested by this examination of mountainous landscapes, an experiment was carried out with an eyemark recorder, which indicates shifts in the point on which a person's vision is focused.[13]

Figure 4.22
Mount Nantai seen from
the shore of Lake Chūzenji
(Nikko, Tochigi Prefecture)

Figure 4.23
The eastern mountains of
Nara seen from the *shoin*
of the Jikō-in (Nara
Prefecture)

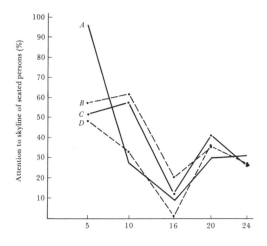

Figure 4.24
Percentage of attention devoted to looking at the skyline (seated informants)

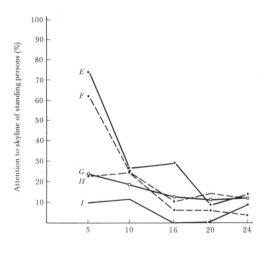

Figure 4.25
Percentage of attention devoted to looking at the skyline (standing informants)

It stands to reason that, when a person views a number of landscapes having different angles of elevation, the point on which his vision is concentrated tends to vary. When the angle of elevation is large, the viewer is likely to focus on the mountainside rather than the part forming the skyline. When, on the other hand, the angle of elevation is small, the tendency is to look at the skyline, which can easily be taken in without moving the eyes up and down. As in the case of Märtens's art object there exists a point at which the whole view can be taken in with maximum facility.

In the experiment undertaken, a number of people were shown mountains with different angles of elevation, and the distribution of the focal points of their vision was analyzed by an eyemark recorder. Because of the difficulty of actually visiting a number of different mountains, the experiment was held indoors with slides, which included four shots of two mountains in the vicinity of Mount Fuji and one of a mountain in the Tsukuba range. The angles of elevation were 24, 20, 16, and 10 degrees in the case of the former and 5 degrees in the case of the latter. The size of the projection was adjusted so that it occupied a visual angle of 62 degrees, or slightly more than the normal 60 degree range of vision, and the slides were varied at random. Four persons were asked to remain seated, and five watched from a standing position. The results, obtained by use of a film analyzer, were as indicated in figures 4.24 and 4.25.

For the seated participants there was a distinct drop in the degree of concentration on the skyline in the vicinity of an elevation angle of 16 degrees, the figure for this angle of elevation being even smaller than for 20 and 24 degrees. The reason for this seems to be that, as the angle approached the higher range, the informants shifted their position, leaning back on their chairs so as to be able to look upward more easily. The tentative conclusion is

method but whether one uses it to analyze the subject or not and whether the result of the analysis can be used as a means of planning a better space."[16] What use is made of the classifications given here will, "of course, depend on the imaginative powers of the person who uses them."[17]

5

Visual Perception of Space

Landscapes, of course, are three-dimensional spaces in which some objects are nearer and some farther away from the viewer. What determines the visual perception of three-dimensional spaces? To answer this and other related questions, it is convenient to set up as an index a property that we call depth. Depth is an effect, first, of a continuous change in the surface of the terrain and, second, of atmospheric perspective or the overlapping of objects viewed. Depth in the former sense has a fundamental connection with all three-dimensional spatiality; in the latter sense it plays a particularly large role in Japanese landscapes.

DEPTH AS A VISUAL RESULT OF SURFACE CHANGES
Gibson's Theory of the Visual Perception of Space

J. J. Gibson's theory of the visual perception of space which attributes the sense of depth to a continuous change in the surface of the terrain is of particular importance to our discussion. His basic idea was stated as follows: "There is literally no such thing as a perception of space without the perception of a continuous background surface."[1] In other words, it is not the object we are looking at that gives us a visual sense of space but the object's background. The idea is reminiscent of the experienced perception and the brain pattern of Gestalt psychology, as well as of the manifest and the nonmanifest in the study of phenomenology.

As was noted earlier in the discussion of the angle of incidence, the surfaces we view can be divided into two types, frontal and longitudinal. The longitudinal planes, parallel to the line of vision, are associated with our perception of depth. Gibson assumed that these planes would be perceived as having a textural density gradient, which is to say, a gradual rise in the density of the texture as the distance from the viewer increases.[2]

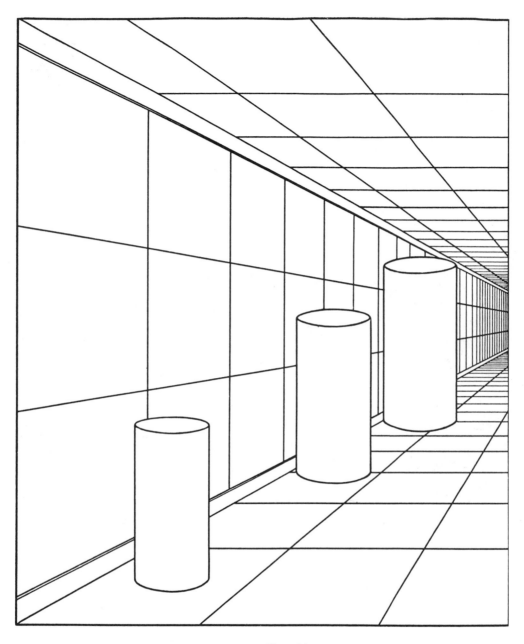

Figure 5.1
Diagram showing how
our sense of three-
dimensionality is governed
by the background, rather
than the principle objects
we see (from J. J. Gibson)

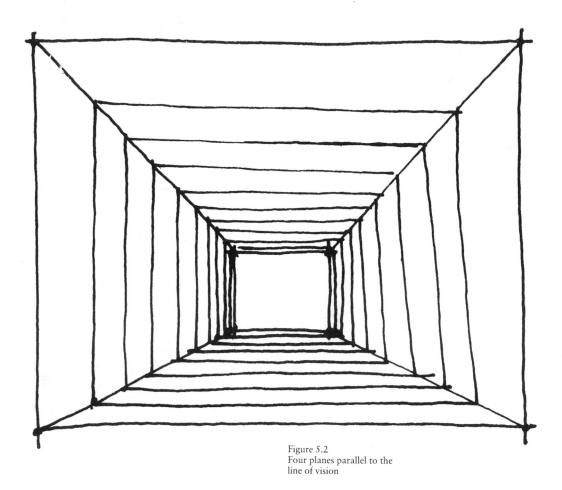

Figure 5.2
Four planes parallel to the
line of vision

In figure 5.1, presented by Gibson as an illustration, if it were not for the floor, ceiling, and wall, all of which are planes with a textural density gradient, what we would see would be no more than three cylinders of identical size. The gradually increasing density of the linear textures in the planes gives a sense of depth and causes the cylinders to cease to appear the same. In short, the background, rather than the objects, has created a spatial order. Gibson's theory is applicable to landscapes, townscapes, and architectural structures, in all of which the background is formed by continuously changing surfaces.

Terrain Surfaces in Landscapes

In a building four planes are parallel to the line of vision—one above, one below, one to the right, and one to the left (figure 5.2). In landscapes, however, we generally consider only three since the upper part of the view is open sky. Exceptions would be caverns or tree-lined vistas in which the branches come together overhead.

If, as in figure 5.3, a plane with an easily discernible textural density gradient is added to the barren space (a), the result is space (b), which has depth. The addition of similar planes on either side yields (c), where the impression of depth is even stronger. Type (c) is found in places where mountains close in on long valleys from either side. Japan, whose numerous mountains tend to have jagged outlines, has countless such valleys, and in many instances the quiet, darkish inner recesses were regarded by the ancients as the concealed abodes of dead spirits. Even today one often finds a shrine or a temple in a deeply receding valley behind a community situated in the foothills of a mountain.

The sense of depth that a landscape evokes, then, is governed by the structural composition of the planes parallel to the line of vision and by the density gradient of the textures of these planes. Even if the physical depth re-

Figure 5.3
Diagrams indicating how a sense of depth is produced by longitudinal planes with textural density gradients

mains the same, the degree of depth perception will depend on whether the landscape is a meadow, a body of water, a dense collection of buildings, a desert, a heavily wooded area, or a snow-covered terrain.

As compared to a body or water or a snowscape, a longitudinal surface covered by trees or rock or houses or large paving blocks will have a more pronounced depth, because the density gradient of the texture is more prominent. On the other hand, if the textural unit is too small, the density gradient becomes difficult to discern. A plaza paved with small cobblestones can become a sea of little rocks, in which the density gradient is not obvious to the eye. In such cases depth can be achieved by arranging the stones in large regular patterns, thus creating a new texture of which the density gradient stands out more clearly (figure 5.4). Similarly, the visual depth of a flat stretch of water becomes more apparent when it is dotted by boats and ships (figure 5.5).

In a photograph furnished by Superstudio (figure 5.6), introducing a grid on the flat surface between the people and the hills in the background produces a scene that seems very different in scale from the same picture without the grid.

To emphasize the depth of the landscape as it actually is, to make the depth seem even greater, or to create illusions of depth and scale, all of these are valuable techniques for the landscape designer. When illusion is desired, the textural surface is all-important.

In this connection mention should be made of longitudinal planes as they appear in perspective drawings. In figure 5.7, an object of width W is placed across a longitudinal plane below the line of vision. As the distance D from the eye to this object increases, the width W in a perspective drawing becomes $w \propto W/D$, and the depth segment V becomes $v \propto V/D^2$. The height H of an object at distance D is $h \propto H/D$. Thus, while the width and height are reduced at the rate of $1/D$, the length of the depth segment is reduced at the rate of $1/D^2$, with the result that the density gradient of the depth segments is very high. This means that the length of the depth segment becomes much harder to perceive with increasing distance than does its width (figure 5.8).

In landscapes the only truly flat surfaces are those of bodies of water. So-called "flatlands" have few stretches of terrain with completely flat surfaces. Even when there are only tiny obstacles along the horizontal surface, at a distance they can easily conceal the terrain beyond and make invisible areas, though the depth of invisibility may be small.

While the surface of the longitudinal plane is a ruling element in depth perception, the surface can be blocked off from view by relatively small obstructions. This helps explain why horizontality and verticality in ordinary landscapes is easier to perceive than depth.

Having seen how the texture of the terrain affects the apparent depth of landscapes on level ground, it remains for us to examine briefly what happens when the ground is sloping, convex, or concave, or when there is a distant borrowed landscape.

Depth and Sloping Surfaces

In our discussion of the angle of incidence we observed a qualitative difference between the visual effect of a gentle slope in front of the viewer and that of a steep one. An angle of incidence of about 15 degrees was taken as the line of demarcation between gentle and steep slopes. In our perception of space this means that, when the slope in front of the viewer inclines at an angle of less than 15 degrees, its surface falls in the general category of longitudinal planes parallel to the line of vision, but, when the angle is greater than 15 degrees, the slope is seen more or less as a frontal surface.

Figure 5.4
Textural density gradient
created by arranging small
paving stones in large regular blocks (Komazawa
Park, Tokyo)

Figure 5.5
Depth created by ships
lying at anchor (Tokyo
Bay)

67　*Visual Perception of Space*

Figure 5.6
Landscape in which scale
has been altered by inser-
tion of a grid (photo by
Superstudio)

Figure 5.7
Perspective character of
longitudinal surface parallel to line of vision (from
J. J. Gibson)

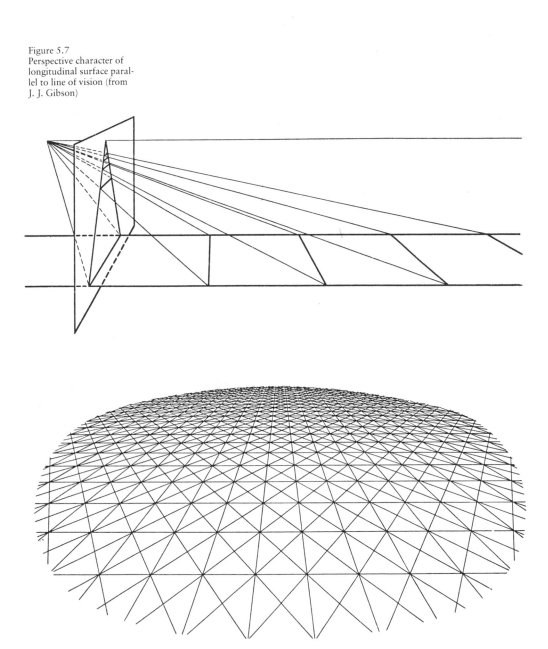

Figure 5.8
Perspective of a longitudinal plane parallel to the
line of vision (from J. J.
Gibson)

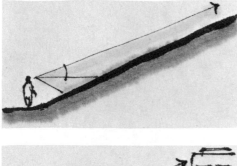

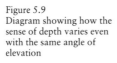

Figure 5.9
Diagram showing how the
sense of depth varies even
with the same angle of
elevation

When the angle reaches 30 degrees, the slope might for all practical purposes be considered vertical.

It follows that, when the slope of the surface exceeds 15 degrees, the viewer feels himself to be looking at a frontal plane, and his perception of depth is minimal. This may very well account in part for the sense of visual oppression that one experiences when climbing mountains.

In figure 5.9 the angle of elevation is the same in (a) and (b), but in (b) the plane in front of the viewer is completely vertical, and, since there exists a plane parallel to the direct line of vision, the viewer feels a sense of depth. There is not therefore as great a sense of visual obstruction as in (a). It is obvious from the drawings that vision is much more limited in (a) than in (b), and that the quantity of visible space (the darkened area) is correspondingly smaller.

The visual tension that mountain climbers experience then is not simply lack of depth caused by the verticality of the slope; this tension is also related to the position of the eye with respect to the surface, so that it is greatly reduced when there exists an intervening plane parallel to the direct line of vision, for this plane produces a sense of depth.

The designs of a number of important Japanese landmarks produce an effect similar to that illustrated in figure 5.9 (a). Noteworthy among these are the Ise Shrine, the Okunoin at Mount Kōya, and temple and shrine stairways in general.

The Ise Shrine, the most sacred of Japanese Shinto shrines, is divided into an outer shrine, dedicated to a food goddess, and an inner shrine, dedicated to the sun goddess. At present ordinary visitors are allowed to penetrate only as far as the south gate in the outermost of four fences surrounding the main building in the inner shrine. From this point they look up toward the sanctuary through a white

Figure 5.10
Entrance to the Inner
Shrine at Ise (Mie
Prefecture)

Figure 5.11
Mausoleum of Kōbō
Daishi, the Okunoin at
Mount Kōya (Wakayama
Prefecture)

cloth hanging in the gateway (figure 5.10). What they can see through the cloth as it flutters in the wind is a graveled path leading up to the south gate in the next inner fence. The angle of elevation is 3.5 degrees, and from a comparison of this figure with the ground plan, it would appear that the slope of the gravel-covered incline is about 6 degrees. A slope of 6 degrees is equivalent to about 1:10, which falls into the category that Kevin Lynch says "appears gentle."[3] It may be assumed that by achieving a delicate balance between visual obstruction and depth, this graveled incline enhances the air of sacredness surrounding the inner shrine.

At the mausoleum of Kōbō Daishi (774–835), which is in the Okunoin at Mount Kōya (figure 5.11), the method employed is similar to that at the Ise shrine. Here the point at which people worship is sunk to about shoulder level, so that the gravel path leading up to the building starts directly before the viewer's eyes. The slope of this path is around 5 degrees (figure 5.12). Even though the incline is gentle, the device of dropping the point of view greatly adds to the spiritual dignity of the mausoleum.

Many Buddhists believe that they can acquire special virtue by making pilgrimages to certain sets of temples (the thirty-three temples to Kannon in the Kansai Region, for example), and, when they undertake a project of this sort, they customarily receive a paper marker or a red seal from each of the establishments in question to prove that they have been there. It happens that such temples are often in the mountains and must be approached by way of steep stone stairways. By use of the diagrams shown in figure 5.13, Ashihara Yoshinobu made it clear how the design of such stairways affects the viewer's sense of depth.[4] In case (a) there is little impression of depth, and the effect is one of high visual tension accompanied by expectancy

(figure 5.14). In case (b) there is less obstruction, and the sense of depth is increased (figure 5.15). A majority of the pilgrimage temples appear to have stairways that belong to type (a). Typically, the angle of elevation is between 20 and 40 degrees, with the result that the stairway rises sharply before the eye and cuts vision off short. Examples are found at the Ishiyama-dera (31 to 34 degrees), the Mii-dera (25 to 28 degrees), the Hase-dera (10, 17, and 20 degrees), the Juntei-dō at Upper Daigo (30 degrees), the Seiganto-ji at Nachi (30 to 40 degrees), and the Main Hall of the Murō-ji (22 degrees). Pilgrims are forced to climb these stairways because the places where they receive their paper markers or red seals are invariably at the top.

Depth and Concave Terrains

The presence of a concave terrain between the viewer and a mountain has a remarkable affect on depth perception. Let us consider first the case in which the longitudinal plane parallel to the line of vision has a relatively slight concavity, as when a mountain is seen across a plain from another mountain (figure 5.16). Clearly, the space viewed from above appears larger than that viewed from below; so more of the terrain separating the viewer from the mountain can be seen. Accordingly, the angle of incidence for this area is larger, while the density gradient of the textural units revealing depth is comparatively small. Individual units are therefore easy to see. The viewer's line of vision naturally descends to the terrain and then rises up to the top of the mountain, so that the transition in the terrain is observed in one continual eye movement. The effect of the concavity is to make the view more majestic.

Kojima Usui (1873–1948), a well-known mountain climber, remarked on the difficulty of choosing the best place from which to view Mount Fuji: "Of the places I have seen in my travels, there are four from which I find it dif-

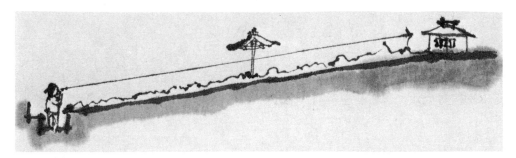

Figure 5.12
Diagram showing the slope
leading up to the mauso-
leum of Kōbō in the Oku-
noin at Mount Kōya

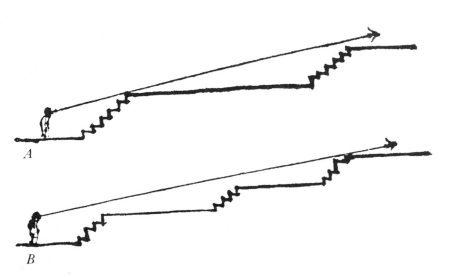

A

B

Figure 5.13
Depth as affected by two
series of stairways (from
Yoshinobu Ashihara)

Figure 5.14
Stairway and depth, case
(a) of figure 5.13

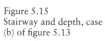

Figure 5.15
Stairway and depth, case
(b) of figure 5.13

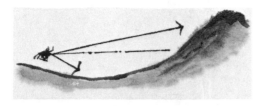

Figure 5.16
Concave terrain

ficult to choose just one. These are Otome Pass in Hakone (figure 5.17), Misaka Pass in Kai (figure 5.18), the Ryūge-ji in Suruga, and Daruma Pass in Izu (the pass between Shuzenji and Heda). The last is the least known, but probably the best."[5] Of Kojima's four viewpoints all save the Ryūge-ji in Suruga are separated from Mount Fuji by concave terrains.

From Misaka Pass, where the novelist Dazai Osamu (1909–1948) found the view so perfect as to be "embarrassing," one looks across Lake Kawaguchi at Fuji.[6] From Daruma the view is across Suruga Bay. In both places the composition of the landscape is tight and pictorially well-organized. At Otome Pass the bathhouse-wall-painting prettiness is missing, but the majesty afforded by the intervening concave terrain is impressive.[7]

Figures 5.19 and 5.20 show the views from Otome Pass and Tagonoura in perspective drawings. While in each case the horizontal distance from the peak of the mountain is about twenty-five kilometers, the vantage point chosen at Otome Pass is 1,101 meters above sea level but at Tagonoura only 20 meters above sea level. The sides of each box in the perspective grid are 500 meters. These are classic views of Mount Fuji as seen across a concave terrain and from level ground. The special features of the intervening continuous terrains are brought out by the way in which the 500 by 500 meter grid units show up in the drawings. The proportion of the visual field taken up by the foreground differs greatly in one view from the other. In the case of the concave terrain the grid units do not all grow larger at once, but instead start large, gradually decrease in size to the point where the slope of the mountain increases sharply, and then grow larger again. This is the reason for the dynamic grandeur of the view. In the same way the angle of incidence of the individual units first decreases, until it reaches a

Figure 5.17
Mount Fuji seen from
Otome Pass (Shizuoka
Prefecture)

Figure 5.18
Mount Fuji seen from Mi-
saka Pass (Yamanashi
Prefecture)

77 *Visual Perception of Space*

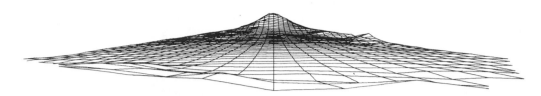

Figure 5.19
Perspective drawing of
Mount Fuji seen from
Otome Pass

Figure 5.20
Perspective drawing of
Mount Fuji seen from
Tagonoura

Figure 5.21
Visual unity with objects
across a deep valley
(Mount Yoshino, Nara
Prefecture)

minimum, and then increases. The charm of the view across a concave terrain derives from the continuous change in the appearance of the unit grid.

The situation is very different when the drop in the concave terrain is very deep, as when the intervening area is a gorge or deep valley sloping sharply upward toward the point where the viewer stands (figures 5.21, 5.22). In this case the base of the concavity is not visible, and one sees the mountainside beyond more or less as a frontal plane. Since the terrain linking the viewer to the mountain is shut off from view, the viewer is able to judge the distance only in terms of the size of known objects on the mountainside, which also is apt to be seriously affected by atmospheric changes. When the weather is fair, the mountain seems nearby; when the weather is poor, it seems remote. Because of the invisibility of the intervening concavity, the foreground is greatly abbreviated, with the rather paradoxical result that the link between the eye and the mountain is strengthened. The viewer feels himself to be face to face with the mountainside across from him. If the mountain is within the middle-distance range and visibility is good, he is apt to feel extremely close to it.

Depth and Convex Terrains

If there is a crest in the landscape relatively near the observation point, an area behind the crest will not be visible, and the continuous terrain needed for depth perception will be cut off at the top of the crest (figure 5.23). The crest itself is likely to be a rising slope of the kind that makes depth perception difficult. Although the mountain constituting the main object of view projects above the crest, it appears illusive. As a result the viewer is not able to judge the distance to this mountain. The viewer's perception of this distance will be influenced further by atmospheric condi-

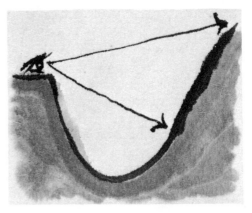

Figure 5.22
Deep drop in a concave terrain

Figure 5.23
Convex terrain

tions: if the visibility is good, the top of the more distant mountain will seem to draw closer to the crest.

Figure 5.24 gives a view of the peak of Mount Fuji as it is seen from an existing road. With only slight changes in the flat plane and section it would be possible to increase depth perception greatly and create a much more tangible view, making the illusory mountain appear real.[8]

Visual Obstacles and Borrowed Landscapes
It has been observed that the viewer's sense of depth and distance is lost when there is an area of invisibility between the viewer and the object. This area might be a deep valley, a crest, or anything that cuts off the longitudinal plane linking the viewer with the view.

Excellent examples of this principle at work are the borrowed landscape gardens at the Entsū-ji and the Shōden-ji, both of which are temples in Kyoto. The Entsū-ji, which is oriented eastward, toward Mount Hiei, is situated on a plain that rises very gradually to-toward the foot of the mountain. The peak of Mount Hiei is six kilometers away and has an angle of elevation of 7.5 degrees, which makes it suitable for viewing. The garden is bordered by hedges less than two meters high but tall enough to conceal the terrain stretching out in the interval between the garden and the lower part of the mountain. Those who have caught glimpses of Mount Hiei on their way to the Entsū-ji are astonished upon entering the garden to find that the mountain looks completely different. The reason is that from the garden side of the hedge Mount Hiei is divorced from distance and depth, so that it constitutes not a distant physical feature of the terrain but a visual part of the garden space.

Valleys and Depth Perception
It was pointed out earlier that the viewer's sense of depth is particularly strong when he is looking through a valley because of longitudinal planes below and on both sides of his line of vision (figure 5.25). This sense of depth plays an important role when the valley, or a valleylike space, serves as an approach to a landmark, as, for example, the mountains at Kumano which press in on the gap leading from Hamanomiya to Mount Nachi. The same effect may be seen on the approach from the Great Gate to the Okunoin at Mount Kōya, though it is obscured today by the presence of many houses along the way. At both Kumano and Mount Kōya the visitor's sense of depth is increased by the fact that the approach is not straight but winding.

Mount Yoshino, famous for its cherry blossoms, has an uncanny ability to entice the visitor farther and farther into its recesses.[9] The reason lies in the heightened sense of depth that results from valleys and mountain ridges running parallel to the path of approach. Since landscape designers have to make use of natural topographical features, it is difficult for them to achieve the reverse perspective seen at Michelangelo's Campidoglio or the intricate optical illusions of Bernini's Scala Reggio. Special depth effects are even more difficult to achieve on flat ground, where it becomes necessary to use buildings or trees to create longitudinal planes not present in the natural terrain. This artificial approach is particularly in evidence in André le Nôtre's park at Versailles.

ATMOSPHERIC PERSPECTIVE
When the air is dry and clear, distant mountains appear to be nearby; when it is misty, nearby mountains appear to be far away. By the law of atmospheric perspective, turbidness in the air causes the appearance of things to change. The farther away an object is, the lower the quantity of visible light coming through from it.

Weather conditions and lighting have a subtle effect upon the way things look. In

 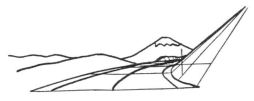

Figure 5.24
Illusionary mountain with
summit projecting above a
crest (left) and the same
mountain made real by a
sense of depth perception
(right)

Figure 5.25
Kurobe Gorge (Chūbu
Mountains National Park,
Toyama Prefecture)

landscapes they bring about constant changes in apparent spatial depth:

When the floating bridge
Of the dream of a spring night
Was snapped, I awoke:
In the sky a bank of clouds
Was drawing away from the peak.
—Fujiwara no Teika (1162–1241)[10]

At the mountain's ridge,
Where the bright moon is rising
Into a clear sky,
A single bundle of clouds
Hesitates, then fades away.
—Eifuku Mon-in (1271–1342)[11]

While the effect of atmospheric perspective on depth perception cannot be determined in any quantitative terms, it, nevertheless, plays an important role in creating mystic or fantastic settings with its constant changes and transformations (figure 5.26).

Shiga Shigetaka observed this to be one of the special features of Japanese landscapes, due to "the presence of large quantities of water vapor."[12] Neither the constant changes of nature nor the distinguishing characteristics of Japanese landscapes can be discussed without reference to atmospheric perspective.

Of the 134 spring poems in the *Kokin wakashū* ("Collection of Ancient and Modern Poems"), 13 mention the mist in spring; in the *Shin kokin wakashū* ("New Collection of Ancient and Modern Poems"), it is 24 out of 174.[13] Whether there is mist or rain, atmospheric perspective makes the scenery seem deeper or more distant than it actually is. It is interesting to observe the effect in a number of specific locations.

In a book called *Kankōchi no hyōka shuhō* ("A Method for Evaluating Scenic Attractions"), Suzuki Tadayoshi and his colleagues list changes caused by the weather as one of thirty-six criteria.[14] In doing so, they point out that there are a number of scenic spots whose beauty is enhanced, rather than obscured, by rain or mist. Among the places given high rating in this respect are Oirase, Yabakei, the Koke-dera, and Nagasaki. In these locations the textures of the treetrunks, boulders, moss, or the stone paving are brought out by the rain, and mist from the rain has the effect of adding a sense of depth and distance.

One has only to go to Oirase to see how effective a rainy landscape can be. Oirase is a narrow valley where depth perception is cut off by the trunks of thickly growing trees—a valley that might be described as being on a human scale. Without water it loses most of its charm. The same, in general, is true of Yabakei, which is physically small but seems to have impenetrable depths.

Nagasaki for its share consists of an inlet with mountains crowding in from both sides. The mountains are in a seeing-and-being-seen relation to each other, and it is difficult to escape a somewhat claustrophobic effect when the weather is fair. But when it rains, the visual depth of the space seems to increase, and psychological oppression is diminished.

Other spots selected as good for viewing in the rain are Sōun Gorge, the part of Toro Gorge known as Torohatchō, Shiraito Falls, Nachi Falls, Matsushima, Shōdojima, the Amakusa Islands, the Chūson-ji, Nikko, and the Ise Shrine. In all these places the atmospheric perspective that results from rain or mist adds depth and awesomeness of a kind that is easy to feel but difficult to describe.

DEPTH RESULTING FROM THE OVERLAPPING OF ELEMENTS

When two objects overlap, the one of which a part is hidden is recognized as being behind and therefore farther away than the others. For this reason overlapping leads to a certain sense of perspective (figure 5.27). In distant landscapes overlap perspective may play an

Figure 5.26
Mount Arashi and Togetsu
Bridge (Kyoto)

Figure 5.27
Overlap perspective

83   *Visual Perception of Space*

important part in depth perception, particularly when, as in Japan, the typical landscape contains mountains that rise in numerous ridges. It is worth mentioning in this connection that a number of words meaning "mountains in layers" or something to that effect are commonly used in Japanese descriptions of natural settings.

Japanese garden designers employ a method called *miegakure*, which means "now you see it, now you don't." This relies heavily on the principle of overlapping perspective and involves making only a part of an object visible, rather than exposing the whole. The purpose is to make the viewer imagine the invisible part and thus create not only an illusion of depth but also the impression that there are hidden beauties beyond. *Miegakure* is, in short, a means of imparting a sense of vastness in a small space.[15]

In ancient Japanese the word *kumade* meant a space hidden behind a bend or curve. *Yasokumade*, "eighty *kumade*," was the name used by the *Kojiki* and the *Nihon shoki* for the road to the land of the dead, Yomi. The boundary between Yomi and the real world was called Yomotsuhira Hill. In other words, the land of the living and the land of the dead were separated only by a hill or mountain, but the approach was a long winding path.

Kumano, in Wakayama Prefecture, has since the medieval period been a mecca for Japanese religious pilgrims. Originally, the name, which is related to *kumade*, signified a hidden place deep in the mountains where dead spirits dwelled. It is generally thought that with the spread of Pure Land Buddhism, in the eleventh and twelfth centuries, this hidden country came to be thought of as the paradise to which the Buddha Amida transported dead believers.[16] The concealed place among "Kumano's 3,600 peaks" thus became the habitat of the all-saving Buddha.

The Pure Land Buddhists developed a form of painting in which Amida is shown flying down on a cloud with a host of attendants to greet a dying believer. A modified version of this type, called "Amida Crossing the Mountain," portrays the Buddha rising over a range of rolling mountains (figure 5.28). Of such paintings, Origuchi Shinobu commented: "Since the ridge of a group of mountains is present, the basic condition for the Pure Land *hensō* [painted representation of Amida's paradise] is fulfilled. We see here then a purely Japanese version of this genre."[21]

Perhaps we might conclude that, if one attempts to envision the other world as occupying an infinitely broad space, one is led to the concept of a heaven in the sky, but, if one tries to find the other world in a mountainous country like Japan, one naturally imagines a Kumano, or *kumade*, hidden among the impenetrable mountains.

The Japanese idea of depth then is not something that extends infinitely into space but something hidden behind the bend, so to speak. In examining Japanese urban spaces, one rarely finds the magnificent straight vistas of Baroque architecture. Even when there are straight passageways, they often terminate, in the fashion of the classic teagarden paths, in a corner beyond which one cannot see.

Figure 5.28
Painting of the "Buddha Amida Crossing the Mountain" (Collection of the Zenrin-ji, Kyoto)

6

Summary of the Visual Structure of Landscapes

Up to this point we have developed the formal procedure to be used in clarifying the visual structure of landscapes in terms of various Japanese landscapes. In this summary we outline an experimental application of this approach and problems that remain for future consideration.

CASE STUDY

By using the visibility index, we can ascertain which parts of a given landscape are visible and which are not. The distance index enables us to classify the visible parts as short-, middle-, and long-distance views. From these indexes we discover the visibility of the landscape's texture.

By reference to the angle of incidence, we can discern which planes should be taken as frontal and which as longitudinal, or, in other words, the relative visibility of the planes in the landsacpe. The same index, set at a value of 0 degrees, tells us where the skylines, ridges, or lake shores that form the boundaries of the landscape are. By examining the angles of depression or elevation of these boundaries, we can determine their visibility in terms of whether or not they fall within ranges that the human eye can see with ease. The depth of invisibility index helps us to clarify further the texture of the landscape as a visual structure, as well as the visibility of surfaces and boundaries. The light index (not discussed earlier) would show the frequency with which sunlight falls on a given object from the front, from behind, and from the sides.

By ascertaining the distances and elevation angles of surfaces having large angles of incidence, we can decide whether the visual space is open or closed. Questions concerning the apparent depth of the visual space can be considered in terms of the textural density gradient of longitudinal planes having low angles of incidence, as well as in terms of atmospheric perspective. By discovering at what points the angle of depression falls to 10 degrees or rises to 30 degrees, we can analyze the space-position relationship between the point of view (here) and the object viewed (there). In short, by combining indexes, we are able to clarify the spatiality of a landscape as a visual structure (figures 6.1 through 6.3).

How these indexes are applied in the actual process of planning is illustrated by an analysis undertaken in the course of reviewing plans for the development of Shiga Heights, part of a national park in Nagano Prefecture.

The area in question, which extended about 5 kilometers on the east–west axis and 10.9 kilometers on the north–south axis, was first reproduced (with the aid of a computer) into a digital terrain model with a 100 meter mesh.

Analysis 1

Within this national park, which is a popular tourist attraction, there are four main lookout points where visitors come to view the scenery. The purpose of the study was to analyze the view from these four stations with an eye toward improving the future plans for the park.

The first step was to delineate the area of visibility from each of the four observation points and determine the visual angles of incidence within these areas. Seen in figure 6.4 are the results for one of the points, indicating areas having angles of incidence of 14 degrees or more and 30 degrees or more. These areas are the most prominent and should therefore be left untouched insofar as is possible. The shaded parts of the map are areas where the old plan called for constructing resort facilities; since these include part of the terrain having a high angle of incidence, the old plan requires revising. Such installations as have already been constructed in this sector should be redesigned and reconstructed in such a way as to harmonize with the natural surroundings. The same applies to areas having a visual

angle of depression of 10 degrees, since they also stand out prominently.

The points at which the visual angle of incidence is zero degrees represent the skyline surrounding the area. This must not be disturbed by the construction of buildings that would alter the natural flow of the contours.

Even in invisible areas, attention must be paid to the depth of invisibility. Where the depth is slight, even a small building might become an eyesore. As it happens, the whole area is subject to a 13 meter height limitation. It should therefore be sufficient to permit new construction only in areas having a depth of invisibility of 15 meters or more.

Analysis 2

A second step is to determine inconspicuous locations for new facilities. By combining the charts showing the areas of visibility from the four observation stations, it is possible to make a map on which possible sites are graded from one to five according to frequency of visibility. By taking into consideration other factors—angle of incidence of visible areas, the number of visitors to each of the lookout stations, distances of sites from stations—the desirability of various sites can be graded even more finely. Figure 6.5 shows the areas whose visibility frequency is zero, which is to say, the areas that cannot be seen from any of the four observation stations. These are obviously the best sites for future construction.

Analysis 3

Whereas the first two analyses were concerned with visibility from the four lookout posts only, in actual fact it is necessary to take into consideration visibility from highways or hiking routes or the resort hotels themselves. To compile the necessary data from all possible points, however, would be a staggering task; it is therefore more practical to select a

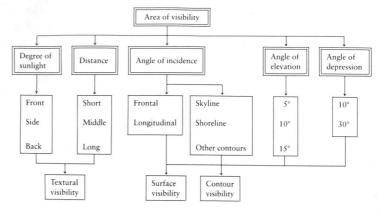

Figure 6.1
Visibility of landscapes

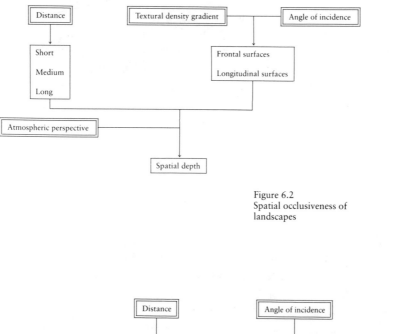

Figure 6.2
Spatial occlusiveness of
landscapes

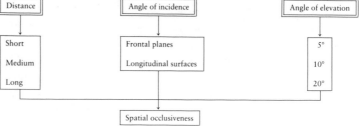

Figure 6.3
Spatial depth of landscapes

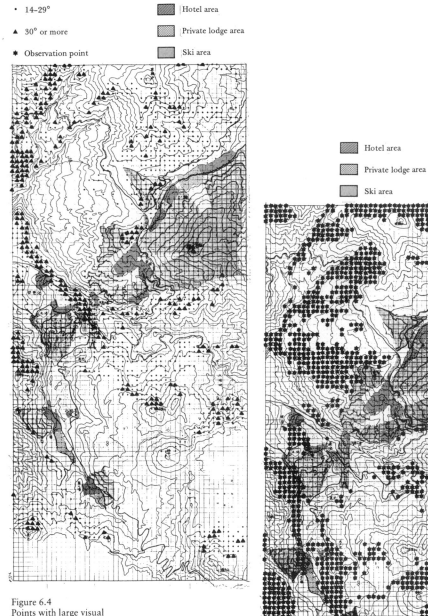

- • 14–29°
- ▲ 30° or more
- ✴ Observation point

- ▨ |Hotel area
- ▦ |Private lodge area
- ▨ |Ski area

Figure 6.4
Points with large visual
angle of incidence as seen
from Mount Tōdate obser-
vation point

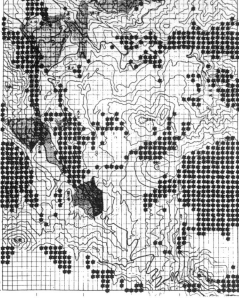

- ▨ Hotel area
- ▦ Private lodge area
- ▨ Ski area

Figure 6.5
Points with zero visibility
frequency

few likely building sites and examine their visual spheres of influence. This is relatively easy, because if point *A* is visible from point *B*, point *B* is also visible from point *A*. To determine the places from which point *A* can be seen, it is necessary only to determine what can be seen from point *A*.

As is demonstrated in figure 6.6, there are sites that, while having a low visibility frequency from the four observation stations, nevertheless have large visual spheres of influence. These should be eschewed in favor of sites such as are illustrated in figure 6.7, which can be seen from only a comparatively small area.

Given that the aim is to preserve the visual purity of the natural setting, the three analytical processes outlined here offer a means of determining the optimum sites for man-made structures in areas such as Shiga Heights.

PROBLEMS FOR THE FUTURE
One of the problems that remain is to examine the affect of color and form on visibility and visual attractiveness. One suspects that the key to the solution in this case lies in applying the principles of Gestalt psychology to landscapes in order to ascertain how different forms and colors alter one's perceptual experience of landscape structure.

Another subject requiring study has to do with visual spatiality. Specifically, more work needs to be done with respect to the illusion of depth created by landscape compositions. A question that is barely touched upon is the relationship of such aesthetic concepts as proportion, symmetry, balance, contrast, harmony, rhythm, and continuity to the visual structure of landscapes.

Our discussion of landscapes in terms of visibility, or ease of vision, which is fundamental to the visual structure, and factors that make landscapes integral visual spaces leads to the larger concept of the landscape as a thing of beauty. Perhaps our findings will serve as a foundation for further study of the aesthetic meaning of landscapes.

A fundamental question is, Just what sort of landscapes do people consider beautiful? We discover certain special qualities in a setting, and from time to time we see places in which these outstanding characteristics have been incorporated in creative fashion into the lives of the inhabitants. It is in such instances that we rejoice not only in the faithfulness of the view to its topographical features but also in its appropriateness to the living needs of human beings.

As Jay Appleton has stated recently in *The Experience of Landscape*, "the satisfaction which we derive from the contemplation of this environment, and which we call 'aesthetic,' arises from a spontaneous reaction to that environment as a habitat, that is to say, as a place which affords the opportunity for achieving our simple biological needs."[1] In considering landscapes, we must regard them as potential habitats and analyze their aesthetic meaning from this angle.

This is not, however, a matter of purely visual structure. It also involves spatial structure and the psychological image evoked by this structure, for the structure is not a thing unto itself but rather a concept or concatenation of concepts taking form in the human mind. By developing the brilliance of the image and harmonizing it with the needs and purposes of mankind, we create aesthetically satisfying habitats.

Japan is a mountainous country where the terrain creates an enormous variety of spaces. The outstanding feature of Japanese landscapes, then, is that they are spaces resulting from topographical variation. In the pages that follow we shall attempt, by adopting a historical approach, to discover the images that the Japanese people have read into various topographical formations and the ways in which they have made these images and formations a part of their everyday lives.

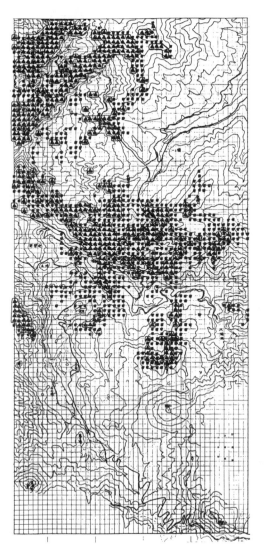

Figure 6.6
Visual sphere of influence
of Hasuike area

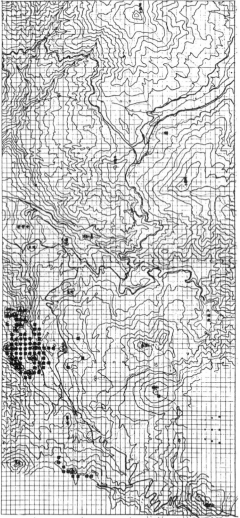

Figure 6.7
Visual sphere of influence
of Ishinoyu area

II

*Spatial
Structure of
Landscapes*

7

Types of
Spatial
Structures

We now turn to examine landscapes as spaces composed of topographical features, to discover what sort of spaces exist, what the character and significance of each type of space are, and what constitutes the spatial structure of the spaces under consideration.

As Norberg-Schulz has pointed out, space exists on several different levels.[1] At the most intimate level comes the interior space of houses and other architecture. Next there is composite space—urban space, for example—formed by buildings and gardens or buildings and buildings. Determining the foundation for such space is landscape space, composed of elements in the natural terrain.

In the past, when human beings were enveloped by nature and subject to its whims, the character of the natural terrain played a decisive role in determining the spaces in which they lived. Even their religious beliefs were governed by the geographical features surrounding them, which overawed them and moved them to worshipful acts and attitudes.

But as man lost his religious feeling toward nature, as he acquired the power to change the natural features around him, he gradually ceased to take deep consideration of the terrain. In his cities houses were crowded together, superhuman structures were raised, and the environment was mechanized; the natural lay of the land was to all intents and purposes forgotten.[2] Insensitivity toward nature led to the deformation of nature.

Yet, though we have lost our deep regard for the terrain, it continues to exist as the ground on which our architectural contrivances are founded. It continues, as it were, to speak to us in terms having spatial significance. If we do not have the ears to hear, we shall doubtless go on despoiling and denuding the land on which we live.

In Japan, which is largely mountainous, the typical natural setting is likely to involve a wealth of variety—elevations and depressions, winding contours, lakes, and forests. In contrast to great plains or deserts, such settings have great significance with respect to spatial composition. Instead of serving merely as the ground or backdrop for man's activities, they tend to function as spatial designs.

In discussing Japan's ancient shrines and temples, farming and fishing villages, or old imperial capitals, it is impossible to describe the spaces involved without reference to the natural terrain. The spatial composition of the Ise Shrine, for example, cannot be explained without taking the surrounding mountains and the Isuzu River into account, any more than Kyoto can be explained without mentioning the mountains on the east, west, and north, and the Kamo River.

In the ensuing pages, we shall deal with a number of landscape types that the Japanese of the past chose as living spaces—spaces where imperial capitals, Shinto shrines, Buddhist monasteries, burial mounds, or gardens were constructed. Our concern will focus on the spatial composition of the terrain and on its significance in the lives of the people. The aim is to discover just how the natural topographical features functioned as part of the spatial environment.

From documentary evidence and direct observation, we have abstracted seven classical types of landscape spaces, for which we have tried to analyze the compositional features and spatial elements:

1. The Akizushima-Yamato type. A valley is enclosed on all sides by green mountains rising in layers. In the valley is a broad, fertile meadow, watered by a clear stream. In Japanese mythology, Jimmu, the first emperor, carried out a military campaign to the east and established his capital in "a beautiful land, surrounded on all four sides by green mountains." Called Akizushima, this area represented a utopian ideal of the ancient Japanese. It was a haven protected from invasion by the mountains and suitable for the cultivation of rice in wet fields.

2. The eight-petal lotus blossom type. In the Womb Mandala, held in particularly high regard by Esoteric Buddhists, the Cosmic Buddha is seated on an eight-petal lotus blossom representing the womb of the universe. A number of Japanese Buddhist establishments are situated in highland valleys which, together with surrounding peaks, suggest the lotus blossom configuration. The great priest Kūkai (774–835) spoke of such a setting as a "secluded plain, surrounded by high peaks and untrod upon by man." The type differs from Akizushima-Yamato in that it is high in the mountains and remote from the everyday world.

3. The Mikumari Shrine type. A river or rivulet flows down through the mountains. At the point where water is first drawn off for use in the wet rice fields below, which normally coincides with the point where the steep slope of the mountains gives way to the gentler slope of foothills, there is a shrine to the god who distributes water. Fields spread out in the basin below in a relatively narrow meadow bordered on each side by mountains. The river divides the fields from the sacred ground occupied by the shrine. This is a classic Japanese image of a small farming community in the mountains, a type of landscape that to most Japanese seems familiar and nostalgic.

4. The secluded valley type. A river flows down through a narrow valley with relatively high mountains on either side. The inner recesses form a secluded space, which is apt to have a mysterious, otherworldly atmosphere about it. In the past settings of this sort were often regarded as the home, or the approach to the home, of dead spirits.

5. The zōfū-tokusui type. The name signifies literally "storing-wind acquiring-water," and the concept, current among ancient Chinese and Japanese geomancers, was of a site where "the vital energy that flows throughout the earth is confined by water and not scattered by the wind." In practical terminology, this amounted to a plain with mountains on the north, hills to the east and west, and open land to the south, with rivers flowing down from northeast and northwest and converging south of the plain. The classic example in Japan is Kyoto, which was the nation's capital

from 794 to 1868, but the same pattern is found in many other Japanese settings. Geomancy aside, a site of this type has certain obvious advantages.

6. The sacred mountain type. A small mountain rising from a plain or projecting into it from a more distant mountain range was often regarded as sacred by the Japanese of the past. Since a mountain of this type can be seen from any point on the plain, it provides focus and order for the surrounding space.

7. The domain-viewing mountain type. As in the case of the sacred mountain type, a small mountain is situated near a plain or juts out into it from other mountains. The difference is that the sacred mountain type is looked up to as an object of worship, whereas the domain-viewing mountain serves as a vantage point from which to look down on the surroundings.

Japan has steep, rugged mountain ranges, down whose slopes run thousands of short, rapidly flowing streams. The roughly 30 percent of the country's area in which the people choose to live are the valleys, basins, and plains through which these waterways run. The characteristics of these flatlands form what the Japanese people regard as proper, or even ideal, places to live.

Our studies have led us to the discovery that the spatial patterns observed in such homelands can be grouped in a definite number of types. Among these the Akizushima-Yamato and eight-petal lotus blossom formations are more or less round basins surrounded by mountains, described in Japanese as tray lands (*bonchi*); the Mikumari Shrine and secluded valley settings are narrow valleys or gorges; the *zōfū-tokusui*, sacred mountain, and domain-viewing mountain terrains lie at points where basins or plains meet the skirts of mountains.

The significance and spatial composition of each of these types are discussed in the following chapters, and an attempt is made to analyze the environment created by each of them. These seven types are considered to be fundamental to the Japanese terrain. Nearly every topographical space in Japan is either a variation of one of these types or a combination of two or more of them.

8

The Akizushima-Yamato Type

The *Nihon shoki* relates how the legendary first emperor of Japan, Jimmu, fought his way toward the east in order to find the proper place to establish his empire. Before undertaking his campaign, the emperor describes his ideal as follows:

Now I have asked the Ancient of the Sea, and he said, "In the east there is a beautiful land, surrounded on all four sides by green mountains. There is someone there who flew down in the rock-strong boat of heaven." I think that this land will surely be suitable for the expanding of our heavenly enterprise, so that its glory will fill the universe. It is no doubt the center of the world, and I suspect that the one who flew down was Nigihayahi. Why do I not go there and make it my capital?[1]

Jimmu thereupon set out toward the east and conquered all the people along the way. When he had acquired the beautiful land in the east and made it his capital, he surveyed it and found it good. The account in the *Nihon shoki* says: "The emperor went up on Hohoma Hill at Wakigami and, having gone around viewing the shape of the country, said, 'Oh, what a magnificent land we have won! Though it is a small country, it looks like a dragonfly licking its tail.' Because of this, the land came to be called Akizushima."[2]

Akizu is an ancient word for "dragonfly," and the words about the dragonfly that the authors of the *Nihon shoki* had the emperor speak were doubtless intended to provide an etymology for a place name that already existed. Akizushima is also called Yamato, and for that reason we have called it Akizushima-Yamato here. Izanagi, the progenitor of the sun goddess, is said to have described Yamato as "the country of inner peace," while the deity Ōanamuchi-no-ōkami is supposed to have called it "a land within beautiful fencelike mountains."

Reference has already been made to the famous poem attributed by the *Kojiki* to Yamato Takeru no Mikoto in which the mountains of Yamato are described as layer upon layer of green hedges (see chapter 3).[3]

Tsuchihashi Yutaka has pointed out that images like 'green hedges lying layer upon layer' were used not only in connection with Yamato, but also of other places, specifically in encomiums spoken by rulers surveying their domains.[4] In the *Izumo fudoki*, for instance, the deity Ōnamochi-no-mikoto says:

The land of Izumo,
Where the clouds rise in layers,
Is the land where I will rest. ·
Encircling it with green-hedge mountains,
I will bestow on it a precious jewel
And protect it.[5]

The repeated references to surrounding green-hedge mountains and the like led Ishida Kazu-yoshi to conclude that the ancient Japanese had a special fondness for closed terrains.[6]

In this connection, the word Yamato, used since time immemorial to refer not only to the district around Nara that still bears the name but also to Japan as a whole, offers considerable food for thought. The great lexicographer Ōtsuki Fumihiko (1847–1929), having dispensed with other etymologies as "dubious," declared that Yamato was probably a contraction of *yama* = mountain, *ma* = interval, and *to* = place. He went on to point out that the province of Yamato (Nara Prefecture today) "has mountains on all sides with a plain in the middle," and that the word might be regarded as contrasting with Yamashiro (modern Kyoto Prefecture), which he construed to mean "behind the mountains."[7]

"Mountain-interval-place" has much to be said for it. Origuchi Shinobu (1887–1953), a poet and scholar deeply interested in Japanese folklore, suggested that Yamato, having originally signified "gateway where one enters the mountains," gradually came to refer to all the territory enclosed within such a gateway. He wrote: "The fact is that the people of old regarded the area within the mountain gateway as being sunny and cheerful. . . . When one descended through the gateway, one came upon a fertile plain, a bright and happy land. It was generally thought that once inside the gateway, one encountered no more barriers. Consequently, attention was focused on the gateway itself, and its name, *yamato*, came to be applied to the land of light and hope within."[8] This idea is connected with what Origuchi and fellow ethnologists called the "eternal-land cult": "The urge to discover and move to a land where the climate was good, food and other supplies were plentiful, and life was pleasant was the wellspring of their ability to continue improving their way of life. Drawn on by visions of riches, they progressed farther and farther toward the east. Their destination was always an unknown land [of abundance]."[9]

When the Japanese tribes pushing eastward had driven out the earlier inhabitants and destroyed their gods, the area that opened up before them was Yamato, the fertile land of light and hope—Akizushima-Yamato, the land surrounded by green mountains. This, to them, was the realization on earth of that unknown utopia toward which their primitive instincts had always impelled them. It is only natural then that their leader, upon surveying his realm, would lift up his voice and cry, "Oh, what a magnificent land we have won!"

At the same time a paradise that is envisioned as a religious ideal cannot actually exist on earth, and it could be argued that the attempt to see a given location as identical with this ideal merely testifies to the smallness of concept imposed on the people by their difficult living conditions. In any case, however, it is evident that this Akizushima-Yamato, a closed space encircled by green mountains, was the land of plenty that the ancient Japanese strove for. It is one classic form of their eternal land.

They thought of the area within the mountain gateway as bright and happy, and they considered it a place where inner peace could be achieved. The mountains formed a wall preventing incursions by outsiders; in a sense the land within was a place to hide. It was, indeed, the Japanese answer to the agoraphobia experienced by the ancient Egyptians, who lived on a vast, defenseless plain.[10] Furthermore it had the added advantages of water supplied by mountain streams and a variety of riches available in the mountain forests.

Ishida Kazuyoshi makes the following pertinent observation:

In ancient Japanese books, the word for land or country, *kuni*, was written with a variety of characters, among them those meaning earth, ground, district, and castle. Motoori Norinaga [1730–1801], in his edition of the *Kojiki* (vol. 7) says, "My teacher's theory was that *kuni* was the name for a place bounded by fixed limits. He said . . . this was why people in the east call a fence *kune*." Norinaga thus tacitly accepted the explanation offered by his mentor, Kamo no Mabuchi [1697–1769]. In fact, place names such as Kuni, Yoshino-no-kuni [the province of Yoshino], and Hase-no-kuni [the province of Hase] all refer to districts surrounded by green mountains and traversed by clear streams.[11]

In sum, the word *kuni* appears to have connoted the topographical features attributed to the ideal land known as Akizushima-Yamato.

Although the earliest written sources of Japanese history, in particular the *Kojiki* and the *Nihon shoki*, mention a number of palaces of ancient emperors, the question of whether these emperors and their palaces actually existed has not yet been answered. It is of sufficient importance here that the supposed locations appear in the records.

PALACES IN THE FOOTHILLS OF MOUNT KATSURAGI

Many historians consider that the earliest Japanese emperor who actually existed was the one known today as Sujin, who is referred to at one point in the *Nihon shoki* as "the first emperor to govern the nation."[12] Some scholars see Sujin as the first of the emperors belonging to a hypothetical Miwa dynasty, which was supposedly preceded by a dynasty known as Katsuragi. Both Miwa and Katsuragi are the names of mountains in the Yamato region.[13]

Of the palaces mentioned as belonging to the nine emperors preceding Sujin, the most interesting are those said to have been built by the Emperors Kōshō and Kōan. The *Kojiki* says that Kōshō lived at the Wakigami Palace in Katsuragi; the *Nihon shoki* calls this the Ikegokoro ("heart-of-the-pond") Palace in Wakigami. What is striking about this is that Wakigami is the place where the Emperor Jimmu is said to have climbed Hohoma Hill and spoken the words that caused the land to be called Akizushima. The Wakigami Palace, or Ikegokoro Palace, if it indeed existed, is thought to have been in the neighborhood of Ikenouchi ("middle-of-the-pond") in the modern city of Gose (figure 8.1).

As for the palace of the Emperor Kōan, both the *Kojiki* and the *Nihon shoki* call it the Akizushima Palace in Muro. This is the only instance in which the name Akizushima is used for an imperial residence. Although Jimmu is credited with originating the name, his dwelling is said to have been the Kashiwara Palace in Unebi.

The Akizushima Palace is traditionally said to have been located next to the Wakigami Palace in what is now Gose. Just to the south there is a string of hills ranging from two to three hundred meters in height. Hohoma Hill is part of a ridge running along the north and east, and the range known as Mount Katsuragi is to the west, extending north and south.

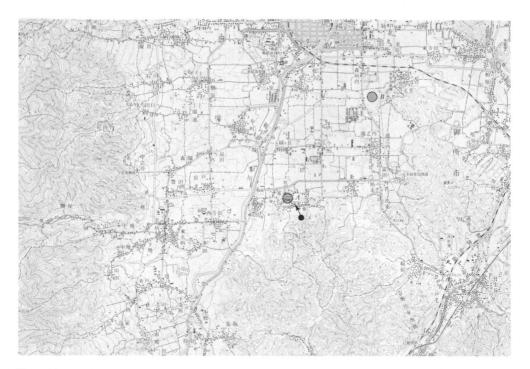

Figure 8.1
Map of the foothills of
Mount Katsuragi where the
Akizushima Palace (*A*) and
the Wakigama Palace (*B*)
are situated

Figure 8.2
View of the Yamato Plain
spreading northward from
Muro, where the Emperor
Kōan's Akizushima Palace
is legendarily said to have
stood (Nara Prefecture)

The Yamato Plain stretches out broadly to the north (figure 8.2) and is considerably larger than one would suspect from the words "small country." It may well be that Akizushima-Yamato, the "small country surrounded by green mountains," existed primarily in the minds of the ancients, rather than in fact.

PALACES NEAR MOUNT MIWA

Most of the palace sites attributed to the Emperor Sujin and the succeeding members of his line are in the general region of Mount Miwa, south of the modern city of Tenri. They include Sujin's Mizugaki Palace in Shiki, Suinin's Tamaki Palace in Makimuku, Keikō's Hishiro Palace in Makimuku, Richū's Wakazakura Palace in Iware, Yūryaku's Asakura Palace in Hatsuse, Seinei's Mikakuri Palace in Iware, Buretsu's Namiki Palace in Iware, Keidai's Tamaho Palace in Iware, Kimmei's Kanazashi Palace in Shikishima, Bidatsu's Sakidama Palace in Osada, Yōmei's Namitsuki Palace in Iware Ikenobe, and Sushun's Shibagaki Palace in Kurahashi. Of these, all save the Asakura Palace, the Namiki Palace, and the Shibagaki Palace are in an area bounded on the south by Mount Kagu and on the east by Mounts Miwa and Torimi. This is a flat district, watered by the Anashi, Hatsuse, Awahara, and Iware Rivers. The location reminds one of a passage in the *Kojiki* that speaks of

. . . a palace where shines
The morning sun,
A palace where gleams
The evening sun.[14]

Stretching out to the north and west is the whole Yamato Plain, and again it is difficult to say that the area fits the description "small country."

ASUKA

In the interval between 592, when the Empress Suiko (r. 592–628) ascended the throne, and 710, when the capital was moved to Nara, nearly all the palaces were in Asuka, a relatively small area surrounded by mountains (figures 8.3, 8.4). Exceptions were the Emperor Kōtoku's Toyosaki Palace at Nagara in Naniwa (present-day Osaka) and the Emperor Tenji's Ōtsu Palace in Ōmi (modern Shiga Prefecture). The move to Naniwa was shortlived, because the crown prince and the abdicated Empress Kōgyoku abandoned the emperor there and returned to Asuka, where, owing to the emperor's death in 654, the empress resumed the throne in the following year (figure 8.5).

Of the temporary shift to Ōtsu, which occurred in 667, an entry in the *Nihon shoki* says, "At this time the common people of the empire did not desire the removal of the capital. Many made satirical remonstrance, and there were also many popular songs. Every day and every night there were numerous conflagrations."[15] In 672, when the Emperor Temmu (r. 672–686) overthrew the Emperor Kōbun (r. 671–672, if indeed he reigned at all), the capital again returned to Asuka.

Naniwa, which commanded a view of Osaka Bay, and Ōtsu, which looked out over the broad expanse of Lake Biwa, were both very different as landscapes from the capitals in Asuka. If one stands on the remains of the Ōtsu Palace today and compares the view of the lake with the mountain-locked small country idealized as Akizushima-Yamato, one can only conclude that the Emperor Tenji, who chose this spot, was a man of exceptional spirit and vision. Yet the poet Kakinomoto no Hitomaro (active in the late seventh and early eighth centuries) was probably voicing the sentiments of most of the people when he wondered what motives had caused the emperor to move to Ōmi. From the

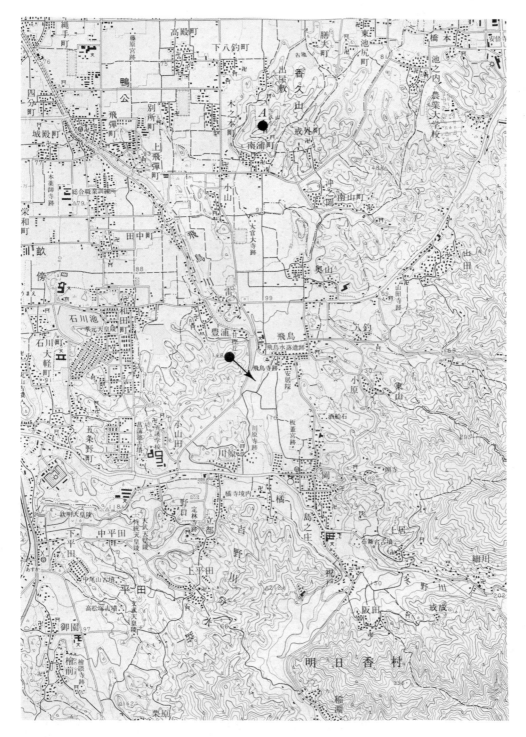

Figure 8.3
Map of Asuka where
Mount Kagu is situated
(arrow indicates the direction from which photo in
figure 8.5 was taken)

Figure 8.4
The Asuka district seen
from Mount Kagu (Nara
Prefecture)

Figure 8.5
Asuka, the "mountain-
interval-place" (Nara
Prefecture)

viewpoint of the people living in Asuka, Tenji's capital must have indeed seemed beyond the horizon, as Hitomaro described it.[16] It was certainly not Akizushima-Yamato in aspect or feeling, and this may well be the reason why it remained the capital for only five years.

From 694 to 710 the capital was located at Fujiwara, north of Asuka, where the Empress Jitō (r. 686–697) attempted to construct a city similar to the great planned capitals of China. On the east, north, and west of Fujiwara were the famous three mountains of Yamato, Kagu, Miminashi, and Unebi; the mountains of Yoshino were visible in the distant southwest. But, as is suggested by the "Well Poem" in the Man'yōshū, the three Yamato peaks were little more than high hills.[17] They appear almost to have been brought from somewhere else and set down in the Yamato Plain, and it can hardly be said that the new capital accorded with the Akizushima-Yamato ideal. Perhaps Fujiwara is best explained as representing a transitional stage between Akizushima-Yamato and the zōfū-tokusui type exemplified by the later capitals at Nara and Kyoto. After 710, when the government was transferred to Nara, the capital never again returned to the Asuka district.

THE CAPITAL AT KUNI

Though Nara remained the capital during most of the time from 710 to 784, there was a restless interval of about five years, beginning in 740, when the Emperor Shōmu (r. 724–749) moved his palace from place to place at a bewildering pace. During most of this time, his principal abode was in Kuni (figure 8.6), northeast of the present city of Nara. The Man'yōshū contains quite a few poems about this new capital, many of them praising its scenery highly.

The emperor's aim in moving to Kuni has never been adequately explained, but for our purposes the transfer may be regarded as a reversion to the earlier ideal, for, to a much greater degree than Nara, Kuni resembles the Akizushima-Yamato type. Surrounded on all sides by mountains, it is definitely a "small country," by comparison with Nara, and the "green-hedge mountain" effect is prominent. Kuni, in sum, is a relatively tiny valley watered by the Kizu River, which flows through it from east to west (figure 8.7). Concerning it, the poet Ōtomo no Yakamochi (716–785?) wrote:

When I see the pure beauty
Of the mountains and rivers
At the new capital,
Abuilding at Kuni, I think
This is a natural choice.[18]

In other poems we find Kuni described as "a district with lovely mountain ranges" and "a village where the waves of the river vie with each other." The setting of Shōmu's Futagi Palace, said to have been located where the remains of the Yamashiro Provincial Temple are to be seen today (figure 8.8), was lauded as follows:

The rivers being near,
Clear comes the sound of the running waters;
The mountains rising close by,
The clamorous voices of birds are heard.
When the autumn comes,
The stags call loudly to their mates,
Their voices echoing through the mountains.
When the spring comes,
Thick over hill-sides and amid rocks
The flowers bloom bending the sprays.[19]

There exist poems written in praise of Mount Kasuga, Mount Ikoma, and other landmarks near Nara, but they lack the freshness and inspiration of the poems about Kuni. "The rivers being near . . . The mountains rising close

Figure 8.6
Map of Kuni where the Ya-
mashiro Provincial Temple
is situated (arrow indicates
the direction from which
photo in figure 8.7 was
taken)

107   *The Akizushima-Yamato Type*

Figure 8.7
General view of Kuni
(Nara is beyond Mount
Kase, marked here by an
arrow)

Figure 8.8
Remains of the Yamashiro
Provincial Temple, where
the Futagi Palace is thought
to have been located (Kuni,
Kyoto Prefecture)

by"—there is a sensitivity in these poems that comes from sheer proximity to the beauties of nature. While Mount Kasuga is about five kilometers from the site of the Nara palace, and Mount Ikoma more than ten kilometers, at Kuni, the nearer mountains were only one kilometer or so from Futagi Palace, and the farthest ones no more than two kilometers. Moreover, the Kizu River at Kuni is much larger and consequently more conspicuous than the Saho and Tomio rivers at Nara. The very closeness of the view at Kuni gave it an immediacy and a freshness that appealed to the poets of the Nara period (710–794), whose ability to describe what they had seen objectively was already highly developed.

In 744 the courtiers and merchants were asked whether they preferred Kuni or Naniwa as the capital. The courtiers were slightly in favor of Kuni, and the merchants overwhelmingly so, but the emperor nevertheless made a "progress" to Naniwa and soon issued an edict naming it the new capital. Though he changed his mind a year later, he returned not to Kuni but to Nara, and the still unfinished capital at Kuni was abandoned.

The *Man'yōshū* poet Tanabe no Sakimaro (dates uncertain) wrote the following lines upon seeing the deserted capital in later years:

At the capital in Kuni,
On the plain called Mikanohara,
The mountains are lofty,
The flow of the river clear.
People called it a good place to live;
I thought it a good place to be.
Now it is a deserted village:
Though one looks out over the land,
There is no one coming and going;
Though one looks toward the village,
The houses are broken down.
Alas, is this the way life goes?
On the edges of Mount Kase,
The mountain where the gods are worshiped,

The colors of the blossoming flowers are beautiful,
The voices of innumerable birds are nostalgic.
I wish it still existed!
I bewail the decline
Of a place that was good to live in.[20]

By the mid-eighth century the Japanese imperial state, with its Chinese-style bureaucracy, could no longer make do with a capital city hidden away in a small secluded valley. A larger, more accessible site was necessary for the workings of government. The attempt at Kuni to recover the Akizushima-Yamato ideal was but an abortive throwback to an outmoded ideal.

STRUCTURE AND COMPOSITION OF THE
AKIZUSHIMA-YAMATO TYPE
As a spatial structure, the Akizushima-Yamato type had features that may be summarized as follows:

1. It was surrounded by green-hedge mountains, which formed a wall of sorts, cutting the area off from the outside and creating a cozy place where it was possible to enjoy peace of mind. The boundary was what Bollnow has described as a means whereby men could "resist the destructive force of invading chaos."[21] Both figuratively and literally, it was the "strong demarcation needed so that man does not dissolve in that which is without essence."[22] It offered the promise of inner tranquility and security. It is worth emphasizing that in Japan this boundary took the form of mountains covered with trees.

2. The flatlands within constituted a land of light and hope, nestled in protective surroundings. This was a distinct district unto itself, subdivided by waterways that functioned as lifelines for agricultural activity (figure 8.9). It is of significance that this enclosed area was a "small country," for, as Minkowski has noted, a certain degree of smallness is necessary in order for a space to seem intimate and livable.[23] The green-hedge mountain concept is closely connected with man's visual sense of distance. It may be taken as an

illustration of the typical Japanese feeling of intimacy with such natural features as rivers, mountains, and trees. Compactness is essential to the Akizushima-Yamato space. Expanded, it loses its meaning.

3. The space is oriented toward the east, as is implied in the statement "In the east there is a beautiful land." The fact that the early Japanese pushed farther and farther toward the east may be largely a matter of historical coincidence, but Ōno Susumu has made the following observation:

In the Indo-European languages, words for "east" reveal two basic concepts. In one, the east is thought of as the place where the sun rises, the location of dawn or morning. In the other, it is connected with the idea of what lies forward or ahead. In ancient times, when it was necessary to spend long hours amid the black terrors of the night, people longed in their hearts for the rising of the sun. Their attention was directed toward the east, where this event took place.[24]

The Japanese word for east, *higashi*, is thought by some to derive from elements meaning "directed toward" and "sun." In seeking a place where the climate would be good and supplies plentiful, the ancient Japanese looked toward the direction from which the sun rose. This was "dawn"; it was also "forward." It must have seemed obvious to them that this was the direction in which they must go to find the eternal land of abundance.

9

The Eight-Petal Lotus Blossom Type

A BUDDHIST IDEAL

Of particular importance in Esoteric Buddhism is the Mandala of the Womb World (Japanese: *Taizōzai-mandara*; Sanskrit: *Garbhadhātu-maṇḍala*), a schematic picture in which the universe is represented in terms of sacred beings emanating from the cosmic Buddha. In the standard version employed by the Japanese Shingon Sect, this mandala depicts 414 sacred figures grouped in tiers around a central section, in which the universal Buddha (Japanese: Dainichi-nyorai; Sanskrit: Vairocana) is shown at the middle of a crimson eight-petal lotus blossom, with four directional Buddhas and four Bodhisattvas occupying the petals around him (figure 9.1). At some undetermined time Japanese Buddhists began to see in certain landscapes a manifestation of the sacred eight-petal lotus blossom and consequently a topographical embodiment of the center of the universe.

In the *Taiheiki* ("Record of Great Peace" —despite its title, a saga of fourteenth-century civil wars) there appears the following passage: "In 1340 . . . he made a pilgrimage to Mount Kōya, where he stayed three days. As he went about making obeisance at the temples and in the valleys, he found them to be more dignified and magnificent than he had heard. The eight-petal peaks soar in the sky; a pedestal for a thousand Buddhas rises high in the clouds."[1]

From the *Taiheiki*, completed in 1370 or 1371, it is clear that by that time the idea that the peaks of Mount Kōya (figures 9.2, 9.3) represent an eight-petal lotus blossom had already taken root. A standard Japanese dictionary of Esoteric Buddhist terms gives under "eight-petal peaks" (*hachiyō no mine*), "one name for Mount Kōya; based on the idea that the mountains there represent the eight-petal lotus pedestal in the Womb Mandala; a great pagoda at the center of the flower form represents the South Indian Iron Tower; there are

Figure 9.1
Central section of the
Shingon-in version of the
"Mandala of the Womb
World" in the collection of
the Tō-ji, or Kyōō Gogoku-
ji (Kyoto)

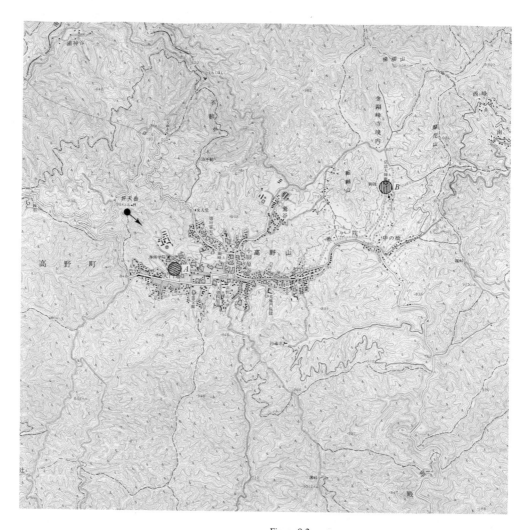

Figure 9.2
Map of the Mount Kōya
region where the central
tower (*A*) and Kūkai's
mausoleum (*B*) are situated
(arrow indicates the direction from which photo in
figure 9.3 was taken)

Figure 9.3
Mount Kōya and the Great
Pagoda (Wakayama
Prefecture)

thus eight petals for the eight directional Buddhas and Bodhisattvas and a central tower for Vairocana."[2] The South Indian Iron Tower, it might be noted, is supposed to have been the place where the sutras on which the two most important mandalas are based were vouchsafed to patriarchs of the Shingon Sect. "Mount Kōya," for its part, is the general name for a mountainous area in Wakayama Prefecture where one of the two chief monasteries of the Shingon Sect is located. The principal temple there, known as the Kongōbu-ji, was founded by Kūkai in 816.

We see in this instance a symbolic meaning read into an actual landscape configuration (augmented, of course, by a man-made tower at the center). According to Itō Teiji, "In Esoteric Buddhism, all things in nature are considered as mandala, literally 'pictures of the Buddhas,' that is, embodiments in reality of the spiritual world."[3] This is the basis for the concept of Mount Kōya as an eight-petal peak.

Physically, the region in question consists of a valley surrounded by a number of mountains. In the Asuka and Nara periods (592–645; 645–794), Buddhist centers were for the most part located in or around the capital, but with the development of a hermit philosophy in the Heian period, Buddhism took to the hills, so to speak, in an effort to divorce itself from the cares and temptations of the ordinary world. A celebrated commentary on three Buddhist sutras, said to have been composed in the Asuka period by Prince Shōtoku (ca. 574–622), says, "he likes to go to the mountains and sit there in Zen meditation, but, if he does only this, how will he find time to spread this sutra to the world? From this consideration, we know that to be fond of meditating in the Zen fashion all the time is not to be in the realm of those who are intimate with the Buddha."[4] This may be re-

garded as a seventh-century attitude; the later appearance of Buddhist monasteries in secluded mountain areas implies a new development in the history of Buddhist thought. An important segment of the priesthood reacted against the secularization of the faith, and the mountain monasteries of the ninth century and later were the spatial expression of this reaction.

It is significant that the eight-petal peaks formed a boundary enclosing the space inside, which itself became a sacred area. The idea is not dissimilar to that of the land of hope and light in the Akizushima-Yamato configuration. Here, however, the secluded valley is conceived of as the residence of the Buddha, a paradise simulating in form the central lotus blossom in the Womb Mandala. The surrounding mountains eliminated agoraphobia, shut out the evil influences of the everyday world, and created a Buddhist capital of peace and tranquility, where a "pedestal for a thousand Buddhas" soared in the clouds.

MOUNT KŌYA

When Kūkai requested that the court grant him Mount Kōya as a place for worship and meditation, he explained that as a young man he had liked to tramp around in the mountains and that in the course of his wanderings he had come across an area in the province of Kii (Wakayama Prefecture) that he wanted. He described it as a "secluded plain, surrounded by high peaks and untrod upon by man." It was called Kōya, or "lofty meadow."[5]

The term translated here as "meadow" is variously pronounced no and ya in Japanese. According to Yanagita Kunio, this morpheme normally refers to an area of gentle slope near the foot of a mountain, where there is plenty of water and sunlight. Such an area, remarks Yanagita, is usually a good place to live and would presumably have appealed to ancient settlers.[6] Kōya differs from the ordinary plain in that it is situated high above sea level. This bowl-like valley walled in by mountains must have been chosen by Kūkai as his city of Buddha because it was both livable and inaccessible—a haven surrounded by steep slopes and lonely peaks where hermit-priests could perform their ascetic rites.

Murō-ji

The Murō-ji (figures 9.4, 9.5), a nunnery in the mountains outside Nara, was first established in the latter part of the eighth century, at the command of the court, by the monk Kenkei (703–793), who rose during his lifetime to the high priestly rank of *daisōzu*. It is of particular interest that the same Kenkei played a part in the selection of the area to which the imperial capital was transferred in 794.

Historians believe that the mountainous district in which the Murō-ji is situated was chosen as the site for a temple because some years earlier, when the crown prince was ill, prayers for his recovery had been successfully pronounced there. Even earlier, this area had been sacred to a dragon god to whom prayers for rain were frequently addressed.

The mountain on which the Murō-ji stands is called Shōjin Peak; the valley below is the crater of an extinct volcano. Together, the peak and valley stand out prominently from among the surrounding mountains and may be regarded as the central landmark. The region has numerous caverns and oddly shaped crags. "The mountains on all sides slant high into the sky; the pond where the dragon resides is connected to the center of the earth. Truly this is a place where the immortals disport themselves—a place where the sages have walked."[7] Or in other words an ideal home for a dragon god or a Buddha with miraculous powers. Though the location is deep in the mountains, the landscape is similar in many respects to the settings observed at the Tsuge Mikumari Shrine and the Uda Mikumari Shrine in Furuichiba.

It is not certain when Shōjin Peak, together with the nearby mountains and valleys, came to be regarded as a manifestation of the eight-petal lotus blossom, but we may safely assume this to have occurred after the nunnery came under the strong influence of Esoteric Buddhism. The Murō-ji first came to be spoken of as the "Women's Mount Kōya"—implying that it was a women's counterpart to the esoteric center for men at Mount Kōya—after 1698, when it ceased to be affiliated with the great Kōfuku-ji of Nara and was absorbed into a branch of the Shingon Sect.[8] To read a symbolic meaning into the totality of a given topographical configuration represents a viewpoint that is peculiar to Esoteric Buddhism, though, as we shall see, there are points of similarity with the *zōfū-tokusui* type, described in the next chapter.

STRUCTURE AND COMPOSITION OF THE EIGHT-PETAL LOTUS BLOSSOM TYPE

The characteristics of the eight-petal lotus blossom type may be summarized as follows:

1. The mountains representing the eight petals shut the interior space off from the outside and make it a distinct district, thus creating what Bollnow has called a "bounded and well-ordered form."[9] Peaks jutting up to form a skyline delineate an integrated space and provide it with landmarks (figure 9.6).

2. The plain surrounded by the peaks becomes a sacred place or district. At the same time it constitutes a quiet, secluded area where "the immortals disport themselves." Although enclosed by high peaks, the flatlands themselves are lofty enough to serve as a "pedestal for a thousand Buddhas." The total space has an upward directionality.

Figure 9.4
Map of the area around the
Murō-ji (*A*) and Shōjin
Peak (*B*) (arrow indicates
the direction from which
photo in figure 9.5 was
taken)

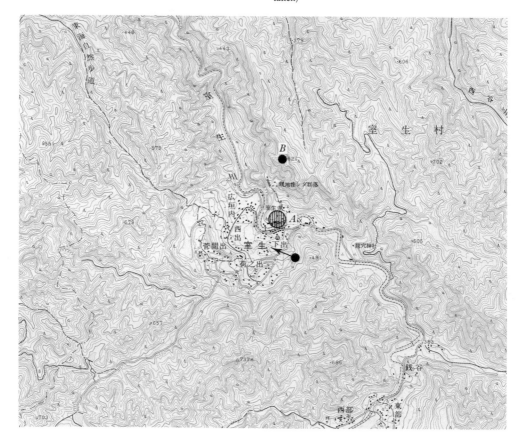

Figure 9.5
The Murō-ji and its environs, Shōjin Peak at right
(Nara Prefecture)

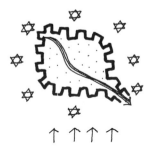

 Boundary: Mountains

✡ Goal (landmark): Eight peaks

Domain: Plain

↑↑↑ Directionality: High rise of mountains

Boundary and directionality: River

Figure 9.6
Structural elements of the
eight-petal lotus blossom
type

119　The Eight-Petal Lotus Blossom Type

Figure 9.7
The Okunoin at Mount
Kōya and its surroundings,
as portrayed in the *Ippen
Shōnin Eden* ("Picture Bi-
ography of Saint Ippen") in
the collection of the Kankikō-ji (Kyoto)

The actual setting at Mount Kōya has certain additional interior features. One is that the path leading from the great gateway on the west to the Okunoin "inner temple," which is Kūkai's mausoleum (see figure 9.7); in the deep forest on the northeast is a passageway space with depth. Nevertheless, the space in which the Okunoin stands has peaks on the north, east, and west, and flowing water on the south—the configuration seen in spaces of the *zōfū-tokusui* type of landscape.

10

The
Mikumari
Shrine Type

For people whose livelihoods are based on the cultivation of rice in wet fields, irrigation is a matter of life or death. It is hardly surprising then that the ancient Japanese believed in a deity whose function was to provide water abundantly and fairly for the rice fields. He was called Mikumari-no-kami, "the water-distributing god," and was worshiped at shrines in many different parts of Japan.[1]

The most logical site for a shrine to this deity would perhaps have been at a watershed high in the mountains, but, since the deity had to be worshiped periodically, a place lower down on the mountainside was more practical. The spot chosen was usually at a point where the mountain changed into foothills, or, in effect, where the slope shifted from steep to gradual. This was the location of the "watergate"—the first opening from which water descending in a mountain stream was drawn off for the fields. From a different viewpoint this was the "mountain gate" leading to uninhabited upper regions. Since the water here was clear and unsullied, it must have excited a feeling of reverence. And since this was the place where the god of the entrance to the mountain was worshiped, that deity tended to become one with the water-distributing god.

The well-known ethnologist Yanagita Kunio had the following to say of shrines dedicated to this being:

With respect also to the eight Mikumari shrines distributed judiciously about in the slopes of the fabled "green-hedge mountains" of Yamato, even today a comparison of terrains brings to mind the primitive organizations that cultivated the fields in earliest times, as well as the cults of water-giving deities around which these grounds clustered. Until the age when great new tracts of land could be reclaimed and put under cultivation, small, gently sloping valleys nestled among the mountains were the units of agricultural production. The ordinary practice throughout the country was for these communities to hold annual festivals dedicated to the deity who apportioned an abundance of water to them.[2]

In his discussion of kaijō no michi ("maritime routes") the same author divides the development of wet cultivation of rice in Japan into four stages, characterized by (1) dependence upon rainwater, (2) dependence upon springwater, (3) use of ponds, and (4) use of dams.

The worship of the water-distributing god presumably belonged to the second stage. As Yanagita writes, "People speak of 'a field of droplets from Mount Tsukuba,' which is to say, fields irrigated with the stingy quantities of water that can be wrung from mountain streams. Such farming areas started with something called a 'small mountain field' at the head and skirted out broadly over a slight downward slope. Today they are pleasant places, with scenery that recalls the aboriginal past."[3]

The Mikumari shrines were built in an age when large-scale engineering was impossible, which is to say, before the introduction of Chinese-style legal and administrative institutions or the land-distribution system that came with them.[4] The spatial characteristics of the terrain on which life was led and production carried on at this early historical stage can be analyzed by referring to a number of these landscape examples.

The Engi-shiki ("Regulations of the Engi Era"), a compilation of legal rules completed in 927, contains a list of shrines referring to the "Four Mikumari Shrines of Yamato," which are stated to be at Katsuragi, Yoshino, Uda, and Tsuge. One of these, the Yoshino Mikumari Shrine, is situated near the top of a mountain, at a point that might be described as a watershed. The other three, however, are all in the foothills.[5]

TSUGE MIKUMARI SHRINE

It is said that the Mikumari Shrine at Tsuge was transferred to its present location in the mid-Heian period (794–1185), when the fields in this area became part of an estate owned by the powerful Fujiwara family. Formerly it had been at Oyamado, farther up the river, where it had served as a shrine to the god of the entrance to the mountain. There seems to have been a tendency for shrines to the water-distributing god to be moved from higher to lower points on the mountainside as time progressed, for such is the case not only with the shrine at Tsuge but also with the shrines at Uda. It is interesting to note that there is now another shrine to the god of the entrance to the mountain at Oyamado today.

The area in which the Tsuge and Oyamado shrines are situated might be described as a small basin. In the past Tsuge was referred to as "Tsuge in the mountains" (yamato no Tsuge). To the south of the Tsuge Mikumari Shrine are fields like the ones described by Yanagita as being "irrigated with the stingy quantities of water that can be wrung from mountain streams." They lie along the banks of the river, and the houses of the farming community are built on higher ground to the east and west. We see here a pattern suited to Yanagita's second stage of rice cultivation, which involved dependence on springwater.

Before discussing the Tsuge shrine, let us consider for a moment the Oyamado shrine, situated where the Tsuge shrine was in earlier times. As can be seen from the accompanying map and photograph (figures 10.1, 10.2), the location is near the first point where water was drawn off the stream, which was also the point of entry into the mountain proper (the point where the slope changes from gradual to steep). From here downward along the stream, or toward the north, "small mountain fields" spread out to form the valley. The slope is no more than 1 to 2 degrees. Since the

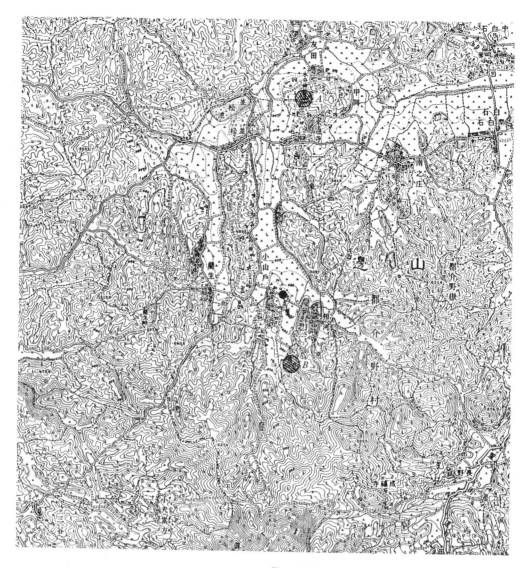

Figure 10.1
Map of the area where the
Tsuge Mikumari Shrine (*A*)
and the Oyamado Shrine
(*B*) are situated (arrow indicates direction from
which photo in figure 10.2
was taken)

Figure 10.2
Shrine to the god of the entrance to the mountain at
Oyamado (arrow) and the
"small mountain fields" below it (Nara Prefecture)

shrine itself is situated on a hill projecting from the mountain side of the slope-change point, it not only commands a good view but is eminently visible from the fields below. The shrine looked down protectively on the fields, and the farmers looked up to the residence of the deity from their slightly inclining meadow. (The subtle obstruction and sense of reverence produced by a gently sloping longitudinal plane was discussed in chapter 5, with the Ise Shrine and the mausoleum of Kūkai introduced as examples.) A visual relationship of seeing and being seen was thus established between the god and his worshipers. In addition the topographical features—ridges on the east and west converging toward the mountain on the south, which serves as the shrine's background—combined to make the shrine the spatial focal point.

In the case of the Tsuge Mikumari Shrine the shrine building itself is on a projecting hill around which the river flows as it turns toward the east. The stream more or less frames the eminence on which the building stands, and the fields on the low ground beyond spread out crescent-fashion. The visual relationship between the fields and the shrine is thus fundamentally the same as in the case of the Oyamado shrine, but the topographical features are quite different. Though there are once again fields in a hollow between mountains, at Tsuge the low flat area is more expansive in feeling, and the site of the shrine juts out into the valley.

We see here no doubt the result of a very natural development. When the farmers had learned to control the flow of the river to some extent, they were able to make fields in the low, humid basin through which the stream had previously wandered at will. The shrine was thereupon moved to the prominent position it now occupies, even though this location is not adjacent to the actual watergate. Horizontally, the topographical setting of the Oyamado shrine is concave, whereas that of the Tsuge shrine is convex. Since at Tsuge the site of the shrine is much higher than the surrounding fields, there is strong emphasis on the shrine's presence, and we are led to suspect that political aims were involved. This is the sort of place in which the owner or ruler of the district might want to erect a symbol of his authority. It is therefore probably no accident that the shrine was moved here around the time that the area was incorporated into an estate belonging to the Fujiwara family.

UDA MIKUMARI SHRINES

It is not clear whether the Uda Mikumari Shrine mentioned in the *Engi-shiki* is the one now in Furuichiba or another farther downstream in Idani. In addition to these two, there is a third shrine upstream from Furuichiba that is definitely not the one referred to in the *Engi-shiki*. (This last is sometimes called the Nakayama Mikumari Shrine.) There are, in sum, three Mikumari shrines in this area, situated in the upper, middle, and lower reaches of the river.

The *Udano-chō-shi* ("Official History of the Township of Udano") says, "The original Mikumari Shrine was in the upper reaches (Nakayama) of the Yoshino River. It appears that, as farming developed and flourished, other Mikumari shrines were built in the middle reaches (Nishidono) and lower reaches (Idani)."[6] The Nishidono referred to here is the same as Furuichiba.

From this statement we may infer that the situation was roughly the same as at Tsuge: the earliest cultivators had "small mountain fields" near the watergate, but as irrigation control improved, settlements appeared farther downstream, where new shrines were constructed.

Furuichiba is a small basin situated at a point where the Yoshino River shifts from a northward to an eastward course. Several other streams flow into the river along here, but farther downstream there are narrows. One is reminded of the "damp, humid little district" mentioned in the *Izumo fudoki*. The course of the river being somewhat uncertain, the basin is susceptible to flooding, but the richness of the soil was attractive to settlers once they had mastered the techniques for harnessing the water supply. The lovely little shrine is situated on a hill projecting into the bend of the river, and the grove in which it is nestled has as high a degree of visibility from the surrounding fields as does the Tsuge Mikumari Shrine (figures 10.3, 10.4).

The village of Furuichiba is on the same side of the river as the shrine. Formerly it was on the opposite bank, but because of frequent floods the inhabitants transferred their houses to the present location and diverted the river to a more southerly course. One supposes that in earlier times the river was a boundary demarking the area sacred to the water-distributing god.

The site of the Uda Mikumari Shrine in Idani (figure 10.5) is similar to the settings observed at Furuichiba and Tsuge. The Yoshino River, flowing northward from Furuichiba, becomes the Uda River in the vicinity of Idani, where, joining with a stream called the Nishi River, it turns again toward the east. The shrine is situated on a low hill extending from the east side into the crook of the river. Here, too, the shrine is high above its surroundings, and its grove can be seen from any point on the plain beneath. As at Furuichiba, the basin is a "damp, humid little district," below which the flow of the river is constricted by encroaching hills.

THE KATSURAGI AND TAKE MIKUMARI SHRINES

The Katsuragi Mikumari Shrine, another of the four mentioned in the *Engi-shiki*, is situated in a deep recess fairly high upon on the Mizukoshi River, which flows down from Mount Katsuragi (figures 10.6, 10.7). It presides over a narrow valley of gentle slope, where the farmland consists of "small mountain fields." Here again the shrine must originally have been built by a community constituting a minimal production unit.

The Mizukoshi River flows down to a broader plain where it joins with the Katsuragi River. This point is at the southwest tip of the Yamato Plain and is the place where a number of legendary emperors are supposed to have held court. Here, for example, were the Takaoka Palace of the Emperor Suizei, the Ikegokoro Palace of the Emperor Kōshō, and the Muro Palace of the Emperor Kōan. The Katsuragi Mikumari Shrine is too far up the valley to have visual unity with the sites where these palaces are said to have stood.

From Mizukoshi Pass, some distance up the mountain from the Katsuragi Shrine, a second branch of the Mizukoshi River flows down to the west. At the point where this stream meets the flatlands, in a situation similar to that on the east slope, stands the Take Mikumari Shrine (figures 10.8–10.10). As in other cases the building stands on a hill at the head of a valley, where it serves as a spatial focal point.

STRUCTURE AND COMPOSITION OF THE MIKUMARI SHRINE TYPE

As indicated earlier, the landscapes associated with the Mikumari shrines are divided into two subtypes. One is the essentially triangular space at the shrine to the deity of the entrance to the mountain at Oyamado, at Katsuragi Mikumari Shrine, and at Take Mikumari Shrine (figure 10.11). The other is the crescent-shaped space seen at the Tsuge Mikumari Shrine and the Uda Mikumari Shrines in Furuichiba and Idani (figure 10.12).

The triangular subtype has the following characteristics:

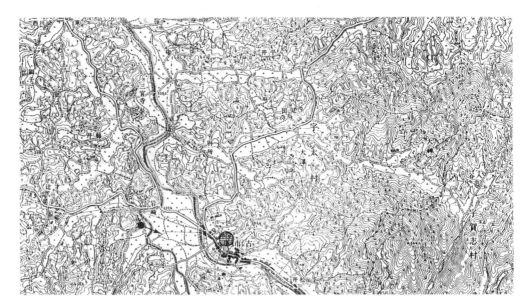

Figure 10.3
Map of the area around the
Uda Mikumari Shrine in
Furuichiba (arrow indicates
direction from which photo
in figure 10.4 was taken)

Figure 10.4
The Uda Mikumari Shrine
in Furuichiba (arrow) and
its surroundings (Nara
Prefecture)

Figure 10.5
Map of the area around the
Uda Mikumari Shrine in
lower Idani

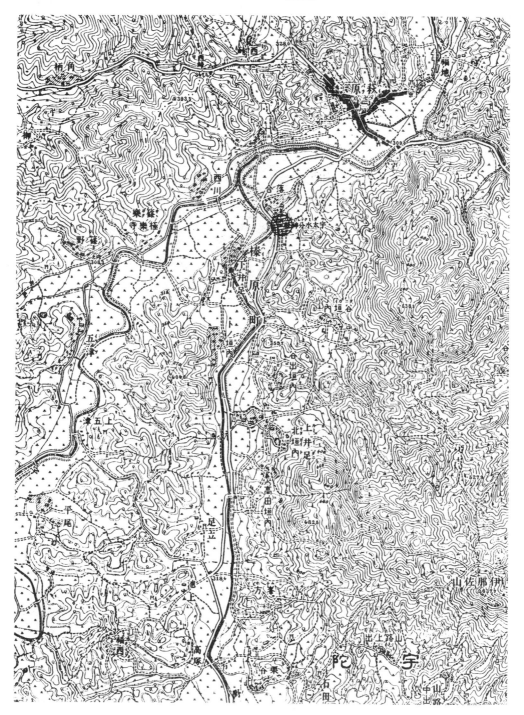

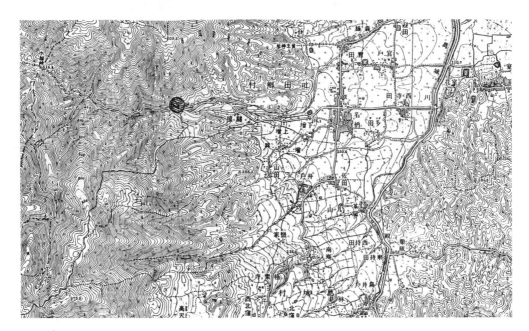

Figure 10.6
Map of the area around the
Katsuragi Mikumari Shrine

Figure 10.7
Mikumari Shrine at Kat-
suragi (Nara Prefecture)

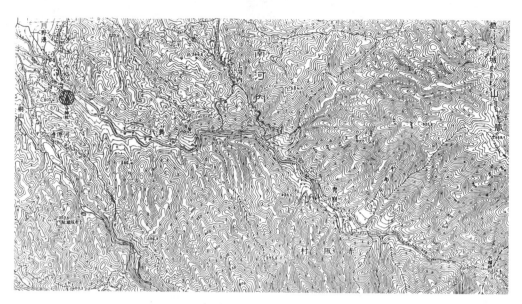

Figure 10.8
Map of the area around the
Take Mikumari Shrine

Figure 10.9
Plain below the Take Miku-
mari Shrine (Osaka
Prefecture)

Figure 10.10
View of the Take Mikumari
Shrine (arrow) showing the
high visibility of the hill on
which it stands, as seen
from the basin below
(Osaka Prefecture)

 Focus: Shrine

 Boundary: Mountains and hills

Boundary and directionality: River

↙ ↘ Directionality: Slope of ground

Domain: Fields, basin

Figure 10.11
Structural elements of the
first Mikumari Shrine
subtype

Center: Shrine

Boundary: Mountains and hills

Boundary and directionality: River

↙ ↘ Directionality: Slope of ground

Domain: Fields, basin

Figure 10.12
Structural elements of the
second Mikumari Shrine
subtype

1. Mountains close in on the valley toward the upper reaches of the river. The mountains serve as walls, or edges, setting the farmlands between them off as a distinct region unto itself. This area narrows in the upper reaches of the stream and broadens in the lower reaches. As a longitudinal surface, it gives both depth and directionality to the space as a whole.

2. The valley is of the "small mountain field" type, sloping only slightly from upstream to downstream. With the mountains on either side, the gentle slope gives the region the directional relationships of up and down.

3. The shrine is situated at the point where the slope shifts from steep to gentle. The building is at the pivot of a fan-shaped space; together with its forest, it enjoys a high degree of visibility and functions to concentrate the space toward a focal point. The sacredness of the shrine is reinforced by the upward slope of the land and by the mountains coming in on either side.

4. There is a river flowing down from the mountain behind the shrine. This serves not only as an edge separating the area that is sacred from that which is not but also as a waterway on which the deity can descend from the shrine to the fields at the time of his annual festival. As the path along which the water granted by the deity flows, it also enhances the upstream–downstream directionality.

The features of the cresent-shaped subtype can be summarized as follows:

1. Mountains separate the flat area from its surroundings, creating a closed basin.

2. The shrine is situated on a point jutting out into the flat area. The projecting mass enjoys high visibility and functions as a central focal point. It serves to organize the spatial structure.

3. The river runs like a belt around the hill on which the shrine stands. It is therefore an edge separating the sacred area from the nonsacred. Flowing from one end of the basin to the other and gathering the water from tributaries along the way, it provides a sense of directionality, while at the same time serving as a pathway for the deity.

4. The basin, bounded by mountains, brought together by the central hill, divided into sacred and profane sectors by the river, and given directionality by the downward-sloping riverbed, is a distinct region, a definite place discrete from all others.

Though there may be differences in scale, the crescent-shaped landscape is structurally quite similar to the Piazza del Campo in Siena. We may also see here the elements that Lynch abstracted from his analysis of urban spaces: landmark, path, node, edge, and district.[7]

11

The Secluded Valley Type

TERMINOLOGY

The expression "secluded valley" is employed here as a translation of the ancient Japanese *komoriku*, which might also be rendered as "hidden land." In early Japanese writings *komoriku* is usually found as a pillow word for Hatsuse, an elongated valley in the mountains east of the Yamato Plain. A pillow word is an epithetical modifier conventionally used with a particular word or group of words in both poetry and prose. Often its original meaning is obscure, but it appears that before *komoriku* became locked into the pillow word function, it was used more generally to refer to a narrow, secluded district with mountains pressing in closely on both sides.[1]

Hatsuse follows this description. With respect to the Yamato Plain it is a hidden valley running up the Hatsuse River to a point deep in the mountains. The significance of such a topographical space to the ancient Japanese can be inferred from a cursory examination of several specific examples.

HATSUSE

Located in what is now the city of Sakurai in Nara Prefecture, Hatsuse (figure 11.1) is said in ancient times to have been the site of the Asakura Palace of Emperor Yūryaku (r. 456–479) and the Namiki Palace of Emperor Buretsu (r. 498–506). The *Nihon shoki* contains a passage describing the former ruler's reaction to the landscape in this district:

The emperor visited a small meadow in Hatsuse. Upon viewing the mountains and fields there, he reacted with great feeling and spoke the following poem:

The mountains of Hatsuse,
The secluded valley—
If I go out, I see excellent mountains;
If I run forth, I see excellent mountains.
The mountains of Hatsuse,
The secluded valley—

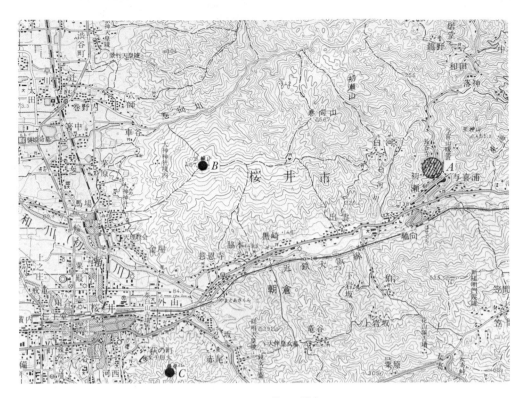

Figure 11.1
Map of the secluded valley
of Hatsuse where the Hase-
dera (A), Mount Miwa (B),
and Mount Tomi (C) are
situated

Mysterious, heart-warming beauty!
Mysterious, heart-warming beauty![2]

The mountains, in other words, are so close that the minute one walks out of the house, one is overcome by their beauty.

There is more to Hatsuse than this, however. Compare the following passage from the *Man'yōshū*:

Poem composed by Kakinomoto no Hitomaro at the cremation of the Maiden of Hijikata

The cloud drifting over the brows
Of the hills of secluded Hatsuse—
Can it, alas, be she?[3]

Other *Man'yōshū* poems were inspired by the burial of a certain Prince Iwata in the mountains of Hatsuse, and a burial ground for an ancient crematorium has been discovered there.[4] Hatsuse thus appears to have been a place where the dead were buried or cremated—a place where their departed spirits floated about like clouds. The word *hatsu* can have the adjectival meaning "first," or "beginning," but as a verb it can mean "to end" or "to be exhausted." Hatsuse appears to have been thought of as an abode for those whose lives had ended. It could hardly have been a site for cremation before 700, when the custom of burning the dead was introduced, but it was very likely regarded as a home for dead spirits in earlier times.

As one approaches Hatsuse from the Yamato Plain, two mountains, Miwa on the north and Tomi on the south, flank the entrance to the valley like a gateway. Beyond this point the Hatsuse River forms a passageway leading farther and farther inward. Close to the innermost point stands the Hase-dera (figure 11.2) which Yasuda Yojūrō described as "a most beautiful monastery whose buildings are in perfect harmony with their natural setting."[5] The Hase-dera is recorded to have been founded by a monk named Dōmyō (dates uncertain) at the behest of the Emperor Temmu (r. 672–686). It was intended as a place of mourning for those who had died in the civil war of 672.

The road from the Yamato Plain to Hatsuse leads almost straight east. As the mountains close in and the sound of the river begins to be audible, the road turns sharply to the north. Straight ahead, in a sequestered area embraced by the mountains, is the Hase-dera. It is both the destination and a node from which a deeper valley beyond is entered. At the same time it is the terminal of the passageway space formed by the secluded valley between the mountains.

After capitals were built at Asuka and Fujiwara, the Hatsuse district was regarded nostalgically as a place where earlier emperors had reigned. As Yasuda Yojūrō has pointed out, "Its mysterious atmosphere, which resulted from its being locked inside a deep valley, made it all the more awesome and at the same time brilliant."[6] It was recognized as a country of the dead—"a valley over which the sun and moon climb boldly, yet charmingly, morning and night."[7]

KUMANO

Gorai Shigeru, who described Kumano as "the land of the dead," explained his reason as follows:

All places deep in the mountains, where the spirits of the dead conceal themselves, are suitable to be called "Kumano." When the gods of Izumo died, they were said to betake themselves to the "eighty road-bendings," *yaso-kumade*. This *kumade*, along with the similar *kumado* and *kumaji*, signified a place where dead spirits hide. It is an old word for the kingdom of departed spirits and is the same as *komoriku*, which is used a number of times in the *Man'yōshū* to refer to the place where the spirits of the dead hide. Kumano, which is related to all these words, may be a shortened version of *komorino*, "hidden meadows."[8]

Figure 11.2
View from the main hall of
the Hase-dera (Nara
Prefecture)

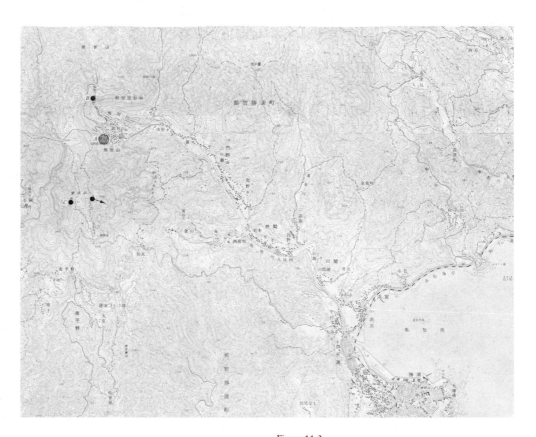

Figure 11.3
Map of the Kumano-Nachi
district where Nachi Shrine
and the Seiganto-ji (*A*), Nachi Waterfall (*B*), and
Mount Myōhō (*C*) are situated (arrow indicates the
direction from which the
photo in figure 11.5 was
taken)

There is considerable justification for this idea. We read in the *Nihon shoki*, for example, that the creator goddess Izanami was buried at the village of Arima in Kumano, that the god Sukunabiko-no-mikoto proceeded from Cape Kumano to the Eternal Land, and that Susanoo-no-mikoto dwelt on Kumanari Peak, said to be in Kumano, before proceeding to the Nether Land.[9] Whatever relationship these myths might have to historical fact, it would appear that Kumano was thought of as a country of the dead.

There is a Mount Kumano in the province of Izumo (modern Shimane Prefecture), and many scholars of the past thought this was the Kumano referred to in the *Nihon shoki*. The reference to the burial place of Izanami, however, states that Kumano was in Kii Province, and it is the Kumano in Kii (modern Wakayama Prefecture) that is best known as a religious center today. The area is south of Yamato and is so mountainous that some sources speak of the "3,600 peaks of Kumano."

Particularly famous among the mountains of Kumano is Mount Nachi, which is sacred to both Shinto and Buddhist cults. No doubt Mount Nachi gained religious significance because of its proximity to the Nachi Waterfall and Mount Myōhō (figures 11.3–11.5), both of which were objects of nature worship in very ancient times. The waterfall, framed by mountains with virgin forests, is at the head of the Nachi River, which flows from this point down through a narrow valley to Hamanomiya, on Nachi Bay. The topography is essentially the same as that observed at Hatsuse, though here the valley opens on the seashore and the inner extremity is an impressive cataract, falling straight down from a ledge high above and serving as a spatial focal point. Beyond Nachi Fall rises Mount Myōhō, where the spirits of the dead reside.

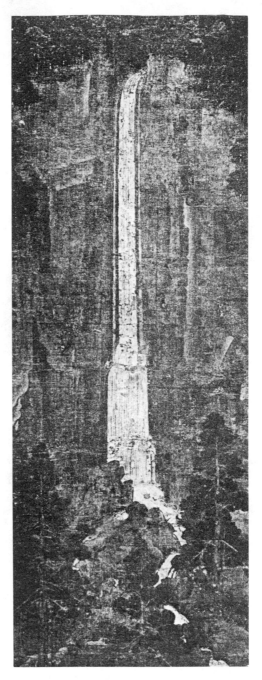

Figure 11.4
Painting of "Nachi Waterfall," in Kumano, in the collection of the Nezu Museum of Art (Tokyo)

Figure 11.5
The Nachi River valley and
Nachi Bay seen from the
Amida-dera on Mount
Myōhō (Wakayama
Prefecture)

From Mount Myōhō, it is possible to see both the "secluded valley" approach to the waterfall and the ocean. Of the view toward the ocean, a poet once wrote:

The sea at Nachi,
Stretching out brightly to the south—
The boats of Potalaka
Show the true Way of the Law[10]
Counted as the first of thirty-three places in Western Japan sacred to Kannon, the Kumano-Nachi district has a landscape density that would be difficult to match.

OTHER EXAMPLES

Mention has already been made of the Yoshino area, of which Kamei Katsuichirō wrote, "It has the power to draw one farther and farther into its recesses and, when one is there, to entice one still farther." Secluded valley configurations of this sort are found here and there all over Japan. As a rule they are marked by the presence of a Shinto shrine, a Buddhist monastery, or some spot sacred to both Buddhists and Shintoists. There may be some connection between spaces of this type and what Yanagita Kunio called "mountain shrines." Of these, he said: "Formerly it seems to have thought that at the end of our lives we would be sent to the inner recesses of a quiet, darkish valley, where we would take leave of all contamination and begin to climb ever and ever upward."[11] The "mountain shrine," according to Yanagita, was regarded as "a gardenlike spot deep in the inner reaches of a valley, used on a temporary basis for festivals."[12] Like the beach of the river Sai, which was a sort of limbo for the spirits of dead children, these lonely, shaded valleys used for occasional festivals were boundaries between this world and another, points from which one entered the realm of the spirit (figure 11.6).[13] Spaces of this kind probably existed near all communities where a nearby mountain was regarded as sacred territory. A topo-

Figure 11.6
"Manifestation of Amida at Mount Nachi" in the collection of the Dannō Hōrin-ji (Kyoto)

graphical map of Kyoto reveals that in the upper reaches of the streams descending from the surrounding mountains, there is invariably a famous Shinto shrine or Buddhist temple. Not all of the valleys receding into the mountains were used as burial grounds, but spaces of this type were regarded as sacred enough to serve as sites for religious establishments.

Landscapes in general have a tendency toward diffuseness, but the "secluded valley" type is noteworthy for its spatial density. Other famous examples of this configuration are to be seen at Nyūkawakami Shrine in Nara Prefecture, the Sūfuku-ji and Ishiyama-dera in Shiga Prefecture, and the Kiyomizu-dera, Jingo-ji, Daigo-ji, and Kurama-dera in Kyoto Prefecture.

STRUCTURE AND COMPOSITION OF THE SECLUDED VALLEY TYPE

The features of the secluded valley landscape can be summed up as follows:

1. Mountains on both sides not only serve as boundaries but also form parallel planes leading the eye farther and farther into the inner reaches of the space (figure 11.7). As a rule there is a stream flowing through the valley, and this gives two kinds of directionality at once, one leading upstream and inclining upward toward the sacred region and the other leading downstream and declining toward the entranceway. As can be seen from the specific examples cited, a space of this nature may function as a passageway to the other world or to the land of the gods.

2. The innermost point in the valley is not only the destination of the passageway but also the point from which the spirits of the dead climb on to higher ground. It is both a boundary and the node from which the world beyond is entered. It is here that we normally find a temple or shrine.

3. Downstream from the valley is an open plain which, by providing contrast, gives the valley its meaning. The valley is felt to be hidden and mysterious precisely because it is so different from the plain without, which is typically the place where people actually reside.

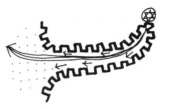

⊓⊔⊓	Boundary: Mountains
⟿	Boundary and directionality: River
→→ →→	Directionality: Slant of land surface
✡	Focus, goal: Inner recesses of valley
⠂⠒⠂	Domain: Flatlands

Figure 11.7
Structural elements of the secluded valley type

12

The Zōfū-Tokusui Type

PRINCIPLES OF CHINESE GEOMANCY

In China, since ancient times a type of geomancy involving directions, seasons, signs of the zodiac, and the elements has played a large part in determining the location of cities, buildings, and tombs. The rules that have evolved are known collectively in Japan by the name *zōfū-tokusui*, which literally means "storing-wind acquiring-water." Although there are many complicated ramifications, the general idea behind this principle is that mankind can avoid calamities and ensure his own well-being by determining heaven's will with respect to various locations and then acting in accordance with it. Chinese geomancy was imported to Japan at an early stage and has exerted a strong influence ever since.

According to Akita Nariaki, "the four directions are considered to belong to the green dragon (east), the crimson bird (south), the white tiger (west), and the black tortoise-snake (north); mountains, streams, buildings, and houses represent these beasts. By studying the configuration of mountains and rivers, one selects a site where the vital energy that flows throughout the earth is confined by water and not scattered by the wind, and there one builds houses for the living or tombs for the dead. It is held that if one follows this principle, one's descendants will partake of the earth's vital energy and obtain riches, happiness, and long life."[1]

The green dragon, crimson bird, white tiger, and black tortoise-snake are seen in the murals of the Takamatsuzuka Burial Ground, which date from the early eighth century, if not still earlier. With respect to the question of how to amass wind and acquire water, Saitō Tadashi has the following to say:

In concrete terms the mountains come from behind, which is to say from the north, and end at this point [the site selected], overlooking a plain ahead. They occupy the position of the so-called "drooping head of a tortoise-snake." On the left and right, mountain ranges extend southward to protect the area; these are known as the "undulations of the green dragon" and the "deferential bowing of the white tiger." To the south are spreading flatlands or low hills. As a rule water from the three sets of mountains flows down through the area bounded by them. In short, there are mountains behind, lower mountains on either side, and a plain with flowing water in front. Such a location is suitable for *zōfū-tokusui* conditions.[2]

Saitō gives as examples a number of Japanese tombs dating from the beginning of the eighth century.

The *Sakuteiki* ("Record of Making Gardens"), a late Heian-period manual on gardening, says, "Water flowing east of the house is the green dragon"; "the avenue to the west of the house is the white tiger"; "the pond on the south (front) side is the crimson bird"; "the hillock on the north (back) side of the house is the black tortoise-snake."[3] Here, it will be noted, the features corresponding to the four beasts are man-made creations, rather than elements of the natural terrain. The idea that the house must fit into the geomantic plan of things, however, remains intact.

IMPERIAL PALACES

A number of early imperial palaces were cited in connection with the Akizushima-Yamato type of landscape. It would appear that even in the age when these buildings are supposed to have been erected, some form of divination similar to Chinese geomancy (if not Chinese geomancy itself) was employed in choosing the sites. The following entry, for example, appears in the section of the *Nihon shoki* dealing with the Emperor Bidatsu (r. 571–585): "[Fourth year of the reign.] In this year diviners were commanded to divine the site for Prince Ama's dwelling and the site for Prince Itoi's dwelling. The divination was repeatedly propitious, and eventually a palace

was constructed at Ōsata. It was called the Sakidama Palace."[4]

The same work records that in 670 the Emperor Tenji (r. 661–671) "went to the plains of Hisa in the county of Kamafu and looked at a site for the palace."[5] In 682 officials "were sent to Niiki to examine the lay of the land; it was decided that the capital would be built there."[6] Again, two years later, high officials, including masters of astrology, "were sent to the home provinces to decide by divination upon a site where the capital might be built."[7]

From this and several other instances it is clear that divination was employed in determining the proper site for the capital, but these early statements give no clue as to what topographical features were considered propitious.

In 690 the Empress Jitō went to Fujiwara, in the southern part of the Yamato Plain, to inspect the site for a new capital. She was accompanied, if we are to believe the *Nihon shoki*, by "all the courtiers and officials."[8] Fujiwara, which actually became the capital in 694, was mentioned in connection with the Akizushima-Yamato type. Though the *Nihon shoki* gives no information as to the kind of site the empress was seeking, we have already noted that Fujiwara had characteristics of both the Akizushima-Yamato type and the *zōfū-tokusui* type. A poem in the *Man'yōshū* contains the following passage:

The green hill of Kagu of Yamato
Stands at the eastern gate,
A luxuriant springtime hill;
Unebi, with its fragrant slopes,
Rises at the western gate,
Ever fresh and flourishing;
Miminashi, the green sedgy mound,
Rears at the northern gate
Its form divine;
And the mountains of Yoshinu, of lovely name,

Soar into the sky,
Far from the southern gate.[9]

Although the poet makes no mention of water, the Fujiwara capital was bounded on the south by the Asuka River, so that the space in which it stood at least fulfilled the literal requirements of the *zōfū-tokusui* type, even though the mountains in question were mere hills rising from the plain (figure 12.1).

From the time of the Emperor Kimmei (r. 531?–571) the Yamato Plain was traversed from north to south by three highways set at equal intervals from each other and known as the Upper Road, the Middle Road, and the Lower Road. There were also east–west highways creating a rough grid plan and implementing the spatial organization of the plain as a whole.

Less than twenty years after Fujiwara became the capital, the Empress Gemmer (r. 707–715) decreed the construction of a new capital farther north on the plain. Her edict, as quoted in the *Shoku Nihongi* ("Chronicles of Japan, Continued"), said: "Now at the district of Heijō, the four beasts fit the charts, the three mountains provide peace, and the tortoise divinations are favorable. Let our capital be built here."[10] Here we find mention not only of the four beasts of Chinese geomancy but also of the mountains on three sides.

The Lower Road, which coincided with the westernmost avenue of the Fujiwara capital, ran straight north to the new capital at Heijō, or Nara, where it led directly into Suzaku ("Crimson Bird") Avenue, a broad boulevard extending from the imperial palace, in the north, southward down the middle of the city to the main gateway. The Middle Road, which had been the eastern boundary of Fujiwara, connected more or less directly with the avenue forming the eastern border of the rectangular grid that made up most of Nara. In

other words, the two streets forming the east and west boundaries of Fujiwara marked the boundaries of the east half of Nara. Nara was thus twice as wide as Fujiwara.

North of the new capital were the Nara Mountains; to the east was a range called Higashiyama, and to the west lay the mountains of Ikoma. The Saho River cut across the area south of the city. At Asuka and Fujiwara the view to the south had been cut short by hills or mountains, but at Nara the view out over the Yamato Plain to the south was more or less unobstructed. This fitted in nicely with the Chinese idea that the emperor should sit at north center and be able to survey his domains to the south. In short, Nara not only fulfilled the requirements of the geomancers but also occupied a commanding position with respect to the whole Yamato Plain. The construction of a capital here signified the coming of age of the ancient Japanese state, modeled on Chinese principles of government and law (figure 12.2).

In 784 it was decided to move the capital north to a place called Nagaoka, but the construction work there did not go well. It is conjectured that the principal reason was a bad choice of sites.[11] The palace itself was properly situated on an eminence, with mountains to the north, but the Katsura River flowed down that east side of the city, and to the south lay the low, humid plain where the Katsura, Uji, and Kizu rivers flowed together to form the Yodo. Mountains pressed in from the west, and a large swamp known as Ogura Pond was not far away on the southeast. The whole area is subject to periodic flooding, and floods occurred while the attempt to construct a capital was still going on. Despite its having been on key travel routes during the Nara period, Nagaoka was not a suitable location for a city. In the words of the geomancers, it was a place that amassed water rather than wind.

Figure 12.1
The Three mountains of
Yamato: Kagu (right),
Miminashi (center), and
Unebi (left) (Nara
Prefecture)

Figure 12.2
The site of the ancient imperial palace in Nara

Figure 12.3
General view of Kyoto,
originally called Heian-kyō,
the "Capital of Peace and
Tranquillity"

When in 794 the capital was shifted to what is now Kyoto (figure 12.3), imperial edicts were issued saying, in part, "The rivers and mountains at the site of the great palace in Kuzuno are beautiful," and "This province is surrounded by mountains and rivers, which form a natural stronghold. Because of its topography . . . let the name of the province be changed from Yamashiro [meaning 'behind the mountains,'] to Yamashiro [meaning 'the mountain stronghold']."[12]

As suggested in these quotations, the Kyoto area has mountains on the north, east, and west, and rivers to the south, as did Nara. A comparison of the edicts just cited with the one announcing the earlier move to Nara, however, indicates a certain difference in attitudes. The Nara pronouncement seems to express concern over geomantic formulas; the later statement reveals an eye for landscape beauty as such.

Comparative visibility data of microclimatological differences between Nara and Kyoto show that in Nara meteorological visibility is more than ten kilometers 80 percent of the time, while in Kyoto it averages about ten kilometers most of the time. Presumably, this is because the mountains around Kyoto are higher. The effect is that in Kyoto, to a much greater degree than in Nara, one has the feeling of being near the mountains. Nara is found to be satisfactory because "the four beasts fit the charts"—essentially an ideological consideration. Kyoto, on the other hand, is selected because "the rivers and mountains . . . are beautiful" and "form a natural stronghold"—an aesthetic reason coupled with a pragmatic one. We may see here a change in attitude toward landscapes, brought on at least in part by differences between the topographical spaces in which Nara and Kyoto are situated.

GARDENS

The *Sakuteiki* which applies the concept of the four beasts to garden design gives a description somewhat different from Saitō Tadashi's, in that the green dragon and the white tiger are not mountains but a stream and a road, respectively. Yet the other two elements, mountains to the north and water to the south, are the same. As it happens, the hill-behind, pond-before garden is the most classic type in Japan.

From the practical viewpoint, to find a natural setting that fitted the four-beast pattern must have been virtually impossible in Nara or Kyoto, and we may regard the *Sakuteiki*'s statement as a compromise resulting from urbanization. As a matter of fact the same book goes on to say that, if there is no stream on the east, nine willow trees may be planted there; if there is no avenue on the west, seven catalpa trees will do; if there is no pond in front, nine katsura trees should be planted; and if there is no hill on the north, it can be simulated with three Japanese cypresses. Nevertheless, the *Sakuteiki*'s garden must be regarded as an extension of the geomantic way of thinking.

The actual advantages of the four-beast plan can hardly be ignored. It would provide good exposure to the sun, protection against wind from the north, and, thanks to the slope away from the northern hill, a good view toward the south. In addition water from the mountain behind the house could easily be introduced into a pond in front. Geomantic and practical considerations aside, it may be that the *Sakuteiki*'s ideal garden owed something to Confucius's dictum that "the wise man loves the rivers and lakes, the benevolent man loves the mountains."

The Saga-in and the Kinkaku-ji
One of the landmarks of western Kyoto today is Ōsawa Pond which eleven centuries ago

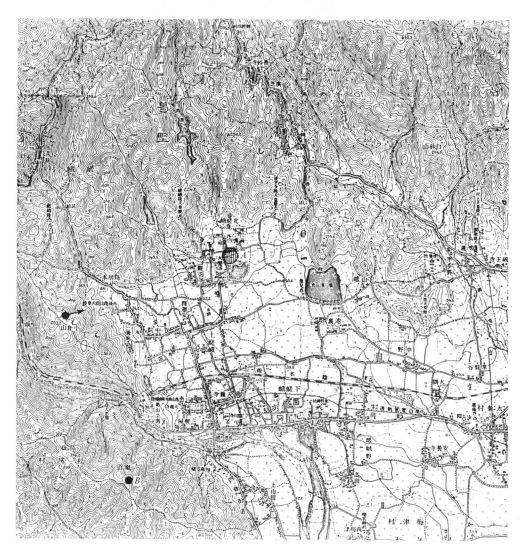

Figure 12.4
Map of the Sagano district
where Saga's Palace (*A*) and
Mount Arashi (*B*) are situated (arrow indicates the
direction from which photo
in figure 12.5 was taken)

was part of the garden of a detached palace belonging to the Emperor Saga (r. 809–823). The small meadow in which it is situated is known as Sagano (figures 12.4, 12.5) and was praised by Sei Shōnagon, author of the famed *Pillow Book*, as the best meadow of all, no doubt because of its beauty as a landscape.[13]

Saga's palace stood in a land pocket formed by high mountains to the north and ridges on the east and west. The plain spreads out to the south, coming to a boundary in the form of the Katsura River. Visible to the southwest are Mount Arashi and Mount Ogura, which form a part of Kyoto's white tiger. The gentle southward slope of the meadow must have made for a pleasant view from the ancient palace, which stood just to the north of the pond.

Another well-known example of the hill-behind, water-before garden is to be seen at the Kinkaku-ji, or Temple of the Golden Pavilion which is situated in a similar pocket-meadow a little to the east of Sagano. In the early thirteenth century this was the site of a dwelling owned by a courtier named Saionji Kintsune (1171–1249), famous for his efforts to cooperate with the military government in Kamakura. Later it passed into the hands of the third Ashikaga shogun, Yoshimitsu (1358–1408), who erected a palatial villa here and retired to it for the last few years of his life. After Yoshimitsu's death the establishment became a temple with the name Rokuon-ji. The reason why it is popularly known as Kinkaku-ji today is that the Golden Pavilion, Kinkaku, a three-story belvedere whose upper stories were covered with gold leaf, is the only part of Yoshimitsu's mansion that survived into modern times.[14]

Of the setting here the fourteenth-century historical romance *Masukagami* ("Mirror of Increase") says:

Formerly there were many fields here, and the feeling was completely rural; but the fields were dug up or filled in, and a glittering garden was laid. Deep, mountainlike stands of trees, a heart-moving pond extolling the gods of the sea—the sound of the waterfalls falling from the peaks moves one to tears; the place is one of deep meditation. . . . The mountain landscape is fascinating, and there is no way to describe the propitiousness of the view, so remote from the atmosphere of the city.[15]

Today the trees in front are so tall and thick that the view to the south has been lost, but otherwise the beauty of the past has been preserved. As at the Saga-in the site was close enough to the mountains for people to hear the sound of "waterfalls falling from the peaks," which implies that there was an amplitude of beauty and variety in the small landscapes observable as one walked through the garden. We see here the essence of the traditional Japanese word for landscapes, *sansui*, which translated character by character means "mountains and water."

Itsukushima Shrine

Miyajima, the island on which the famous Itsukushima Shrine stands, is in the Seto Inland Sea southwest of Hiroshima. Alongside Amanohashidate, an elongated sandbar in Miyazu Bay, and Matsushima, a group of pine-covered islands offshore from Sendai, Miyajima is celebrated as one of Japan's three most beautiful scenic spots. It might be noted in passing that all three of these consist of land masses rising from a quiet sea.

Itsukushima Shrine, on the north shore of Miyajima, is built out over an inlet, and its great *torii* is a fair distance out in the water (figure 12.6). The whole shrine complex is beautifully integrated with its surroundings. South of the shrine rises a mountain, Misen, which is worshiped as a sacred peak (kannabi-yama), and it would appear that the entire island was formerly regarded as sacred. Some hold that it was worshiped from the

Figure 12.5
Sagano, or Saga Meadow,
(Kyoto) seen from Mount
Ogura (arrow points to Ōs-
awa Pond)

Figure 12.6
Itsukushima Shrine (Hiro-
shima Prefecture)

Chigozen Shrine in Hatsukaichi, on the mainland, and that this is why Itsukushima Shrine was built over the water rather than on land.[16]

The shrine area is bounded on either side by promontories, and the sea spreads out broadly in front. Since the shrine faces northwest, the directionality does not suit the *zōfū-tokusui* pattern, but, with Misen looming up in the rear, the landscape as a whole may be regarded as belonging to the lineage of the hill-behind, pond-before garden. To be sure, it is a sacred garden, consecrated to the deities of Itsukushima Shrine, Ichikishima-no-hime, Tagori-no-hime, and Tagitsu-no-hime. Nevertheless, the shrine as a whole is reminiscent of the style of residential architecture known as *shinden-zukuri*, thought to have been employed for the mansions of the nobility in the Heian period. In that style, the main house, *shinden*, occupied a central position facing south toward a pond and was linked by open corridors to other apartments. Among the latter were kiosks called "fishing pavilions," *tsuridono*, which often extended out over the pond. One sees at Itsukushima Shrine the same sense of delicacy and refinement that seem to have characterized the *shinden-zukuri* house and garden, as well as certain temple-garden complexes built by followers of Pure Land Buddhism.

The shrine is said to have assumed a form similar to the one we see today in the latter part of the twelfth century, as a result of the special patronage of the then all-powerful Taira clan. This is probably correct, although the exact circumstances of the construction have been subjected to debate, as have the questions of when, how often, and to what extent the shrine has been reconstructed. It is, nevertheless, generally regarded as typical of late-Heian architecture. In this connection it might be noted that the sea over which the shrine seems to preside was of particular importance to the Taira, whose greatest leader,

Kiyomori (1118–1181), devoted a vast amount of time and money toward developing a trade route to China via the Inland Sea.

The inlet, which is suitable for navigation by small boats, is of a type that, according to Yanagita Kunio, was called *futo* or *futto* in some Japanese dialects. Yanagita related this word with *hoto* or *hodo*, which in ancient Japanese referred to the feminine genitalia, and pointed out that a crotchlike recess in the shore was a point of vital importance to sailors and fishermen.[17] Though the inlet at Itsukushima is too shallow for large vessels, formations of its type had a distinct functional significance to those whose occupations involved the sea.

The Amida Hall at Shiramizu

Located in the city of Iwaki, Fukushima Prefecture, the Shiramizu Amida Hall (figure 12.7) was built in 1160 by the sister of Fujiwara no Hidehira (?–1187) in memory of her husband. Hidehira's branch of the Fujiwara family is famous for having built a flourishing cultural center in the northern town of Hiraizumi during the twelfth century; this Amida Hall, together with its garden, are in the same general style as the more famous Mōtsu-ji and Muryōkō-in constructed in Hiraizumi by Hidehira and his father. All three temples follow a pattern associated with Pure Land, or Jōdo, Buddhism of the eleventh and twelfth centuries.

North of the Amida Hall is a cone-shaped mountain of the sort that might well have been sacred in the past. To the east and west are mountains known respectively, as the Evening-sun Fudō and the Morning-sun Fudō, Fudō being the name of a Buddhist deity of frightening mien. The Shiramizu River flows to the south, completing the classic *zōfū-tokusui* pattern. According to a reconstruction carried out by Fujishima Gaijirō, the Amida Hall originally stood on an island in a

Figure 12.7
The Shiramizu Amida Hall
and its surroundings (Fu-
kushima Prefecture)

pond.[18] If so, it must have been even more beautiful than it is today, although in its present condition it ranks as an excellent example of Jōdo temple art, which sought to reproduce on earth the glories thought to exist in the western paradise of the Buddha Amida.

KAMAKURA

In the year 1185 the forces of Minamoto no Yoritomo (1147–1199), whose power base was in the eastern region of Kantō, defeated the Taira in the Inland Sea and brought an end to their thirty-odd years of dominance over the court in Kyoto. With his defeat of the northern Fujiwara four years later, Yoritomo became the undisputed military master of Japan. Rather than remain near the decadent imperial government in the traditional capital, he chose to rule the country from Kamakura, about 350 kilometers to the east (as the crow flies), where he set up a military government of his own. The Kamakura *bakufu*, or "tent government," as it was known, was to rule the nation for nearly a century and a half. Its presence, superimposed on that of the ancient court in Kyoto, represents a transitional phase of dual authority between the age of Chinese-style imperial rule and the age of mature feudalism.

Earlier, in 1063, Minamoto no Yoriyoshi (988–1075), Yoritomo's great-great-great-grandfather, had established himself in this area and constructed, near a beach called Yuigahama, a shrine sacred to the deities of the Iwashimizu Hachiman Shrine outside Kyoto. Yoriyoshi, who had gained fame as the victor in the famous Nine-Year War of the mid-eleventh century, had done much to strengthen the control of the Minamoto clan over the eastern provinces. Why he chose Yuigahama for the shrine is not clear; sources inform us merely that "it fitted in with his desires."[19] Yet it seems significant that the location was by the sea. The beach at Kamakura is, in fact, on an inlet of the *futo* type, opening on Sagami Bay and usable as a haven for boats (figure 12.8). Moreover it is situated at the eastern end of the bay, at a point from which a main highway led north toward the past communicating with other parts of the eastern region. It was a perfect place from which to carry out an attack against the surrounding area and consequently a logical spot in which to build a shrine to the god of war (as embodied in the three Iwashimizu deities).

According to the *Azumakagami* ("Mirror of the East"), when Yoritomo had suffered a setback in 1180 and been forced to flee to the province of Awa (the southern part of modern Bōsō Peninsula), one of his followers, Chiba Tsunetane (1118–1201), advised him as follows: "The place where you are staying now has no stronghold to speak of, and there are no traces of your ancestors. You ought to go to Kamakura in Sagami Province as quickly as possible."[20]

Yoritomo followed this advice, and, once in Kamakura, moved the Hachiman Shrine to a village called Kobayashi, where he renamed it Tsurugaoka Wakamiya. The new location was a typical *zōfū-tokusui* setting, with mountains on the north, east, and west, and the ocean on the south. As boundaries, the mountains and sea here are of the sort that Bollnow described as means whereby man might "resist the destructive force of invading chaos."[21] They represent a return, at the hands of the newly arisen warrior class, to the original function of boundaries, as opposed to the more aesthetic concept observed in the case of Kyoto ("the mountains and rivers are beautiful"; "the mountains and rivers of this province form collar and belt").[22]

A thoroughfare was built from the Tsurugaoka Wakamiya to the ocean, and it became the central axis of the shogun's capital. Unlike Suzaku Avenue in Kyoto, which had extended

Figure 12.8
Map of Kamakura where
the Tsurugaoka Hachiman
Shrine (*A*) is situated

south from the imperial palace, Wakamiya Highroad emanated from the house of the god of war. This fact in itself symbolized the spirit of the warrior class, as well as the relationship between political authority and religious authority under the Kamakura *bakufu*.

Apart from its Shinto connections the Kamakura government made an important contribution to the development of Japanese religion by affording protection to Zen Buddhism, which was introduced to Japan in the late twelfth century by the priest Yōsai (or Eisai; 1141–1215). Spurned at first by the clergy and nobility of Kyoto, Yōsai met with a warm welcome in Kamakura, where in 1200, with the aid of Yoritomo's widow Hōjō Masako (1157–1225), he established a temple called Jufuku-ji. In the succeeding century many more Zen temples were constructed in this area, the most important being a group known as the "five mountains," *gozan*.

A common feature of the Kamakura Zen establishments was that they were built in pocket valleys extending from the plain into the mountains and thus having mountains behind and on either side. One reason for the selection of such sites was that the temples were for the most part laid out in accordance with an oblong, symmetrical plan imported from China. The archetype is the layout of the Kenchō-ji, which was completed in 1253 under the auspices of the regent Hōjō Tokiyori (1227–1263), and which was modeled on the Ching-shan-ssu in Hangchow. Here the principal buildings are lined up precisely along a central axis, beginning with a large gate and continuing through the hall of Buddha and a lecture hall to the priest's quarters. Only the last, because of its residential character, was allowed to depart from strict left–right symmetry. Other buildings were set to left and right of the axis in a more or less balanced plan. The general arrangement did not differ greatly from that seen in an early drawing of the Engaku-ji (figure 12.9), the second-

ranking of Kamakura's "five mountains," which was built in 1282 by the regent Hōjō Tokimune (1251–1284).

The little valleys of Kamakura, of which it is said that there are sixty-six in all, fitted the Zen temple layout admirably. Moreover they fulfilled another Zen requirement, which was that they provide landscape beauty. It was the custom at Zen monasteries to pick out a number of streams or bridges or crags, give them fanciful names, and regard them as boundary points. This practice made the presence of outstanding scenic features desirable, if not absolutely essential, in the selection of sites. It was also customary to find the highest spot available in the temple grounds and build a small pavilion from which visitors could view the surroundings. It is said that the desire to look out over the scenery from a high point became quite pronounced in the Kamakura period (1185–1333).[23]

Though the valleys of Kamakura did not invariably open toward the south, as was considered best, they had the advantage of providing quiet, secluded spaces, cut off from each other by ridges. Normally they were watered by streams flowing down from the mountains. The abbot's residence was near the head of the valley, where it commanded the best view of all. At the Kenchō-ji, it was provided with a second story, called the "moon-viewing tower," which looked out over a large pond toward the recesses behind. From the top of the mountain beyond the pond, it was possible to view the entire monastery and its setting.

Despite variations in directionality the valleys in which the Kamakura monasteries stood may be considered to belong to the general category of *zōfū-tokusui* spaces.

EDO

One wonders what sort of space Edo (modern Tokyo) was for Tokugawa Ieyasu (1542–1616), the founder of the shogunal dynasty

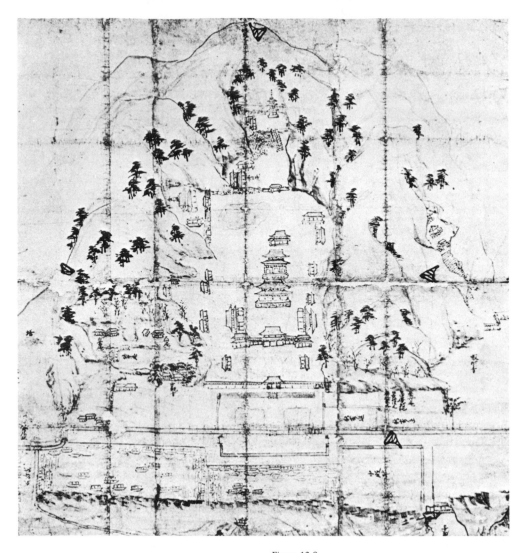

Figure 12.9
Early drawing of the En-
gaku-ji in Kamakura,
showing how neatly the
plan has been fitted into a
long narrow valley

that made its capital there for two and a half centuries. Shortly after Ieyasu established his government in Edo, the neo-Confucianist Fujiwara Seika (1561–1619) visited the place and remarked that there were four remarkable sights in the eastern provinces: Mount Fuji, the large grassy flatland known as Musashino, the Sumida River, and Mount Tsukuba.[24] Of these, Mount Fuji and Mount Tsukuba are quite distant from Edo and have a low angle of elevation when seen from there.

In speaking of Musashino, Seika was probably not referring to its more distant reaches to the north, but it seems likely that, when Ieyasu chose Nikkō, more than a hundred kilometers north of Edo, as the site for his mausoleum, he was thinking in terms of the entire Kantō Plain as a sort of *zōfū-tokusui* configuration, with Mount Fuji on the west, Mount Tsukuba on the east, and Mount Nantai, Nikkō's most famous peak, on the north. His spatial consciousness, however, was no doubt based primarily on political considerations rather than on visual impressions, for the Kantō Plain is much too large to be regarded as a landscape except in a purely conceptual way.

Ieyasu's mental picture of this area may have been similar to that of the agricultural scientist and economist Satō Nobuhiro (1769–1850). "In order to rule over the whole nation," wrote Satō, "it is necessary first to build a royal capital. Since the capital is the nucleus of the empire, it should be located in a beautiful place." But Ōsaka would not do, because "its area is too small, and there are so many people that the rice and grain grown there would probably be insufficient to feed them." The Kantō Plain, however, was a different matter. "The land is broad, and both damp fields and dry fields [exist]. . . . Water routes are plentiful, so that grains, fruits, and the special products of all

the provinces can conveniently be transported there. All commodities are plentiful, and there is little chance of famine." Satō added, "There are sacred mountains on three sides, forming boundaries and offering protection from outside threats. On the east is the vast ocean. In advancing, it is easy to control other provinces; in retreating it is not difficult to stand in defense." Accordingly, "Edo is the best place in which to build a royal capital. The capital ought to be fixed there and not moved for long years."[25]

Yet it remains true that Edo and the Kantō Plain formed too large a space to be experienced directly from many points within it or on its boundaries. It could, for most purposes, only be viewed indirectly, in the mind's eye. In short, it was close to space at what Norberg-Schulz has called the "geographical level." Even so, it is remarkable that men like Ieyasu and Satō Nobuhiro visualized this as a vast landscape with mountains on three sides and water on the other. That the largest flat area in Japan (except Hokkaido) could be thought of as a single space created by its topographical surroundings is proof of the vast importance of the landscape in the Japanese idea of space.

MORIOKA

A few years ago a competition was held for designs suggesting the ideal way of accommodating human beings to their surroundings at the beginning of the twenty-first century. A group called the Twenty-first Century Research Society submitted a futuristic design for the city of Morioka, in Iwate Prefecture, which it regarded as a potentially good example of the medium-sized Japanese urban complex of, say, thirty years from now. The theme of the design was "Mountains, Rivers, and Forests—Then People and Poetry."[26]

Interestingly enough, the city of Morioka has mountains on three sides and is open to the south. Watered by the Kitagami River and the Shizukuishi River, it is definitely in the lineage of the *zōfū-tokusui* type of natural environment. In the course of adopting mountains, rivers, and forests as their theme, the designers had unwittingly lit upon a site that agreed in general configuration with the traditional sites chosen for the Japanese capitals of the past.

STRUCTURE AND COMPOSITION OF THE ZŌFŪ-TOKUSUI TYPE

The features of the *zōfū-tokusui* landscape, as delineated by Saitō Tadashi, are as follows:

1. Mountains loom up on the north, like the drooping head of a tortoise-snake, with the undulations of the green dragon and the deferential bowing of the white tiger extending southward on the east and west. These mountains form barriers for the area they embrace, thus causing it to be defined as a definite district or domain.

2. There is flowing water on the south; there may also be low hills. The flowing water, like the mountains on the other three sides, forms a boundary or edge (figure 12.10).

3. Because of the foregoing characteristics the district slopes gently toward the south. The slight incline provides directionality.

4. The configuration gives a sense of north, south, east, and west. This directionality is directly linked with the movements of the sun and the resulting light effects, as well as with the directionality of the wind, which is not allowed to disperse the vital spirit.

In contrast to the classical pattern, the configuration for gardens outlined in the *Sakuteiki* calls for flowing water on the east, a thoroughfare on the west, and a pond on the south. In other words, the elements forming the edges on these three sides are different. Nevertheless, the area defined by these boundaries has north–south–east–west directionality and constitutes a distinct domain. It is therefore to be regarded as belonging to the *zōfū-tokusui* lineage.

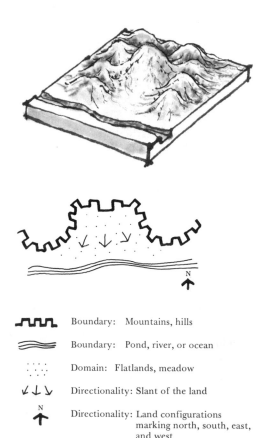

Boundary:	Mountains, hills
Boundary:	Pond, river, or ocean
Domain:	Flatlands, meadow
Directionality:	Slant of the land
Directionality:	Land configurations marking north, south, east, and west

Figure 12.10
Structural elements of the
zōfū-tokusui type

13

The Sacred Mountain Type

TERMINOLOGY

The term "sacred mountain" is used here to refer not to all the many mountains regarded as sacred in Japan but to a particular type known as *kannabi-yama*. In a study of ancient religious practices Ōba Iwao defined the *kannabi-yama* as "a small mountain or hill adjacent to the flatlands." Ōba distinguished this from the other principal type of sacred mountain, which he described as "a majestic peak soaring above the clouds."[1]

Kannabi, sometimes written *kamunabi*, is an ancient word whose meaning is undoubtedly "godly," but whose etymology is not certain. Most likely it derives from elements meaning literally "vicinity of the gods." The ancient sources employ it both as a modifier and as the name of several specific mountains. Not even all sacred mountains that are small and situated near plains are called *kannabi-yama*, but the number that are is noticeably large.

Although no one knows for certain how mountains of this type came to be regarded as sacred, the process is not difficult to conjecture. Yanagita Kunio argued, convincingly enough, that in the development of the Japanese concept of deities, there was a gradual upgrading of dead spirits to ancestral spirits and ultimately to godly spirits. In the beginning communities living in the neighborhood of small mountains buried their dead on the mountainsides, which thereupon became sacred, first as the home of the dead, then as the home of ancestral gods, then as the misty residence of the earthly gods.[2] It would seem only natural that, when the gods of heaven descended to earth, as we are told they did in the *Nihon shoki* and the *Kojiki*, they chose to land on sacred eminences of this sort. The exact manner in which these religious concepts developed, however, must have been very complicated.

Representative of the *kannabi-yama* type are the famous Mount Miwa in Yamato (figures 13.1, 13.2), four mountains in Izumo Province (modern Shimane Prefecture) that are actually called Kannabi-yama, and another in Yamashiro Province (modern Kyoto Prefecture) that goes by that name. Belonging to the same general category are Mount Mimuro in Yamato-Tatsuta (Nara Prefecture), Mimuro Peak at Musashi-Kodama (Saitama Prefecture), Mount Mikasa at Kasuga Shrine in Nara, Mount Kami at the Upper Kamo Shrine outside Kyoto, Mount Ushio at Hie Shrine (Shiga Prefecture), Mount Mikami at Mikami Shrine (Shiga Prefecture), and Misen at Itsukushima Shrine (Hiroshima Prefecture).

Ōba lists the following as the chief characteristics of the *kannabi-yama* type:

1. The mountain is near a community and is sufficiently clean and pure to serve as a place for worship.
2. The form of the mountain stands out conspicuously from the surroundings and gives the impression of being a place that the gods might inhabit.
3. The mountain is covered with trees, so that it appears to be enveloped in greenery.

Mountains of this type have, in the words of Lynch, "visual qualities . . . that make them the inevitable subjects of attention, despite the selective power of the eye."[3] They have a high degree of visibility, which makes them one of the most important elements in a landscape. The frontal surface they present to a viewer on a plain has a high angle of elevation, and they are close enough for the awe-inspiring texture of their luxuriant growth of green trees to be sensed. Moreover, they are girdled by rivers that share their godly nature and set them off as strongholds of the gods. There is no lack of the cleanness and purity needed to make them qualify as sacred places.

In speaking of outstanding landmarks, Lynch observed that "most often, sacredness is concentrated in the more striking natural features." As an example, he cites a hill in Assam regarded as the site of the Buddha's death

that rises "directly from a plain to which it is in contrast."[4] It is not difficult to see here a sacred mountain of the *kannabi-yama* type. Mentioning Waddell as his source, Lynch observed that the Assam eminence "was worshiped by the aborigines long before and has become holy for Brahmans and Muhammadans as well."

MOUNT MIWA

The qualities of our sacred mountain type are well illustrated by Mount Miwa, which is often offered as an example in discussions of Japanese mountain worship as a whole. Gracefully conic in form Miwa stands out from the surrounding hills. Though it is not completely "free-standing," its shape sets it apart, as does the physical border formed by the Hatsuse River, which flows down from the "secluded valley" of Hatsuse on the north. To the subjective eye Mount Miwa appears as an independent entity.

This in itself is not enough to make the mountain a sacred landmark. It must also present its best face to the plain below. In this case the conic form can be seen from any point on the broad Yamato Plain lying to the west. Princess Nukada, a seventh-century poetess, is said to have written the following lines:

O that sweet mountain of Miwa—
I would go lingering over its sight,
Many times looking back from far upon it
Till it is hidden beyond the hills of Nara
And beyond many turnings of the road.[5]

According to a note in the *Man'yōshū*, this was composed at the time when the Emperor Tenji moved the capital to Ōtsu and the princess was obliged to move with the court. On her journey inland she paused at the Nara mountains to take a last fond view of Asuka, where she had lived thus far. To her, Mount Miwa was clearly the symbol of her former

Figure 13.1
Map of Mount Miwa (*A*)
and vicinity (arrow indi-
cates the direction from
which photo in figure 13.2
was taken)

Figure 13.2
Mount Miwa (Nara
Prefecture)

home. From our viewpoint it should be noted that the Nara mountains, which form the entire northern boundary of the Yamato Plain, are about twenty kilometers from Mount Miwa. From a point this far removed, the mountain would have to be classed as a long-range view, but even so it is visible throughout the Yamato Plain.

In much earlier times there existed on the gently sloping skirt of Mount Miwa, where it flattens into the plain, an agricultural community that depended upon mountain streams for its water supply. This is thought to have been the original location of the Miwa dynasty, founded by the semimythical Emperor Sujin, whom the *Nihon shoki* called "the first emperor to rule the nation." The nucleus of his kingdom was presumably the area bounded on the east by Mount Miwa, on the south and west by the Hatsuse River, and on the north by the Makimuku River. The emperor's residence, according to the *Kojiki*, was the palace of Mizugaki in Shiki, Shiki being the name of the region in which Mount Miwa is situated.[6]

The godly rivers, Hatsuse and Makimuku, did not in this case separate the agricultural community from the sacred mountain. Instead, the whole area bounded by the natural features became a single unit. Within it the most distant point from Mount Miwa is about three kilometers from the summit and two kilometers from the foot. The texture of the forest on the mountain can be seen from here except when bad weather reduces visibility; the mountain's angle of elevation is about 8 degrees. Horizontally, the face of the mountain spreads over an angle of from 55 to 60 degrees, which means that it nearly fills the normal range of vision. This then is an integral part of the space that includes the mountain.

IZUMO PROVINCE

The eighth-century gazetteer of Izumo Province noted the presence of four mountains going by the name of Kannabi-yama. Their locations were stated to be Ou County, Aika County, Tatenui County, and Izumo County.[7] Among them, the one in Ou (figures 13.3, 13.4) is of most concern to us here. Known also as Mount Chausu, it juts from the north into the plain lying between the point where the Ou River exits from the mountains and the point where it empties into Lake Naka-noumi. In this position the mountain is highly visible from the surrounding land below.

In recent years the ancient site of the provincial government of Izumo has been discovered at Ōkusa, on the banks of the Ou below Mount Chausu. Seen from this point, the mountain has an elevation angle of 9.5 to 10 degrees, and its face occupies a visual angle of about 60 degrees. Its distance from the early site varies between 500 and 1,000 meters, so that at most it would be classed as a middle-distance view. Its wooded textures are visible from all points on the plain. Like Mount Miwa, then, Mount Chausu may be regarded as typical of the sacred mountain class.

MOUNT MIKASA

Behind Kasuga Shrine in Nara is a beautifully shaped hill called Mount Mikasa, which, though separate in appearance, is a part of Mount Kasuga rising to the rear. The whole area around here is covered by virgin forests, protected by law from woodcutters since ancient times. Growing on Mount Mikasa are many laurysylvan trees, which offer a striking revelation of Japanese plant life in prehistoric times. There exists, in the collection of the Shōsō-in Repository, a map made in 756 of the Tōdai-ji and its environs. On this, the foot of Mount Mikasa is marked as "sacred territory." It is safe to assume that the mountain was an object of nature worship in even earlier times.

Figure 13.3
Map of Mount Chausu
(Kannabi) in Ou (*A*) and
the ancient site of the provincial government (*B*) and
vicinity (arrow indicates
the direction from which
photo in figure 13.4 was
taken)

Figure 13.4
Mount Kannabi in Ou, in
the former province of
Izumo, seen from the site of
the provincial seat of ancient government

169 *The Sacred Mountain Type*

Figure 13.5
"Kasuga Mandala" in the
collection of the Atami
Museum of Art (Shizuoka
Prefecture)

According to the earliest historical sources, the seventh emperor, Kōrei, took as one of his wives a woman from the Kasuga district, and the ninth emperor, Kaika, lived in a palace there. In somewhat less mythical times the region was held by the Wani and Kasuga clans, both of which are recorded to have furnished wives for a number of emperors. Kasuga Village, the stronghold of the Kasuga clan in early historical times, is said by Kishi Toshio to have been situated in the east-central part of the ancient capital at Nara, which corresponds to Byakugōji-chō in modern Nara.[8] This is southwest of Mount Mikasa and separated from it by a stream called the Noto River. Most likely the mountain was sacred to the ancestors and tutelary deity of the Kasuga clan, and the river was the sacred river dividing the mountain from the area where people lived.

After 710, when the capital was moved to Nara, the land passed into the hands of the Fujiwara family, who constructed Kasuga Shrine on it. Mount Mikasa ceased to be the sacred mountain of the Kasuga clan and became an object of worship for the far more powerful Fujiwara, if not for the people of Nara as a whole.

There is an entire genre of Shinto paintings known as Kasuga Shrine mandalas, which depicts the shrine and its surroundings (figure 13.5). In every example great care has been taken to depict individual trees standing on Mount Mikasa. We see not only the treetops but the trunks and branches and leaves as well. The mountain is thus treated as what we have classed earlier as a short-distance view. Unlike the "majestic peaks soaring above the clouds," the *kannabi-yama* derives its awesomeness in part from its abundant foliage, which to the Japanese mind suggests the presence of sacred spirits. As in the case of Mount Miwa and Mount Kannabi in Ou, Mount Mikasa forms a unit with the space lying immediately before it.

STRUCTURE AND COMPOSITION OF THE SACRED MOUNTAIN TYPE

The principal characteristics of the sacred mountain landscapes are as follows:

1. The mountain stands out distinctly from its surroundings, more shapely and beautiful than other mountains in the vicinity, and its face is visible as a short-range view from the flatlands around it. Appearing independent and massive, it serves as a location indicator or landmark and gives organization to the space around it, drawing the flatlands into a single spatial entity (figure 13.6). It also provides directionality by virtue of its height, which draws attention upward toward that which is superhuman. It is the symbol of that which is permanent and abiding in what would otherwise be empty space. It is perceived as a nearby view, or at most a middle-distance view, and the texture of its greenery can be sensed from any point within its "sphere of influence."

2. The flatlands around the mountain are drawn by the mountain's centripetal force into a definite district or place. The pyramids of Egypt function in similar fashion, drawing the area immediately around them into a definite spatial entity distinct from the vast openness of the surrounding desert.

3. In the vicinity of the sacred mountain there is a sacred river, setting off the holy precinct associated with the mountain from the surrounding area. This boundary enhances the oneness of the district as a landscape. The sacred mountain type and the domain-viewing mountain type to be discussed next differ from the previous five types in that they are what Goldfinger has described as plastic or convex, whereas the earlier types are "spatial" or concave (figure 13.7). These last two types fall into the category Ashihara Yoshinobu calls "N spaces," as opposed to "P spaces."[9]

 Goal (landmark): Mountain, hills

Directionality: Rising mountains

Domain: Flatlands

Boundary: River

Figure 13.6
Structural elements of the sacred mountain type

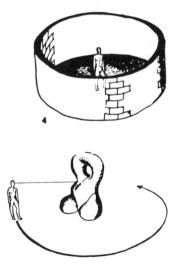

Figure 13.7
Spatial and plastic spaces as conceived by Goldfinger

14

The Domain-Viewing Mountain Type

INSPECTING THE REALM

Countless are the mountains in Yamato,
But perfect is the heavenly hill of Kagu;
When I climb it and survey my realm,
Over the wide lake the gulls are on the wing;
A beautiful land it is, the Land of Yamato![1]

This famous poem from the *Man'yōshū* is supposed to have been composed by the Emperor Jomei (r. 628–641) on an occasion when he climbed to the top of Mount Kagu to view his domain. One question the poem poses is what the significance of the emperor's sightseeing trip was. Was he merely looking at the scenery, or did he have some other purpose?

According to Tsuchihashi Yutaka, the practice of viewing domains, which is called *kunimi* in Japanese, began as a ceremonial part of the annual first trip to the mountains in the spring, a custom practiced by agricultural communities all over the country. Gradually, it seems, the domain-surveying part of the ritual became the sole prerogative of the community patriarch and afterward of the emperor.

As noted earlier, in the chapter on Akizushimaya-Yamato, the element *kuni*, here rendered "domain," was written with a variety of Chinese characters and signified a territory enclosed within certain boundaries. Later it came to be the general term for "province" or "country," but in the earlier states it referred to the property belonging to a particular agricultural community and consequently to the political sphere controlled by its leader.

The element *mi* in *kunimi*, which means generally "to see," is the subject of an interesting observation by Tsuchihashi. "We may suppose," he writes, "that this is not seeing in the vague sense of looking at nature in general but rather seeing or looking at some well-defined object or natural phenomenon. . . .

One notices that the subjects found in poems regarded as domain-viewing poems are such specific things as rising clouds, smoke, or 'heat waves.'" With regard to Emperor Jomei's poem quoted here, Tsuchihashi remarks, "It is fairly clear that the poet has seen what he takes to be the spirit of the land and water. For him, the smoke wreaths and gulls were not merely sights his eye has fallen upon but fetishes associated with poems of the domain-viewing type. The very pronouncement of such a poem was calculated to aid the activities of nature." [2]

Spring is the most active of the seasons. It is the time of the year when the natural life forces of the universe are revived. By praising the rising mist or the flying gulls, which symbolize the annual reawakening, the singers of the domain-viewing songs hoped to ensure an abundant harvest in the fall.

In ancient times "seeing" was not merely a sensory act but one connected with the spirits and with life itself. The domain spreading out before the eyes was perceived as an object of nature worship, and much time had to pass before it ceased to be that and became instead merely a natural landscape. [3]

Gaston Bachelard has stated that, when a person looks out on the sea from a high point or views a city from a tower or gazes out over the vast earth from a mountaintop, he feels a sense of power and authority over all he surveys: "Looking down upon a plain, a dreamer can receive a strong impression of domination. To reach a lofty spot is to experience spiritual recovery. We at least control the fields and meadows. For a person who seeks a dream within nature, even the lowest hill can provide inspiration." [4]

George Sand said that the dream of farmers, bound day in and day out to the soil, was to gaze out over a long distance. In ancient Japan the practice of making a first trip to the mountains in the spring entailed viewing the land below, and this experience must have been an exhilarating one for the ancient Japanese farmers. The process whereby domain viewing by the ruler became a separate ritual no doubt had something to do with the "strong impression of domination" mentioned by Bachelard. Where ordinary farmers might "experience spiritual recovery" from observing their land from above, their leader would be affected by more autocratic sentiments when surveying the same property.

From the scientific viewpoint, when one looks out over a plain, which is essentially a longitudinal surface, the visual angle of incidence increases with the height of the viewpoint. The plain can thus be seen more easily from a higher point than from a lower one. But the meaning of domain viewing involves physological factors that go beyond the realm of optics. The placement of the Usa (Oita Prefecture) and Iwashimizu (Kyoto Prefecture) Shrines, as well as that of the castles of late medieval times, may be regarded as falling in the tradition of the ancient domain viewing, because the same principles of spatial structure and psychological significance are apparent.

Ishikawa Hideaki, who emphasized the importance of hills and waterfronts as elements in urban beauty, wrote the following:

The contribution of hills to urban beauty is my secret discovery. It is obvious that green hills sprinkled with buildings form a beautiful background, but what I would like to stress is the importance of hills as points from which cities can be seen and loved. Only by viewing a city from a hill can one grasp its full beauty or the true flavor of its life. Nurtured by its natural surroundings, constantly shifting and moving, the beauty of the city stretches out objectively before one's eyes. A true sense of love for the city can be felt only when one views it from a hill. [5]

Ishikawa goes on to argue that a city's hills ought to be protected, and protected specifically as places from which the urban populace can observe their surroundings as an everyday experience. What he is driving at is akin to the "experience of spiritual recovery' that the ancients gained from their annual first trip to the mountains rather than the sense of domination inherent in domain viewing. The key point in Ishikawa's argument is the idea of seeing and loving the city in which one lives.

MOUNT KAGU IN NARA

Mount Kagu, the "heavenly hill" mentioned in the poem at the beginning of this chapter, is one of the three mountains of Yamato, the other two being Mount Unebi and Mount Miminashi. Kagu is smaller than either of the others, and, whereas they are independent rises, it is backed up by larger mountains (figure 14.1). Of the three mountains Kagu is the least prominent when viewed from the plain.

Origuchi Shinobu suggested that the reason for including Mount Kagu among the three mountains was that "it was very much an object of worship and was praised for that reason." He added that "the topography here—deep mountains behind, lower mountains in front, and a promontorylike mountain in foremost position overlooking a broad and fertile plain—was suited to be considered as a sort of stairway" by which the gods could descend from heaven to the place where their worshipers lived.[6]

From Mount Kagu it was possible to look out over the site of the Fujiwara capital, bounded on the north by Mount Miminashi and on the west by Mount Unebi. In the distance to the south lay the "green hedge mountains" and the *kuni* they enclosed. Most likely Mount Kagu was chosen as a place for viewing the domain in an age when agriculture, having originated in the foothills, had not yet spread beyond the middle of the valley.

DOMAIN-VIEWING MOUNTAINS IN HARIMA

The following three entries appear in the eighth-century gazetteer for the Province of Harima (modern Hyogo Prefecture):

Ōtachi Mountain. The reason why this is called Ōtachi ["large stand"] is that the Emperor Homuda stood here and looked down upon the lay of the land.[7]

Ōmi Mountain. The reason why it is called Ōmi ["big look"] is that the Emperor Homuda climbed this mountain and looked in the four directions.[8]

Mitachi Mountain. The Emperor Homuda climbed this hill and inspected the country. Therefore it is called Mitachi ["honored stand"].[9]

The personage referred to in these three accounts as the Emperor Homuda is better known as Emperor Ōjin, who is said in traditional chronologies to have reigned from 200 to 310, but who probably lived around the end of the fourth century. The three mountains are all in or near the city of Himeji, overlooking a plain bounded on the east by the Ibo and Hayashida Rivers and on the west by the Ōtsumo River. Ōtachi Mountain (86.8 meters) is what is now called Maeyama in the district of Mitachi; Ōmi Mountain (165.1 meters) is now Mount Dantoku; and Mitachi Mountain is now said to be Mount Tachioka (109.2 meters) in Taishi-chō Tachioka (figure 14.2).

The space defined by these three hills is startlingly similar to that formed by the three mountains of Yamato. Even the mountains themselves are of the same general shape. One wonders if Emperor Ōjin's reason for selecting these three mountains in Harima as vantage points for viewing his possessions was not that they reminded of the three Yamato mountains.

Figure 14.1
Mount Kagu, with higher
mountains behind (Nara
Prefecture)

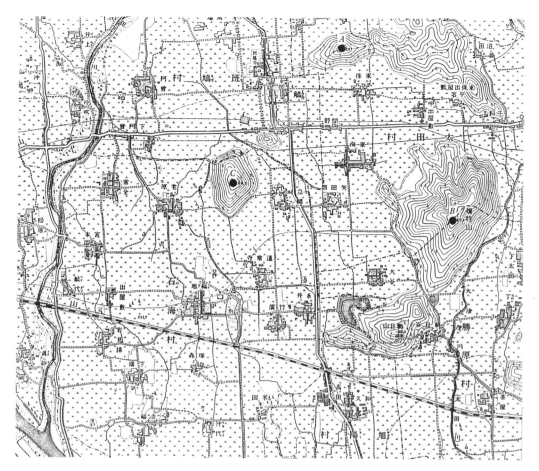

Figure 14.2
Map of domain-viewing
mountains in Harima re-
gion where Maeyama (*A*),
Mount Dantoku (*B*), and
Mount Tachioka (*C*) are
situated

It is generally considered that agriculture, having first been practiced in the small mountain-fields referred to earlier, gradually spread out into the foothills and thence into the plains. One would suppose therefore that the viewing of the domains would have begun on a mountain projecting from a higher range and later have been transferred to independent mountains rising from the plains. The case of the three mountains in the Harima gazetteer seems to corroborate this theory.

As noted earlier, the ritual of viewing the domain seems in its earlier stages to have been a fetishistic observance, calculated to lead to a good harvest. Gradually, it became a more politically oriented practice in which the ruler was actually inspecting the lands under his control. It seems logical to suppose then that in the early stages the gods came down from the mountains to view the fields from projecting hills like Mount Kagu but that, as the fields spread out farther into the plains, earthly rulers chose the more centrally located free-standing mountains as spots from which to survey their territories.

A similar phenomenon occurred much later in Japanese history. During the fifteenth century, when the country was divided into numerous more or less autonomous states, feudal lords built their castles in the foothills of mountains or on projecting rises. But, as the country was unified and peace restored, the castles were more often constructed on high ground amid surrounding plains. In passing, it might be noted that Himeji Castle (figure 14.3), built by Toyotomi Hideyoshi in 1581 and expanded in 1608 by Ikeda Terumasa (1564–1613), stands on an independent hill called Himeyama, about eight kilometers to the east of the domain-viewing mountains of Harima. It is the most impressive and beautiful of the feudal castles still in existence. (Most of the fairly numerous castles to be seen in the Japanese countryside today are modern reconstructions.)

ARAHARA HILL

Arahara Hill is in Ibaraki Prefecture, east of a large lake known as Kasumi-gaura. The eighth-century gazetteer of this area quotes the great (mythical) general Yamato Takeru no Mikoto as saying, upon arriving at the hill and looking about in the four directions: "I stopped the palanquin and took a walk. When I lifted my eyes and looked around, [I saw that] the bends of the mountains and the inlets of the sea wound in and out with one another. Clouds floated on the tops of the peaks, and mist was embraced in the bosoms of the valleys. The sight was very beautiful; the contours of the land were extremely lovely." [10]

This description is more specific than any we have heretofore encountered in ancient sources. Allowing for a certain artificiality of expression, this is an objective description of a landscape as such. It matters little that the statement could not possibly date from as early as the second century, when Yamato Takeru no Mikoto is said by the traditional histories to have conquered the eastern part of Japan. The important point is that the presence of this legend in the early local records indicates that at some time in the course of early history the domain-viewing ritual began to take on the aspect of sightseeing—which is to say, going to the top of a hill or mountain simply to enjoy the view.

In earliest times then "seeing" had connotations of nature worship. Later it referred to political inspection by the ruler and also took on a certain fetishistic meaning. In the final stage it is used merely in the sense of "looking" at a natural setting.

EARLY BURIAL MOUNDS

At some stage in Japanese prehistory, probably the first half of the fourth century, it became the practice to erect large burial mounds for dead leaders or rulers. The earliest of these mounds are characterized by the fact that

Figure 14.3
Himeji Castle (Hyōgo
Prefecture)

Figure 14.4
The Ōtsukayama Burial
Mound, overlooking what
was once a feudal lord's
domain (Kyoto)

their builders took advantage of the natural terrain and chose for their mound sites hills that jutted out into relatively flat areas and consequently had a high degree of visibility. One authority has stated, "We may probably assume that, although there are differences in the height of the hills from place to place, within the area most closely associated with the deceased, the hill from which his territories could best be seen was selected."[11]

In some ways the spaces created by the burial mounds of this type might be classed together with the domain-viewing mountain type, for the idea of control by a ruler is present in both. Yet the being looking down from the mound was dead, and the hill used for his tomb automatically became sacred ground, not likely to be used for the domain-viewing ritual. Perhaps it would be best to consider the mound landscapes as falling somewhere in between the domain-viewing mountain type and the sacred mountain type.

The Ōtsukayama Burial Mound in Tsubai, Yamashiro-chō, Sagara-gun, Kyoto Prefecture, may be offered as an example (figure 14.4). At present a part of it has been shorn off to make way for railroad tracks, and houses have been built on the upper section, but the mount is nevertheless highly visible from the surrounding flatlands, of which it has a commanding view. It therefore fulfills the requirements stated by Ōtsuka Hatsushige.[12] One may suppose that it provided a focal point and gave organization, as well as concentration, to the area visible from its summit.[13]

STRUCTURE AND COMPOSITION OF THE
DOMAIN-VIEWING MOUNTAIN TYPE
The characteristics of the domain-viewing mountain type of landscape may be summarized as follows:

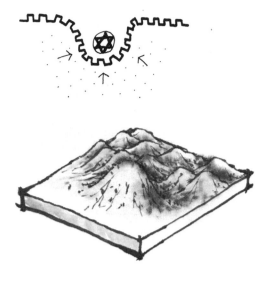

Boundary: Mountains, hills

Center: Mountaintop of hilltop

Directionality: Rising mountain or hill

Domain: Plain

Figure 14.5
Structural elements of the domain-viewing mountain type

Figure 14.6
Piazza del Popolo (from
Sigfried Giedion)

1. The domain-viewing mountain consisted of an independent hill or a projecting hill overlooking a broad flat area. To survey his lands, the ruler naturally chose a hill jutting out from the mountains into the fields or an independent hill amid the fields, either of which would provide a high angle of incidence. Aside from furnishing a vantage point, the hill also offered the sense of domination spoken of by Bachelard.

Unlike the sacred mountain type, which was regarded as the residence of a god not to be trespassed on by mortals, the domain-viewing mountain could be climbed and could therefore serve as a place for ceremonies, including not only the domain-viewing ritual itself but also harvest festivals and the like (figure 14.5). In this respect it fulfilled one of Lynch's conditions for nodes: it was a strategic focus "into which the observer can enter." [13]

In speaking of the Piazza del Popolo (figure 14.6), Sigfried Giedion said: "Its air of modernity is owing much more, however, to the way in which different levels are brought within the same composition . . . Valadier embodies a hovering sensation in the total effect produced by his design by bringing into relation with each other two horizontal areas of different levels: the terrace on the Pincio and the *piazza* proper. A proportion in three dimensions . . . is developed." [14] Similarly, in the domain-viewing mountain type one may consider the interaction of two levels, for the top of the hill becomes a "place" or node bearing a special relation to the plain below. Thus directionality is achieved through the relationship between upper and lower. The same type of spatiality is to be observed in the shrines of the Mount Otoko lineage and the castles-amid-plains of the late sixteenth and early seventeenth centuries.

2. The domain-viewing mountain is surrounded wholly or partially by flatlands. The plains constitute the ruler's territory in which the spirits of earth and water are active. This territory is given spatial organization by the mountain, which serves as a center and focal point.

15

*Elements of
Spatial
Composition
in Landscapes*

In a broader sense the seven types of landscape spaces that have been abstracted are
composed of four elements: boundary, focus-
center-goal, directionality, and domain—
which give landscapes their structural identity.
These elements can be used to analyze natural
settings, to achieve harmony with them, and
in developing land and carrying out construction programs. By understanding the function
of these compositional elements in our surroundings, we may perhaps also be able to
avoid the sense of homelessness and alienation that troubles modern life.

Our discussion is indebted to the work of
Kevin Lynch in *The Image of the City* and
Christian Norberg-Schulz in *Existence, Space,
and Architecture*.[1] Although it happens that
the results given here are in some ways a veri-
fication of Norberg-Schulz's theories, the dis-
tillation of the seven types was carried out
before they became known to the author, and
no deliberate attempt was made to adhere to
the framework of his concepts.

BOUNDARY

A physical spatial enclosure can keep man
from dissolving in the midst of things that are
not essential or from falling before destructive
invading forces.[2] The boundary, in short, protects man's very existence psychologically and
physically. To be effective, it must be difficult
to penetrate. It must also shut the outside
world off from view, while at the same time
have a high degree of visibility within the domain it protects. Lynch pointed out that continuity, no less than visibility, is crucial to the
formation of boundaries, which he described
as "strong edges."[3]

The type of boundary that best fits these requirements is a running string of mountains
or hills (figure 15.1). To serve their purpose
properly, the mountains must have considerable mass and be close enough to occupy a
fairly large vertical angle of vision.

Lynch also offers rivers as possible edges or boundaries, but, insofar as rivers do not cut the opposite bank off from view, they are less efficacious than mountains. This is particularly true in Japan, where most rivers are narrow. Yet it often happens in Japan that a small river functions as a barrier separating an inhabited area from the sacred ground on which the local temple or shrine stands. In this case the stream may be regarded as a symbolic edge that hampers penetration but does not cut the opposite side off from view. This aspect of the river as an edge is particularly interesting from the psychological viewpoint.

In the Mikumari Shrine type, the Akizushima-Yamato type, the eight-petal lotus type, the *zōfū-tokusui* type, and the secluded valley type of landscape spaces, the boundaries are formed by chains of mountains or hills. Rivers or bodies of water function as boundaries in the Mikumari Shrine type, the *zōfū-tokusui* type, and the sacred mountain type.

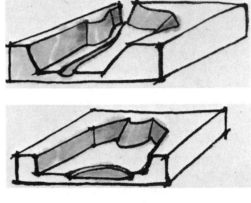

Figure 15.1
Types of boundaries

FOCUS-CENTER-GOAL

Lynch lists three desiderata for landmarks: they must have a "clear form"; they must "contrast with their background"; and they must be endowed with "prominence of spatial location."[4] Beyond this, in order for them to serve as centers or goals, they must have sufficiently solid mass to emphasize their presence; in other words, there must be an element of sheer bigness.

It hardly need be said that mountains and hills as seen from nearby flatlands usually meet these qualifications. Eminences projecting into or rising from plains are the focus-center-goal elements in the Mikumari Shrine type, the domain-viewing mountain type, and the sacred mountain type (figure 15.2). As centers or goals that attract and concentrate attention, mountains give coherence and stability to the otherwise diffuse spaces around them.

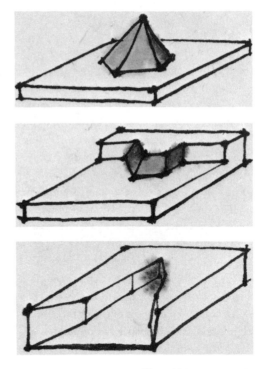

Figure 15.2
Types of focus-center-goal elements

In order for such elements to create spatial order, they must be seen, sensed, and constantly recognized, not merely as geographical entities, which, as Norberg-Schulz has said, is "thought" (in the verbal sense), but as identifying features of the landscape. For this reason they must have qualities of visibility in short- or middle-distance views and physical presence, with an angle of elevation in the range of 10 degrees, or certainly no less than 5 degrees.

In addition to the plastic (convex) features identified by Goldfinger and the N spaces described by Ashihara Yoshinobu, we include among the possible focus-center-goal elements the deep recesses with mountains on both sides that are found in the Mikumari Shrine type and the secluded valley type.

DIRECTIONALITY

Directional relationships are created in landscapes by mountains rising from flat terrain, by sloping ground surfaces, by valleys or basins that either spread out or become narrow at one end, by configurations calling attention to the four directions, or even by prevailing winds. Examples of features producing directionality are the upward-sweeping eight-petal lotus blossom type observed at Mount Kōya where the "pedestal for a thousand Buddhas" rises high above the world of mortals as a sacred capital in the sky, in the various sacred mountain landscapes where the spirits of ancestors sleep on peaks soaring in the clouds, atop domain-viewing mountains from which the emperor could look out over the farmlands and enjoy the sense of domination, in areas surrounding the burial mounds of ancient territorial magnates, in the settings of shrines of the Mount Otoko type where the spirit of the god of war resided, in the plains overseen by the castles of feudal lords during the civil wars of the fifteenth and sixteenth centuries. Directionality was provided in a different fashion by the sloping terrain leading up to the inner shrine at Ise or the Okunoin at Mount Kōya or the several Mikumari Shrines, by mountain-walled valleys with remote and mysterious inner reaches, by river basins reaching up into the mountains, by the eastward or sunward orientation of the Akizushima-Yamato type, by the directional nuances of the cardinal features in the zōfū-tokusui type (figure 15.3).

Sometimes spaces creating a sense of directionality are of the nature of physical passageways, corridors of a sort. This is not a necessary condition, but directional order can be achieved by means of an image that exists only in the mind's eye.

DOMAIN

A domain is the total space that is brought together and given order by the conditions of boundary, focus-center-goal, and directionality. A certain domain may, for example, be bounded by mountains, rivers, or the ocean; furnished with a focal point by an independent peak, a projecting foothill, or a valley extending into the mountains; and endowed with directionality by a soaring peak, a sloping terrain, topographical enclosure or openings, or the flow of a river.

The elements that determine the spatial structure and nature of landscapes thus inform us of design options within a given landscape; they tell us what we ought to look for in that landscape and what features we ought to try to develop or at least preserve.

In planning a site, we must ask first, What are its boundaries as a landscape? What is its focus-center-goal? Is there some feature that gives the space directionality? When we have answered these questions, we can consider the spatial entity created by the various components, compare them with the seven spatial types defined in this book, and attempt to adjust our plans in such a way as to convert the space into a coherent domain. Next we must analyze, in accordance with the standards and indexes set up in part I, the visual structure of the landscape in conjunction with the manmade elements to be introduced in the course of development. Having reconsidered the form, scale, materials, textures, and colors involved in the natural setting and in the proposed development project, we must then assess the impact of the project on the landscape and consider means of achieving harmony between the two.[6] This process will involve conservation plans, which should be devised not only in new development, but also in urban redevelopment.[7] Both in protected scenic areas remote from human habitation and in the populated regions, more and more effort must be devoted to the task of determining what sort of plan makes effective use of landscapes or what sort of project harmonizes with the background.[8]

Partly because of our desire to clarify the basic spatial structure of landscapes, we have for the most part confined our attention in this volume to landscapes in which the density of land utilization is low. The next step might be to collect a maximum number of examples in which land utilization harmonizes with the landscape (the examples should include urban areas), classify them in accordance with the type of landscape and the type of utilization program, and then attempt to abstract from them certain abiding principles, such as those arrived at by Camillo Sitte in his study of urban beauty. When we have done this, we shall be able, by means of visual models and the like, to make accurate advance assessments of the degree of harmony that can be achieved between a given project and its natural setting.

LANDSCAPES AND HOME

The spaces that have been discussed in the previous seven chapters are landscapes of the kind that Norberg-Schulz might have had in mind when he wrote: "People affix their idea

Rising mountain

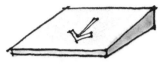
Sloping terrain

Flowing water

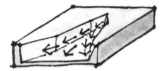
Opening or closing
of space

Figure 15.3
Types of directionality

of the land to the actual land they have found—they impose their image of the setting upon the actual physical setting. Thus an actual landscape and an image that exists only within the mind become one."[9] These spaces are also sites and localities that fit in with Lynch's dictum: "The words *site* and *locality* should convey the same sense that *person* does; a complexity so closely knit as to have a distinct character, worthy of interest, concern, and often of affection."[10] Representing in a sense the "climate" mentioned by Bollnow, a landscape "makes the space lived in a mirror image of the people who live in it and endows this space with its particular and unique aspect."[11] In another sense a landscape connotes "home," as described by Karaki Junzō: "The mountains and rivers and trees and plants, the houses and the streets and people and forests are there in immovable form; we have memories and reminiscences of each; they converse back and forth with us."[12]

The foregoing landscape types fit the Japanese people's image of the setting, arousing interest, concern, and often affection. They are mirror images of the people who live in them. They converse back and forth with the people to whom they are home. When the Japanese think of their homeland, they envision settings with mountains and rivers. But the relationship between the homeland that the Japanese see in their minds and the landscapes types abstracted here remains to be clarified.

In discussing means of overcoming the homelessness and alienation, Bollnow envisaged a new residentialization (*Wohnhaftwerden*) of man—a matter of housing (*Behausung*) in a very broad sense, a new sort of protectionism:

The task is to enable mankind in general to find a new haven—what might be called, in ordinary parlance, a new homeland. We must change the relationship of the human being to the world in such a way as to have the world

seem safe and secure to the human being—at least within certain areas and limitations—instead of confronting him always as an ominous threat. In making this new beginning, it is essential that, instead of allowing the human being to be sucked inexorably into an infinity where there is nothing concrete to hold onto, we must provide him with a new foundation within the finiteness of this world and give him a firm footing against oppressive forces.[13]

What manner of thing is this "new homeland," which represents the new protectionism? What is it in terms of space, which is what interests us here? Bollnow described it as follows:

Homeland [*Heimat*] in this case is quite similar to what was already stressed during our discussion of spatial order. It is not only the spatial concept of a particular regional environment in which people are brought up. It also includes the total life-style in which man feels at home, the entire area of his intimate life relations.[14]

Modern man's sense of homelessness does not result merely from the fact that he has left the narrow territorial confines that he knew as a child. It is caused by his having been driven out of the life system that once sustained him. As to the spatial nature of the home or homeland, Bollnow derives a number of clues from a consideration of the house as an environment. With these in mind, let us now outline the features of the home, or homeland, as they pertain to landscape spaces of the sort that have been examined in this book.

1. The home is a space that has been given form and order by human life. Bollnow described it as an "experienced space." Norberg-Schulz's recent contribution has been to try to explain, in terms of perceptual schemata, just what elements give form and order to "experienced space." Since his theories do much to clarify the five elements Lynch observed in ur-

ban space, as well as the elements of spatial structure outlined for the seven landscapes types, they seem to point the way toward a better understanding of the structure of "experienced space" as a whole.

2. The home is a space that is given form and order by boundaries. Citing Martin Heidegger, Bollnow points out that human beings are by nature "residents," that they cannot realize the true nature of their existence without residing in some definite place. By "residing" is meant being at ease within a peaceful surrounding. Being at ease (Bollnow uses the word *Friede*) means being protected from danger and threats. Bollnow points out in this connection that the German word for "surround with a border" (*umfrieden*) incorporates the meaning of "putting at ease."

3. The home is a space with an atmosphere of intimacy. In defining the special character of a space enclosed by boundaries, which give people a sense of being safe and at ease, Bollnow cites Eugène Minkowski's concept of an "atmosphere of intimacy" (*Atmosphäre des Vertrauens*). The infinite space that opens up before a person observing a very distant view has a fascinating quality, but at the same time its immeasurability tends to be oppressive to the human psyche. "Within these various spaces," writes Bollnow, "there arises the problem of partitioning off a special domain for human beings—a space in which people can feel protected and can resist the oppression of unlimited spaces."[14] Among the landscape types discussed in this book, the Akizushima-Yamato type, the eight-petal lotus blossom type, and the *zōfū-tokusui* type seem to correspond most closely to this idea. The "domain for human beings" is an "experienced space" endowed with a "human flavor," a place where "intimacy" prevails. The next question is, What gives certain spaces "intimacy"?

4. The home must have a certain degree of smallness; we must live in it constantly; and it must offer "clear evidence that we reside here and like it." The space in question is our "image of the setting," as Norberg-Schulz called it. It is what Lynch described as "worthy of interest, concern, and often of affection." It is Bollnow's "mirror image of the people who live in it"; in Karaki's words, it can "converse back and forth with us." The degree of smallness required to give a space an "atmosphere of intimacy" is the smallness of a "small country," such as that mentioned in our discussion of the Akizushima-Yamato type of landscape.[15] There is intimacy when the elements of the landscape are near enough for the sound of rustling leaves and gurgling brooks to be heard. "Clear evidence that we reside here and like it" is the aggregate of those highly visible elements within a landscape that are close enough to become an intrinsic part of daily life. Each person creates his own evidence, but, in general, there is what Lynch calls a "public image," held in common by the majority of the people and composed of the five elements Lynch considered basic to landscapes.[16] The "clear evidence" may also be the mountains and rivers and other features that constitute the four compositional elements we have observed in the seven basic types of Japanese landscapes.

Thus far, we have examined the nature of the home, or homeland, in accordance with Bollnow's theories and applied this interpretation to landscape spaces. Bollnow goes on to cite both the dangers to the existentialist adventurer who forsakes the home and the risks facing the "permanent resident" who remains within it. The homeland that has been recovered, he observes, is in a state of tension that can lead to its destruction; invariably there are stresses making for the loss of the homeland. "The homeland is always relative."[17]

Since Bollnow takes the house as the object of his consideration, he has little occasion in the course of his argument to touch upon the relationship between the home, or homeland, and the natural surroundings. Let us therefore revert for a moment to his general concept of the home, as stated at the beginning of this discussion.

Bollnow says that the home includes "the total life-style in which man feels at home, the entire area of his intimate life relations." To have no home—to be alienated from one's homeland—is to be expelled from the life system that has sustained one.

What *is* "the total life-style in which man feels at home"? What is "the entire area of his intimate life relations"? Bollnow's answer is, "The concept of home includes working at a job with which one is familiar, living within a fixed social and legal order, and being rooted in a fixed system of morality."[18]

Can we not say, however, that nature, the land we live in, and the setting around us function on an even deeper level as a life-sustaining system? Karaki Junzō, in the epilogue to his *Nihonjin no kokoro no rekishi* ("History of the Japanese Heart"), has the following to say on this subject:

It is said that science knows no national barriers, and it is indeed true that our technological civilization is gradually creating a race of universal human beings in whom racial and individual characteristics are minimized. But culture is different from civilization; culture, as can be seen from its etymology, is closely related to the earth, to the land we live on, to the natural surroundings, to the roots of our souls. Not only do the land and the natural setting form and nurture human beings; they also place certain limitations on otherwise independent human beings. Since these limitations are external, they are not absolute, and to regard them as that is extremely dangerous, as is amply demonstrated by history. We seek, by denying these limitations once, and then again and again, to achieve freedom, self-sustenance, self-satisfaction. But the "limitless" state we arrive at is still colored by the land, by our roots, by the place we regard as home.[19]

Where Bollnow decrees that the home is always relative, Karaki asserts that it is inevitably colored by its natural setting.

What is it about the natural setting that "colors" our concept of the homeland? Is it not the beauty of nature itself? We remember the mountains, forests, valleys, and streams not merely because they are landmarks of our childhood but because we regard them as aesthetically satisfying. Shiga Shigetaka said, "The pure beauty of these rivers and mountains, the proliferation of plants and trees—these are the original forces that nurture the Japanese sense of aesthetics, have nurtured it in the past, and will nurture it in the future."[20] Any number of dissertations and treatises have demonstrated how sensitive the Japanese people are to the beauties of nature; how deeply their philosophy and culture are influenced by their love of nature; how important the role of nature is in everyday Japanese life.[21]

That natural beauty is important in Japan does not necessarily mean that nature is more beautiful in Japan than in other places. It is just that traditional Japanese life and traditional Japanese living spaces are so closely, so intimately, connected with nature. To come in contact with nature, to love nature, is a part of everyday Japanese experience. And because of the accumulation of such daily experience, natural beauty becomes the "clear evidence that we reside here and like it."

The Japanese of the past felt life itself to be a part of nature. People, too, were regarded as being a part of the great natural whole. Japanese residential spaces were spaces in which, in Norberg-Schulz's terminology, the landscape level dominated. Japanese production and Japanese ways of life were stable and sedentary, because they were founded on agriculture. In spaces where the landscape level is dominant, topographical features are not a matter of cognizance; they are not "thought." Instead, they are "lived" or "experienced" as landscapes. This is what happens in a country where 80 percent of the land is mountainous, where there is lots of rain, where beautiful scenery abounds, where there is a surrounding ocean, where the climate and the sea currents are varied, where there are many volcanoes, where the air is frequently vaporous, where flowing streams erode dramatically. From the structural viewpoint, it is no accident that the elements forming the boundaries, focus-center-goals, and directional vectors of Japanese landscapes are mountains, rivers, and oceans.

With the advance of urbanization our everyday living space has come to be filled with buildings and other man-made structures. We have nearly lost sight of the landscape as something that is lived or experienced. Only when a flash flood brings the water up under our houses do we remember the little drainage ditch down the block—that is about the extent to which modern Japanese city-dwellers are conscious of their relationship with nature.

Yet ecology tells us that human beings are subsumed within nature's life relationships. No matter how mechanized and structuralized our environment might become, the fundamental sustenance for human existence is the order that nature imposes on life. It is when we feel at home within this order—when it becomes the "clear evidence that we reside here and like it"—that we have found our true homeland.

Bashō enjoined us to return to nature and follow nature. Karaki spoke of conforming "both naturally and of one's own accord" to the natural order of life.[22] It is man's task to create spaces in which this can be done and to make these spaces our everyday environment. We must have spaces that are unified with the beauty of nature. As Nakai put it, "When human beings sense their own personal freedom within nature, that is beauty."[23]

The conclusion we reach is the most fundamental support for human existence is the order of natural life. This does not mean that man-made structures or implements or other cultural artifacts cannot become "clear evidence that we reside here and like it." What it means is that these things must be colored and regulated by the natural order of life.

Norberg-Schulz writes, "Let us repeat that landscape always has the function of forming the continuous background of our environmental image (as well as of our visual field). If this condition is corrupted, we stop talking about landscape."[24] Landscape is defined as the ground upon which cities, architecture, and other structures of the "lower level" appear, but it can also be said that this ground is the natural order of life, which is the most fundamental support for human existence.

16

Conclusion

In the ancient past, when the cultivation of rice in wet fields spread through Japan, many areas that had been covered with laurisylvan forests had to be cleared to make way for farmlands. But the technical level was low, the population small, and the recuperative power of the natural surroundings very strong. In a country where forests are the natural climax of plant life, the ecological damage was relatively slight even when the methods employed by the settlers were rough and unthinking.

When, in much later times, people developed the habit of going to the country on picnics and outings, the landscapes they invaded were still too hardy to be spoiled by nature-lovers who broke off a cherry branch here or there or carried away bunches of reddened maple leaves. Even when pilgrims visited famous temples and shrines in great throngs, they usually refrained from despoiling the natural settings in which these buildings were situated, because these areas were regarded as holy ground and were protected by both custom and regulation. After the ninth century Buddhist sects, particularly the Esoteric schools, often chose to build their monasteries in mountain forests. They valued the scenery to begin with but in any event were not technically equipped to level hills and fill in valleys to achieve some visionary plan. They sought out the flattest sites they could find, and the buildings they set up required a minimum of ground work.

The absence of ground-moving equipment was not the only factor. The ancient Japanese read spiritual meaning into the natural rise and fall of the land and were more eager to interpret it than to alter what they saw. Often valleys or remote recesses were regarded as the homes of dead spirits or of deities, and, in some instances, the hills that set such places off were considered as barriers within which evil spirits were confined.

The Buddhist choice of mountain settings was based ultimately on ancient mountain worship; the conviction that to practice asceticism in the deep mountains was a means of acquiring the power of the gods who dwelt there was always very strong. Yanagita Kunio (1875–1962), the father of Japanese ethnology, believed that Japanese religion as a whole was conditioned by topography, and there is no doubt but that a deep spiritual relation existed between the early Japanese and their natural surroundings.

Reverence for nature is by no means confined to Japan, of course. As Lynch describes it, "In most cultures land is sacred, not to be violated by mere human beings. It is enduring, powerful, extensive, the home of the spirits and the dead, the productive mother on whom human life depends." Yet Lynch goes on to say, "As we discard these religious ideas and increase our power to impose site changes, we lose these restraining attitudes. We no longer unconsciously achieve development in harmony with its setting, nor do we achieve structures expressive of locality."[1]

We have ceased to be able *unconsciously* to develop land in such a way as to conform to nature. We continue to develop, often in depredatory fashion. Nature no longer overpowers us; we take it for granted and forget that it is not inexhaustible. Lacking the reverence that men once had for their natural environment, we have developed instead the technical ability to flatten mountains and valleys alike. Retrospectively, it appears that we know all too little about nature, and what we know amounts to theories that enable us to deform it. As Ōyama Haruo has written,

The more we have sought to discover the proper relationship between man and nature, the more we have spread pollution. Modern civilization, which is unable to produce without ignoring mankind's deeper needs, has achieved industrial marvels, but one cannot avoid the feeling that it is still at a primitive level.[2]

A similar conclusion might be drawn with respect to the way landscapes have been desecrated by environmental designers.

We must make a conscious effort to discover the proper relationship between ourselves and nature. It may be that mankind is by nature foolish, but we must force ourselves to believe that there will come a time when we will cherish the beauties of nature and consider them as part of ourselves. We must be willing to exert ourselves steadily and repeatedly toward the achievement of this goal. Until we can *unconsciously* carry out development projects in harmony with the natural setting, we must continue *consciously* to do this. We have only begun to create a new order in which man and nature coexist. This book is intended as a small effort to realize that new order.

To discover the personality hidden in a given landscape and then build in such a way as to emphasize this personality is the way not only to make the most of the setting but also to achieve harmony between it and the life that goes on within it.

We have dealt in this book with the visual aspects and the spatial aspects of natural landscapes. In every natural setting these two elements—visual and spatial—combine to create a distinctive view. The landscape designer must have a firm grasp of the visual and spatial character of the setting before he can begin to develop it.

The seven indexes introduced in the first five chapters of this book should be of assistance in analyzing the special visual features of the setting. We have indicated in chapter 6 how these indexes might be used in an actual reconstruction program at Shiga Heights.

In "reading" the spatial characteristics of a setting, the seven types of space described in the latter chapters of this book should serve as a valuable reference. Since, however, there is a danger that some readers outside Japan might conclude that these types are peculiar to Japan, I would like to add here a few comments on spatial characteristics in general.

I believe that a space having a given physical terrain has the power to cause human beings to form a particular type of mental image or images. A small valley surrounded by mountains, for example, actually caused the Japanese of the past to conceive of the Akizushima-Yamato conformation, which was basically a well-protected area where man could find peace, and of the eight-petal lotus blossom pattern, which was their mental image of a location where Buddhist enlightenment could be found. In China, Lao-tse saw the ultimate source of life in a female deity residing in the deep recesses of a valley; the ancient Japanese imagined in similar locations a deity who distributed an abundance of water to the fields below and thus created the Mikumari Shrine pattern. In the deeper, darker reaches of valleys the early Japanese saw a suitable place for their dead, who would then find peace in the white mountains beyond. Thus we find the secluded valley type of landscape.

Sometimes our ancestors preferred to live not in the middle of a plain or saucer-land but up closer to the foothills of the mountains. The classic type in this case is the *zōfū-tokusui* formation, where mountains form a protective barrier on three sides. In such places as Mount Miwa, the ancient Japanese saw the conical mountain as a suitable residence for the gods and arranged their habitation around it in the sacred mountain configuration. Or else they viewed a mountain as a suitable place for the ruler to go and look out over his lands, thus giving rise to the domain-viewing mountain type.

The point in all these instances is that the spatial pattern in question is suited to the mental image that people formed of it. Even today we can understand why our ancestors

interpreted these landscapes as they did. True, a small plain surrounded by mountains might evoke images other than that of a safe, peaceful place to live in. Nevertheless, we can see even now that it has the power to inspire an image of that particular sort.

Designers must develop the ability to feel and visualize the sorts of images that the spatial characteristics of a setting are able to call forth. They must then work out designs that are not only suitable to these images but cause the images to grow and be enhanced. Perhaps my description of the seven types of landscapes given here will be helpful in the task of learning how to discover and develop spatial images.

It is true that seven is a small number of types. In my opinion, we need to approach the problem on an international level and attempt to make more or less comprehensive collection of the types of landscapes that people regard as beautiful and pleasant to live in. We must classify the spatial forms and the images they call forth. This book is a first attempt to do this for Japan and Japanese landscapes.

But I do not think the types outlined here are confined to Japan or even to natural landscapes. There is, for example, something about the narrow streets of Venice that dimly suggests a narrow Japanese valley—something about the plaza these streets open upon that brings to mind a small valley encircled by mountains. And the churches and towers facing on this plaza are in some odd way like sacred or domain-viewing mountains of the types described in this book. When I see people at work and play in the porticos and terraces around the plaza, I do not find them completely different in my mind from the people who live in a *zōfū-tokusui* formation in Japan.

In other words, when we consider the spaces that people live in and find beautiful, we can find similarities in the spatial configurations even when the external appearance is completely different. Similarities also exist in the atmosphere created or in the mental images evoked within the inhabitants. For this reason, I believe it would be possible, if a thorough study were made of the type of settings people favor and regard as beautiful, to arrive at a certain number of archetypes that would be universally applicable.

Jung discovered a similarity between common dream images and ancient myths and was able to devise a system of classification. This led him to the concept of the universal unconsciousness, which provides all human beings with certain common tendencies and potentialities. I wonder if the tendency of people to draw certain mental images from certain spatial formations is not connected in some way with Jung's universal unconsciousness. If it is, it would not be surprising to find a number of spatial archetypes that might exist anywhere and everywhere. The question that is in my mind is whether the seven Japanese types of landscapes described in this book are not related to something more universal. I hope to go into this subject in greater detail in a separate study.

Appendix

Concepts and indexes introduced in earlier research papers		
Publication	Analytical or operational concept	Analytical or operational index (Quantitative)
Märtens, *Optisches Mass für den Städtebau*. 1890.	Eyesight Visual range as an elliptical cone	Distance & angle of vision Angle of elevation
Sitte, *Der Städtebau nach seinen künstlerischen Grundsätzen*. 1889.	Positions of monuments & principal buildings in plaza Closed character of space Size & form of plaza	Width and depth of plaza & height of surrounding buildings
Shiga, *Nihon fūkei-ron*. 1894.	Sea currents Water vapor Rocks Flowing water	
Doxiadis, *Raumordnung in Griechischen Städtebau*. 1937.	12-part system 10-part system	Horizontal angle Distance
Uehara, *Nihon fūkeibi-ron*. 1943.	Observation point Visual range Direction Principal view Distance	
Lynch, *The Image of the City*. 1960.	Identity Structure Meaning Imageability (legibility, visibility) Path Landmark Edge Node District	
Cullen, *Townscape*. 1961.	Serial vision existing view and emerging view Place here/there Content this/that	
Ashihara, *Exterior Design in Architecture*. 1962.	P space N space	Angle of elevation (*D/H*) Horizontal angle Distance & texture
Toshi Dezain Kenkyu-tai, "Nihon no toshi kūkan." 1963.	Principles of formation (direction, weight, placement, etc.) Techniques of structure	
Tokyo Daigaku Toshi Kōgaku Kenkyūjo, *Bandai · Inawashiro chiiki kankō kihon keikaku*. 1966.		Visibility, invisibility

Tokyo Daigaku Zōen-gaku Kenkyūshitsu, *Shizen keikan no kaiseki.* 1966.		Quantity of visible space
Tokyo Daigaku Yasojima Kenkyūshitsu, *Hakone · Yugawara kankō kaihatsu chōsa.*		Frequency of appearance
Litton, *Forest Landscape Description and Inventories.* 1968.	Distance Observer position Form Spatial definition Light Sequence	
Norberg-Schulz, *Existence, Space and Architecture.* 1971.	Center-place Direction-path Area-domain	

Notes

CHAPTER 1

1. The English translation is not from the original, but from a standard Japanese version. See Takeuchi, Toshio, transl., *Bigaku*, vol. 1 (*jō*), p. 6.

2. Nakai, Masakazu, *Nakai Masakazu zenshū*, vol. 3, p. 7.

3. Uehara, Keiji, *Nihon fūkeibi-ron*, pp. 394–401.

4. Litton, R. B., Jr., *Forest Landscape Description and Inventories*, p. 2.

5. Märtens, H., *Optisches Mass für den Städtebau*. Unfortunately, this important work has been available to the author only in a Japanese adaptation by Kitamura Tokutarō, entitled "Toshi keikakujō shiryoku hyōjun," *Toshi kōron*, vol. 10, nos. 4, 7, and 9. Later references to Märtens in the present volume should be interpreted as references to Kitamura's rendition.

6. Mizuno, Ichirō, "Keitai to hassei," p. 115.

7. See, for example, Tsuda, Sōkichi, *Bungaku ni arawaretaru kokumin shisō no kenkyū*; Watsuji, Tetsurō, *Fūdo*; Ienaga, Saburō, *Nihon shisō-shi ni okeru shūkyō-teki shizenkan no hatten*; Kamei, Katsuichirō, *Nihonjin no seishinshi kenkyū*; Karaki, Junzō, *Nihonjin no kokoro no rekishi*.

8. Sitte, Camillo, *City Planning According to Artistic Principles*, p. xv.

CHAPTER 2

1. See Kudō, Harumasa, et al., "Taishūka to kyodaika jidai ni okeru shikakuteki mondai (2)," *Glass and Architecture* (May 1967), pp. 12–8.

2. See Nakamura, Yoshio, et al., "Shizen keikan keikaku no tame no jōhō shori to sono ōyō," *Doboku Gakkai dai-nijūshichikai nenji gakujutsu kōenkai gaiyōshū IV* (1972), pp. 251–252.

3. Märtens, *Optisches Mass für den Städtebau*.

4. Blumenfeld, Hans, "Scale in Civic Design," *Town Planning Review*, vol. 24 (1953–4), p. 35.

5. Hall, Edward, *The Hidden Dimension*.

6. Ashihara, Yoshinobu, *Exterior Design in Architecture*, pp. 50–62.

7. Takahashi, Takashi, et al., "Shikibetsu shakudo ni kansuru kenkyū," *Nihon Kenchiku Gakkai rombun hōkokushū*, special issue (1966), pp. 500–501.

8. Blumenfeld, "Scale in Civic Design," p. 37.

9. See *Kishōgaku handobukku*, p. 780

10.Nakamura, Teiichi and Ishihara, Shūji, "Shinrin embō shikibetsu-do to shikibetsu genkai kyori no santei-hō," *Nihon Ringakkai-shi*, vol. 46, no. 8 (1964), pp. 274–280.

11.Ihara, Usaburō, "Kōzu," *Sekai bijutsu daijiten*.

12.Kira, Tatsuo, *Seitaigaku kara mita shizen*, p. 72.

13.The following relies to a large extent on Litton, R. B., *Forest Landscape Description and Inventories*.

14.*Shin kokin wakashū*, p. 82.

15.*Gyokuyōshū*, p. 113. Also see chapter 5, note 12.

16.Ōoka Makoto wrote: "The basic form of life here involved belonging to a communal group who worked a small piece of land. The land was surrounded by forest and shut off from the outside. There was little opportunity for people to develop a feeling of distance even in human relations. Thought and communication were based on the assumption of nearness and consequently relied heavily on abbreviation and intuitive response—as, for example, in such works as *The Tale of Genji*, where on first reading we are astonished by the lack of sentence subjects and the vagueness of verbal objects." See Ōoka, *Ki no Tsurayuki*, p. 120.

17.Rinya-chō Keikaku-ka, Ed., *Kūchū shashin handoku kijun kaado*.

18.Takahashi, "Shikibetsu shakudo ni kansuru Kenkyūo."

19.Ueyama, Shumpei, *Shōyō jurin bunka*, pp. 79–80.

20.See *Fudoki*, pp. 225–257. The word *nita* appears to be related to *nuta*, which is a sort of salad consisting of fish or vegetables mixed with bean-paste and vinegar. The idea is that the soil in the "damp, humid little district"' is of a soft, muddy consistency.

21.Yanagita, Kunio, "Yamamiya-kō," p. 346.

22.According to the *Kojiki* and the *Nihon shoki*, Jimmu was the great-grandson of the sun goddess Amaterasu Ōmikami. He is mythical, but it is assumed by many historians that stories concerning him and other mythical emperors may often have had some basis in fact. Specifically, when the *Kojiki* and the *Nihon shoki* record that the Emperor Jimmu built his palace in Kashihara, near Mount Unebi, it may safely be supposed that one or another of the early Japanese rulers or chieftains resided in that location, or might have resided there.

For the purposes of our discussion, it is not necessary that the palaces mentioned here actually existed but merely that certain places were considered by the eighth-century writers of the historical sources named to have at one time been sites of imperial palaces. We are dealing here not so much with specific landscapes as with a concept of landscapes.

23.The translations are taken, with minor alterations, from Philippi, transl., *Kojiki*, p. 183. In reference to the poems quoted here, Origuchi Shinobu wrote, "We cannot but be surprised at the quiet overflow of feeling experienced as man confronted nature. . . . If there had been no emotional reaction toward nature, lyric poems with metaphorical implications would have been impossible." See "Jokeishi no hassei," p. 423.

24.Horiguchi Sutemi and Hayakawa Masao both remark on the naturalness of the view at the garden of the Sekisui-in. Horiguchi speaks of "a view of nature in the raw" (*Niwa to kūkan no dentō*, p. 10), while Hayakawa writes, "The relation between architectural space and natural views at the Sekisui-in can only be called direct. . . . Without the intermediary effect of any garden-design techniques, obvious planning, ponds, or clay walls, the architectural spaces are suddenly and startlingly connected with the natural vista." See *The Garden Art of Japan*, p. 57. The "direct" link with nature at the Sekisui-in results largely from the fact that the mountain forming the view straight ahead from the usual point of observation has an angle of elevation of 15 degrees and is very close by.

25.Karaki, Junzō, *Nihonjin no kokoro no rekishi*, vol. 2, p. 123.

CHAPTER 3

1.Gibson, J. J., *The Perception of the Visual World*, p. 76.

2.See Goldfinger, "The Sensation of Space," *Architectural Review* (November 1941). Goldfinger considered that the field of vision was a cone having an apex angle of 60 degrees. Ashihara adopts the same figure in his *Exterior Design in Architecture*.

3.Yoshida, Tōgo, *Nihon chimei jisho: Kamigata*, vol. 2, p. 181.

4.Shigemori, Mirei, and Shigemori, Kanto, *Nihon teien-shi taikei*, vol. 4. According to this work, the quotation is from vol. 7 of the Ōnin-ki ("Record of the Ōnin Era"), though it does not appear in the *Gunsho ruijū* edition of that document. The repetition of the word "good" is occasioned by the fact that the name Yosino means "good meadow."

5.*Masukagami*, vol. 6., p. 151.

6.*Kokin wakashū*, p. 246; see Honda, H. H., *The Kokin Waka-shu*, p. 163. This poem is included in the second section of the *Kokin wakashū*, among the love poems, but it is not certain that the lines were addressed to a lover. The implied meaning is that the author, unable to meet the person in Yamato, has news of him (or her) only by word of mouth and is consequently disappointed.

7.*Kokin wakashū*, p. 81; see Honda, *The Kokin Waka-shu*, p. 31.

8.*Man'yōshū*, vol. 1, p. 79. According to a note in the *Man'yōshū*, this was composed when the Emperor Temmu made a trip to his detached palace in Yoshino in the fifth month of the year 679. The emperor was in the company of his empress and a number of his children, and it is supposed that the exhortation was addressed to them.

9.De Wolfe, Ivor, *The Italian Townscape*, p. 69. Toshi Dezain Kenkyū-tai, *Nihon no toshi kūkan*, p. 52. In speaking of the port town of Murotsu in Hyogo, for example, this book comments, "As one goes along the streets (which have deformation), one comes upon the inn where daimyo stayed, then shops, then the inn where there were bath girls, and so on. The scene is constantly changing. With an urban texture like this, it is possible to walk down quite a long street without getting bored."

10.*Kojiki*, p. 127; the translation is adopted with minor changes from Philippi, *Kojiki*, p. 248.

11.Tsuchihashi, Yutaka, *Kodai kayō to girei no kenkyū*, p. 281.

12.Takahashi, Masayoshi, *Kūchū shashin no mikata to tsukaikata—Kūchū shashin handoku.*

13.Lynch, Kevin, *Site Planning*, p. 194.

14.Crowe, Sylvia, *The Landscape of Power*, pp. 35, 38.

15.Cullen, Gordon, *Townscape*, p. 143.

CHAPTER 4
1.Dreyfuss, Henry, *The Measure of Man: Human Factors in Design*. Christopher Alexander says, in a proposal submitted in an international competition for the design of community housing in Peru, "The height of the human eye is usually between 1.30 and 1.60 meters. The height of an automobile, on the other hand, is 1.40 meters. A tall person can look down on an automobile, but in this instance, too, the automobile fills his range of vision. The reason is that the line of vision of a standing man is usually about 10 degrees lower than the horizontal." This is quoted in Dreyfuss's work. In order for a person to see the top of an automobile at a distance of 4 meters, the automobile must be from 50 to 80 centimeters below him. *Toshi jūtaku* (October 1970), p. 64.

2.Shinohara, Osamu, Graduation Thesis for the Department of Civil Engineering at the University of Tokyo, 1971. See also Shinohara, Osamu, and Higuchi, Tadahiko, "Shizen chikei to keikan."

3.Satō, Hironori, Graduation thesis, Department of Civil Engineering, University of Tokyo, 1973. Or see Higuchi, Tadahiko, and Satō, Hironori, "Koshō keikan ni kansuru kenkyū."

4.Cullen, *Townscape*, p. 12.

5.Sitte, *City Planning According to Artistic Principles*. The criticism appears in Kitamura Tokutarō's adaptation into Japanese of Märtens, H., *Optisches Mass für den Städtebau.*

6.Märtens, *Optisches Mass für den Städtebau*, p. 14.

7.Ibid.

8.Blumenfeld, "Scale in Civic Design," p. 37.

9.Hegemann, Werner, and Peets, Elbert, *The American Vitruvius: An Architect's Handbook of Civic Art*, p. 44.

10.*Masukagami* ("Mirror of Increase"), p. 131.

11.Ōta, Hirotarō, *Kinkaku to Ginkaku, Nihon no kenchiku*, p. 147.

12.Hayashi, Razan, ed., *Seika-bunshū*, vol. 2, p. 10.

13.This is a device that determines the center of attention by aiming a beam of light at the eyeball and measuring the reflected light. The center of attention is recorded by a movie or television camera through fiber optics. Valuable advice as to the operation of the equipment was furnished by Murata Takahiro of the Police Institute of Science.

14.Shiga, *Nihon fūkei-ron*, p. 86.

15.Wada, Yōhei, et al., *Kankaku + chikaku shinrigaku handobukku*, p. 609.

16.Ashihara, *Exterior Design in Architecture*, p. 37.

17.Ibid.

CHAPTER 5
1.Gibson, *The Perception of the Visual World*, p. 6.

2.Ibid., pp. 75–6.

3.Lynch, *Site Planning*, p. 49. Lynch considers a slope of 10 degrees the maximum that can be classed as "gentle." He points out that, if the slope is greater, people usually consider it difficult to climb.

4.Ashihara, *Exterior Design in Architecture*, p. 105.

5.Kojima, Usui, *Nihon sansui-ron*, pp. 327–9.

6.Dazai, Osamu, *Fugaku hyakkei*, p. 52. Dazai writes, "I am told that the view of Fuji from here is counted among the three best views of the mountain, but I did not like it very much. Not only did I not like it, I felt it was contemptible. The whole thing is so contrived—Fuji right there in the middle, the bleak, white waters of Lake Kawaguchi spreading out below it, nearer foothills crouching neatly around the lake. The first glimpse threw me into consternation. My face turned red. I felt as though I were looking at a sign painter's rendition of Fuji on a bathhouse wall, or maybe the backdrop for a play. A regular made-to-order landscape—too embarrassing for words."

7.In "Sansui shōki," Tayama Katai says of the view of Mount Fuji from Otome Pass, "It's magnificent, but there's nothing profound about it."

8.Nakamura, Yoshio, and Higuchi, Tadahiko, "Dōro keikan kōsei gihō to sono hataraki," *Doboku Gakkai dai-nijūnikai nenji kōenkai gaiyōshū IV* (1967), p. 122.

9.In *Yoshino no yama*, Kamei Katsuichirō wrote, "It [Mount Yoshino] has the power to draw one farther and farther into its recesses, and, when one is there, to entice one still farther. This is because of Saigyō." Kamei thus attributes the mountain's charms to the influence of the great poet Saigyō (1118–1190), but the terrain itself certainly contributes to the effect observed. It has a definitely "inviting" quality.

10.The poem, one of Fujiwara no Teika's most famous, is from the *Shin kokin wakashū* (see note 17). The translation is from Keene, Donald, ed., *Anthology of Japanese Literature*, p. 194.

11.Eifuku Mon-in was the consort of the Emperor Fushimi (r. 1287–1298). The poem quoted here is included in the *Gyokuyōshū*, an imperial anthology completed in 1313.

12.Shiga, Shigetaka, *Nihon fūkei-ron*, pp. 35, 284.

13.The *Kokin wakashū*, completed in 905, is the first of twenty-one collections of poetry compiled on imperial command and consequently known as imperial anthologies. See Keene, *Anthology of Japanese Literature*, pp. 76–81; Honda, H. H., transl., *The Kokin Waka-shū*. Two of the twenty volumes in the collection are devoted to poems on the subject of spring. The *Shin kokin wakashū*, completed in 1205 by a committee of which Fujiwara no Teika was the chief member, was the eighth of the imperial anthologies. It is considered by many critics to be the best. See Keene, *Anthology of Japanese Literature*, pp. 192–196.

14.Suzuki, Tadayoshi, *Kankōchi no hyōka shuhō*, p. 26.

15.Toshi Dezain Kankyūtai, *Nihon no toshi kūkan*, p. 60. According to this work, *miegakure* is achieved by one of three methods: utilizing a barrier, distributing the elements of the garden in a special way, or taking advantage of the particular form of certain elements.

16.Gorai, Shigeru, *Kumano mōde*, p. 108.

CHAPTER 6
1.Appleton, Jay, *The Experience of Landscape*, p. 70.

CHAPTER 7
1.Norberg-Schulz, Christian, *Existence, Space, and Architecture*, p. 28.

2.Ibid., pp. 27–28. Norberg-Schulz comments that "urban people in our time have lost most of the landscape level, although they usually possess some geographical images learnt in school."

CHAPTER 8
1.*Nihon shoki*, vol. 1, pp. 188–189. See Aston, *Nihongi*, vol. 1, pp. 110–111.

2.*Nihon shoki*, vol. 1, pp. 214–215. See Aston, *Nihongi*, vol. 1, pp. 134–135.

3.In the *Nihon shoki*, vol. 1, pp. 292–293, the same poem is spoken by the Emperor Keikō, who is supposed to have been Yamato Takeru no Mikoto's father. See Aston, *Nihongi*, vol. 1, p. 197, for a different translation.

4.Tsuchihashi, Yutaka, *Kodai kayō to girei no kenkyū*, p. 328.

5.*Fudoki*, pp. 102–103.

6.Ishida, Kazuyoshi, "Nihon kodai kokka no keisei to kūkan ishiki no tenkai," *Nihon Bunka Kenkyūjo kenkyū hōkoku*, vol. 2 (March 1966), p. 86.

7.Ōtsuki, Fumihiko, *Daigenkai*, vol. 4, p. 693.

8.Origuchi, Shinobu, *Origuchi Shinobu zenshū*, vol. 9, pp. 171–173.

9.Ibid., vol. 2, p. 7.

10.See Kusanagi, Masao, transl., *Chūshō to kanjō inyū*, by Wilhelm Worringer, pp. 33–35. The original of this work has not been available in the writing of the present text.

11.Ishida, "Nihon kodai kokka," pp. 87–88.

12.*Nihon shoki*, vol. 1, pp. 248–249. See Aston, *Nihongi*, vol. 1, p. 161. Although the emperors and palaces named may be completely mythical, the point is that the writers of the earliest Japanese histories were prepared to believe that the places named were possible or likely sites for imperial palaces.

13.Hayashiya Tatsusaburō states that Jimmu, referred to earlier in the *Nihon shoki* as "the first emperor to govern the nation," probably ruled around A.D. 100, while Sujin set up the Miwa dynasty around A.D. 250. See his *Nihon no kodai bunka*, pp. 24–29. There are many divergent theories, however.

14.*Kojiki*, p. 193. The translation is from Philippi, *Kojiki*, p. 363.

15.*Nihon shoki*, vol. 2, pp. 366–367. Translation from Aston, *Nihongi*, vol. 2, p. 286.

16.The poem, entitled "On Passing the Ruined Capital of Ōmi," is in *Man'yōshū*, vol. 1, pp. 92–93. As translated by Earl Miner, in his *An Introduction to Japanese Court Poetry*, p. 46, the pertinent section reads as follows:

It was Mount Unebi,
Fair as a maiden gird with lovely scarf,
Where from the first age
Of our sun-sovereigns there rose up
Kashihara Palace;
And there each of our divinities
Ruled in a line unbroken
Like a column of many evergreens,
Beginning their sway
Of this nation under the heavens
In Yamato province,
Which adds its brightness to the sky.
What purpose was there
To leave it, to cross the hills of Nara,
Rich in colored earth,
To establish a new capital in a land
Beyond the horizon,
To choose a palace site off in the country?
But it was in Ōmi province,
Where the water rushes over the rocks,
In Sasanami
At this lofty Ōtsu palace,
Where our ruler
Began his rule over all our nation;
Here beneath the heavens
Yes, here it was our sovereign lord
Made his imperial court. . . .

The passage rendered as "beyond the horizon" could be more literally translated as "remote from heaven." The meaning is "outlandish."

17.*Man'yōshū*, vol. 1, pp. 92–93. See Nippon Gakujutsu Shinkōkai, *The Manyōshū*, p. 69, for a translation.

18.*Man'yōshū*, vol. 2, p. 183.

19.*Man'yōshū*, vol. 2, pp. 188–189. The translation is from Nippon Gakujutsu Shinkōkai, *The Manyōshū*, p. 230.

20.*Man'yōshū*, vol. 2, 192–3.

21.Bollnow, O. F., *Neue Geborgenheit*, p. 179.

22.Ibid., p. 179.

23.From Minkowski, E., *Espace, intimité, habitat*, as quoted in ibid., p. 173.

24.Ōno, Susumu, *Nihongo o sakanoboru*, p. 160.

CHAPTER 9
1.*Taiheiki*, vol. 2, p. 379.

2.*Mikkyō daijiten*, vol. 4, p. 1818.

3.Itō, Teiji, *The Japanese Garden: An Approach to Nature*, p. 159.

4.Hanayama, Shinshō, ed. *Hokke gisho*, vol. 2, p. 190.

5.Kūkai, *Shōryōshū*, p. 398.

6.Yanagita, Kunio, *Chimei no kenkyū*, in *Teihon Yanagita Kunio zenshū*, vol. 20, p. 84.

7.Kitagawa, Momoo, *Murō-ji*, pp. 14–15.

8.Women were not allowed within the monastery precincts of Mount Kōya until 1872.

9.Bollnow, *Neue Geborgenheit*, p. 218.

CHAPTER 10
1.This explanation is based on the *Shintō daijiten* ("Great Dictionary of Shinto").

2.Yanagita, Kunio, "Densha-kō taiyō," *Teihon Yanagita Kunio shū*, vol. 11, p. 539.

3.Yanagita, Kunio, "Kaijō no michi," *Teihon Yanagita Kunio shū*, vol. 1, pp. 32–33.

4.Furushima, Toshio, *Tochi ni kizamareta rekishi*, p. 41.

5.Kunio Yanagita in "Densha-kō taiyō" mentions eight Mikumari shrines, but it is not clear where the four not discussed here were.

6.Udano Town Office, *Udano-chō-shi*, p. 882.

7.Lynch, Kevin, *The Image of the City*, pp. 47–48.

CHAPTER 11

1.See the *Iwanami koten bungaku taikei* edition of *Man'yōshū*, p. 33.

2.*Nihon shoki*, vol. 1, pp. 471–473. See Aston, *Nihongi*, vol. 1, p. 346. This poem illustrates the use of *komoriku*, "secluded valley," as a pillow word for Hatsuse.

3.*Man'yōshū*, vol. 1, pp. 264–265. The translation of the poem is taken from Nihon Gakujutsu Shinkōkai, *The Manyoshu*, p. 51. Again *komoriku* is used as a pillow word for Hatsuse, although the translator has rendered it simply as a modifying participle.

4.*Man'yōshū*, vol. 1, pp. 260–263. Translated in Nihon Gakujutsu Shinkōkai, *The Manyoshu*, pp. 23–5.

5.Yasuda, Yojūrō, *Yamato Hase-dera*, p. 25.

6.Ibid., p. 47.

7.Ibid., p. 68.

8.Gorai, Shigeru, *Kumano mōde*, p. 108.

9.*Nihon shoki*, vol. 1, pp. 90–91. See Aston, *Nihongi*, vol. 1, p. 21. The passage is one of several concerning the death of Izanami that the authors of the *Nihon shoki* with words meaning "one writing says." It is possible that some of the references given were intended to mean Kumano in Izumo Province, as Aston believed, but modern commentators have noted that many place names are found in both Izumo and Kii, and it is therefore impossible in many instances to tell which is meant by the writers of the *Nihon shoki*. *Nihon shoki*, vol. 1, pp. 128–129. See Aston, *Nihongi*, vol. 1, pp. 59–60. The Japanese word for nether land is *ne-no-kuni*, "root country," possibly so called because the early Japanese considered it the home of their dead ancestors, or "roots."

10.Potalaka (Japanese, *fudaraku*) is the name of a mountain on the south coast of India, where the Bodhisattva Avalokitesvara, or Kannon, is supposed to have lived. The name is sometimes applied by Japanese Buddhists to Kumano and other areas considered particularly sacred to Kannon.

11.Yanagita, Kunio, "Yamamiya-kō," *Teihon Yanagita Kunio zenshū*, vol. 11, p. 341. It is not unusual in Japan for there to be a shrine to a particular deity at the foot of a mountain, near human habitation, and another to the same deity farther up on the mountainside. Not infrequently, the upper shrine is no more than a sacred area, marked perhaps by a tree or rock and used only when festivals to the deity are being held.

12.Ibid., p. 317.

13.*Sai-no-kawara* was probably derived from the name of an actual riverbank in Yamashiro Province (modern Kyoto Prefecture) that was a designated place for cremation and burial of commoners in the Heian period. The *Sai-no-kawara* of Buddhist lore was supposed to be in the land of the dead. Children who went there spent their time piling up rocks to build pagodas, but the pagodas were invariably torn down by devils before they were completed. Eventually, it was thought, the Bodhisattva Jizō would come and rescue the children from the demons.

CHAPTER 12

1.Akita, Nariaki, "Fūsui-setsu," *Sekai daihyakka jiten*, vol. 26, p. 221.

2.Saitō, Tadashi, "Jōdai ni okeru fumbochi no sentei," *Rekishi chiri*, vol. 65, no. 6 (1935), p. 24.

3.Tamura, Tsuyoshi, ed., *Sakuteiki*, p. 282.

4.*Nihon shoki*, vol. 2, p. 139. See Aston, *Nihongi*, vol. 2, p. 95. The text specifically mentions two sites but names only one palace. The two princes named are otherwise unknown.

5.*Nihon shoki*, vol. 2, pp. 374–375. See Aston, *Nihongi*, vol. 2, p. 293.

6.*Nihon shoki*, vol. 2, pp. 450–451. See Aston, *Nihongi*, vol. 2, p. 354. The construction mentioned here was not actually carried out.

7.*Nihon shoki*, vol. 2, pp. 461–462. See Aston, *Nihongi*, vol. 2, p. 362. According to the Yōrō Code of 718, there were six masters in the Bureau of Divination (*ommyō no tsukasa*) charged with inspecting and divining the propitiousness of land. See note 31, *Nihon shoki*, vol. 2, p. 461.

8.*Nihon shoki*, vol. 2, pp. 506–507. See Aston, *Nihongi*, vol. 2, p. 401.

9.*Man'yōshū*, vol. 1, pp. 92–93. The translation is from Nihon Gakujutsu Shinkōkai, *The Manyōshū*, p. 69.

10.*Shoku-Nihongi*, vol. 1, p. 34. See Snellen, J. B., transl. *Shoku Nihongi, Transactions of the Asiatic Society of Japan*, 2nd series, vol. 14 (June 1937), p. 220.

11.Suzuki, Mitsuru, "Heiankyō no hensen—Nagaoka-kyō," *Nihon no kōkogaku, Rekishi jidai (2)*, p. 83.

12.*Nihon kiryaku*, p. 268. The first quotation is from an edict issued on the 28th day of the 10th month of 794; the second, from an edict dated the 8th day of the 11th month of 794.

13.Sei Shōnagon, *Makura no sōshi*, p. 344. Not only here but in the famous first paragraph of this work (Ibid., p. 63), Sei Shōnagon seems to anticipate landscape theories of later times: "In spring it is the dawn that is most beautiful. As the light creeps over the hills, their outlines are dyed a faint red and wisps of purplish cloud trail over them. . . . In the summer the nights. . . . In autumn the evenings. . . . In winter the early mornings. . . ." (Morris, Ivan, transl., *The Pillow Book of Sei Shōnagon*, p. 21.)

14.The Kinkaku was burned down in 1949 by an arsonist but was rebuilt in accordance with strictly scholarly methods of reconstruction. It's not certain whether the gold leaf was originally applied to the first floor or not; it was omitted in the reconstructed version.

15.*Masukagami* ("Mirror of Increase"), pp. 130–131.

16.Ōta, Hirotarō, *Nihon kenchikushi josetsu*, p. 78.

17.Yanagita, Kunio, "Chimei no kenkyū," *Teihon Yanagita Kunio zenshū*, vol. 20, p. 114.

18.Fujishima, Gaijirō, *Chūson-ji*, pp. 197–198.

19.*Azumakagami* ("Mirror of the East"), p. 44.

20.Ibid., p. 44.

21.Bollnow, *Neue Geborgenheit*, p. 179.

22.The latter quotation in parentheses is part of the second quotation cited in note 6.

23.Ōta, *Nihon kenchikushi josetsu*, p. 143.

24.Hayashi, ed., *Seika-bunshū*, vol. 2, p. 10.

25.Satō, Nobuhiro, *Unai kondō hisaku*, in *Kojiruien 2, chibu 2, kōto*, p. 174.

26.Nijūisseiki Kenkyūkai, *Kokumin seikatsu to kokudo no miraizō*, pp. 238–261.

CHAPTER 13

1.Ōba, Iwao, *Saishi iseki*, p. 18.

2.Ibid.

3.Lynch, *The Image of the City*, p. 134.

4.Ibid.

5.*Man'yōshū*, vol. 1, pp. 73–74. The translation is from Nihon Gakujutsu Shinkokai, *The Manyōshū*, p. 11.

6.Although the element *mizu* in Mizugaki is usually taken to be no more than an ornamental word suggesting beauty and good fortune, in the *Kojiki*, it is written with the Chinese character for water. In view of the topography in this region, it seems possible that the author of the *Kojiki* actually meant water. It is perhaps idle to split hairs in what is primarily a mythical story to begin with, but there is a possibility that the concept of *mizugaki* once carried the implication that the palace was set off from its surroundings by rivers or moats.

7.*Izumi-no-kuni fudoki*, pp. 117, 159, and 191.

8.Kishi, Nobuo. *Nihon kodai seiji-shi kenkyū*, p. 55.

9.Ashihara, *Exterior Design in Architecture*, pp. 24–28.

CHAPTER 14

1.*Man'yōshū*, vol. 1, p. 64. The translation is from Nihon Gakujutsu Shinkōkai, *The Manyōshū*, p. 3.

2.Tsuchihashi, Hiroshi, *Kodai kayō to girei no kenkyū*, p. 265–294.

3.Interesting in this connection is the following poem from the *Kojiki* (pp. 158, 282; translation from Philippi, *Kojiki*, pp. 306–307):

What a delight
To pick together
With this girl from Kibi
The greens growing
In the mountain field.

Of this, Origuchi Shinobu says: "This and others like it are the earliest writings that reveal a close, intimate examination of nature. The poet suggests the appearance of the terrain and calls attention to the color of the vegetables. Earlier poems pay lip service to nature, have a superficial air that makes one wonder whether the poets were actually viewing a natural setting as they composed. From now on, intimacy with nature gradually becomes more prominent, and, as we approach the Nara period, we begin to find genuinely lyrical landscape poems." See Origuchi, *Yoyo no utabito—Uta no hanashi*, p. 79. Origuchi is talking, of course, about landscape poems expressing feelings that are inspired from a direct view of nature. It may well be that the ability to gaze at nature and appreciate its beauty came earlier than the ability to express this appreciation, but in any case the transition from the concept of a natural scene as an object of worship to the concept of the same scene as simply an example of landscape beauty must have been a long one.

4.The original work being unavailable, this English translation is made from pp. 369–371 of Oikawa, Kaoru, *Daichi to ishi no musō*, which is a Japanese translation of Bachelard, Gaston, *La Terre et Les Rêveries de la Volonté*.

5.Ishikawa, Hideaki, *Toshibi to kōkoku*, pp. 42–43.

6.Origuchi, Shinobu, *Origuchi Shinobu zenshū*, vol. 9, p. 164.

7.*Fudoki*, pp. 274–275.

8.*Fudoki,* pp. 294–295.

9.*Fudoki*, pp. 296–297.

10.*Fudoki*, p. 51.

11.Ōtsuka, Hatsushige, "Kofun no hensen," *Nihon no kōkogaku IV: Kofun jidai (jō)*, p. 42.

12.Ibid.

13.Lynch, *The Image of the City*, p. 72.

14.Giedion, Siegfried, *Space, Time, and Architecture*, pp. 154–155.

CHAPTER 15
1.Lynch's work was published in 1960; Norberg-Schulz's in 1971.

2.Bollnow, *Neue Geborgenheit*, p. 179.

3.Lynch, *The Image of the City*, p. 65.

4.Ibid., pp. 78–79.

5.Cullen, *Townscape*, p. 12.

6.Jacobs, P., and Way, D., "How Much Development Can Landscape Absorb?" *Landscape Architecture* (July 1969), pp. 296–298. See also Faye, Paul, and Tournaire, Michel, "Théorie sur l'Amenagement et la Protection des Sites," *Urbanisme*, no. 125 (April 1971), pp. 26–33.

7.Worskett, Roy, *The Character of Towns*, pp. 75–95.

8.Concerning rivers, see "Sumida-gawa hika," *Toshi jūtaku* (July 1974). There is a need for further work concerning hills. See Tanaka, Seidai, *Nihon no kōen*; Higuchi, Tadahiko, "Chikei kūkan no kōzō to sono kankyō dezain e no tenkai."

9.Norberg-Schulz, *Existence, Space, and Architecture*, p. 39.

10.Lynch, *Site Planning*, p. 10.

11.Bollnow, *Neue Geborgenheit*, p. 174.

12.Karaki, Junzō, *Nihonjin no kokoro no rekishi*, vol. 1, p. 305.

13.Bollnow, *Neue Geborgenheit*, p. 163.

14.Ibid., p. 187.

15.Lynch, *The Image of the City*, p. 7.

16.Bollnow, *Neue Geborgenheit*, pp. 188–189.

17.Ibid., p. 187.

18.Karaki, *Nihonjin no kokoro no rekishi*, p. 317.

19.Shiga, *Nihon fūkei-ron*, vol. 2, p. 147.

20.Mishima Yukio wrote, "I think you can say that in describing landscapes Japanese writers are the best in the world. In their Oriental world, where there is no conflict between man and nature, sometimes the description of scenery sweeps up and overpowers mankind, in much the same way that natural settings in Oriental paintings dwarf the little men who appear in them. In the literature of other countries, if we except travel diaries, we rarely find instances in which the natural setting pours forth from the novel and becomes for a time the novel's chief strength." See *Bunshō tokuhon*, pp. 115–116.

21.Karaki, *Nihonjin no kokoro no rekishi*, pp. 317–318.

22.Nakai, Shōichi, *Gendai geijutsu no kūkan*, p. 6.

23.Norberg-Schulz, *Existence, Space, and Architecture*, p. 29.

CHAPTER 16
1.Lynch, *Site Planning*, p. 10.

2.Ōyama, Haruo, "Riyō kūkan to shite no ryokuchi kankyō," *Randosukeepu*, no. 8, p. 33.

Bibliography

WORKS IN JAPANESE

A. Reference Books and Premodern Writings (by title)

Azumakagami ("Mirror of the East"). *Kokushi taikei* (new rev. & enl.), vol. 32. Tokyo, Yoshikawa Kōbunkan, 1964.

Daigenkai ("Great Sea of Words," dictionary compiled by Ōtsuki Fumihiko). Tokyo, Fuzambō, 1932–1937.

Dai-Nihon chimei jisho ("Dictionary of Japanese Place Names," compiled by Yoshida Tōgo). Tokyo, Fuzambō, 1900–1907.

Fudoki ("Gazetteers"). *Nihon koten bungaku taikei*, vol. 2. Tokyo, Iwanami Shoten, 1958.

Kojiki ("Record of Ancient Matters"). *Iwanami bunko 6576–6578*. Tokyo, Iwanami Shoten, 1963.

Kokin wakashū ("Anthology of Ancient and Modern Poetry"). *Nihon koten bungaku zenshū*, vol. 7. Tokyo, Shōgakkan, 1971.

Makura no sōshi ("Pillow Book," by Sei Shōnagon). *Nihon koten bungaku zenshū, vol. 11. Tokyo, Shōgakkan, 1971.*

Man'yōshū ("Collection of Ten Thousand Leaves"). *Nihon koten bungaku zenshū, vols. 2–5. Tokyo, Shōgakkan, 1971.*

Masukagami ("Mirror of Increase"). *Nihon koten zenshū.* Tokyo, Asahi Shimbunsha, 1948.

Nihon kiryaku ("Abbreviated Chronicles of Japan"). *Kokushi taikei* (new rev. & enl.), vol. 10. Tokyo, Yoshikawa Kōbunkan, 1965.

Nihon shoki ("Chronicles of Japan"). *Nihon koten bungaku taikei*, vols. 67–68. Tokyo, Iwanami Shoten, 1967.

Sakuteiki ("Record of Making Gardens"; modern edition by Tamura Tsuyoshi). Tokyo, Sagami Shobō, 1964.

Sangyō gisho ("Commentaries on Three Sutras," by Prince Shōtoku; modern edition by Hanayama Shinshō). *Iwanami bunko.* Tokyo, Iwanami Shoten, 1975.

Seikabunshū ("Collected Works of Fujiwara Seika," compiled by Hayashi Razan). *Gakken bunko*, no. 2029. Tokyo, Kokkai Toshokan, 1652–1654.

Sekai daihyakka jiten ("World Encyclopedia"), 26 vols. Tokyo, Heibonsha, 1972.

Shintō daijiten ("Dictionary of Shinto"). Tokyo, Heibonsha, 1937.

Shoku-Nihongi ("Chronicles of Japan, Continued"). *Kokushi taikei* (new rev. & enl.), vol. 2. Tokyo, Yoshikawa Kōbunkan, 1966.

Shōryōshū ("Collection of Chinese Poems," by Kūkai). Nihon koten bungaku taikei, vol. 71. Tokyo, Iwanami Shoten, 1965.

Taiheiki ("Record of Great Peace"). *Nihon koten bungaku taikei*, vols. 21–22. Tokyo, Iwanami Shoten, 1960.

Unai kondō hisaku ("Strategy for Unifying the Country," essay by the nineteenth-century economist Satō Nobuhiro). *Koji ruien, chibu 2, kōbu.* Tokyo, Yoshikawa Kōbunkan, 1970.

B. Modern Works (by author)

Dazai, Osamu. *Fugaku hyakkei* ("One Hundred Views of Mount Fuji"). Tokyo, Iwanami Shoten, 1957 (*Iwanami bunko*, nos. 5778–5779).

Fujishima, Gaijirō, ed. *Chūson-ji* ("The Chūson-ji"). Tokyo, Kawade Shobō Shinsha, 1971.

Furushima, Toshio. *Tochi ni kizamareta rekishi* ("History Engraved in the Ground"). Tokyo, Iwanami Shoten, 1967 (*Iwanami shinsho*, no. 657).

Gorai, Shigeru. *Kumano mōde* ("A Pilgrimage to Kumano"). Kyoto, Tankō Shinsha, 1967.

Hayashiya, Tatsusaburō. *Nihon no kodai bunka* ("The Ancient Culture of Japan"), in *Nihon rekishi sōsho* ("Japanese History Series"). Tokyo, Iwanami Shoten, 1971.

Hidaka, Toshitaka, and Satō, Nobuyuki, tsl. *Kakureta jigen* (Japanese translation of Hall, *The Hidden Dimension*). Tokyo, Misuzu Shobō, 1970.

Higuchi, Tadahiko. "Chikei kūkan no kōzō to sono kankyō dezain e no tenkai" ("The Structure of Topographical Space and Its Development Toward Environmental Design"). *Doboku Gakkai dai-nijū-kyūkai nenji gakujutsu kōenkai gaiyōshū IV* (1974), pp. 317–318.

Horiguchi, Sutemi. *Niwa to kūkan kōsei no dentō* ("The Tradition of Gardens and Spatial Composition"). Tokyo, Kajima Shuppankai, 1965.

Ihara, Usaburō. "Kōzu" ("Composition"), *Sekai bijutsu daijiten*, pp. 353–354. Tokyo, Kawade Shobō, 1954.

Ishida, Kazuyoshi. "Nihon kodai kokka no keisei to kūkan ishiki no tenkai" ("The Formation of the Ancient Japanese State and the Development of Spatial Consciousness"), *Nihon Bunka Kenkyūjo kenkyū hōkoku*, no. 2 (March 1966), pp. 85–115.

Ishikawa, Hideaki. *Toshibi to kōkoku* ("Advertisements and Urban Beauty"). Tokyo, Nihon Dempō Tsūshinsha, 1951.

Kamei, Katsuichirō. *Yoshino no yama* ("The Mountains of Yoshino"). *Kamei Katsuichirō zenshū*, vol. 9. Tokyo, Kōdansha, 1971.

Karaki, Junzō.*Nihonjin no kokoro no rekishi* ("History of the Japanese Heart"), 2 vols. Tokyo, Chikuma Shobō, 1970.

Katō, Kunio, tsl. *Jitsuzon · kūkan · kenchiku* (Japanese translation of Norberg-Schulz, *Existence, Space and Architecture*). Tokyo, Kajima Shuppankai, 1973.

Kira, Tatsuo. *Seitaigaku kara mita shizen* ("Nature from the Ecological Viewpoint"). Tokyo, Kawade Shobō Shinsha, 1971.

Kishi, Nobuo. *Nihon kodai seiji-shi kenkyū* ("Research on the Political History of Ancient Japan"). Tokyo, Hanawa Shobō, 1966.

Kishōgaku Handobukku Henshū Iinkai. *Kishō handobukku* ("Handbook on Weather"). Tokyo, Gihōdō, 1959.

Kitamura, Tokutarō. "Toshi keikakujō shiryoku hyōjun," (Japanese adaptation of Märtens, *Optisches Mass für den Städtebau*), *Toshi kōron*, vol. 10, no. 4 (April 1927), pp. 14–17; no. 7 (July 1927), pp. 18–25; no. 8 (August 1927), pp. 33–42; and no. 9 (September 1927), pp. 30–34.

Kojima, Usui. *Nihon sansui-ron* ("Treatise on Japanese Landscapes"). Tokyo, Ryūbunkan, 1905.

Kudō, Harumasa; Nakamura, Yoshio; and Higuchi, Tadahiko. "Taishūka to kyodaika jidai ni okeru shikaku-teki mondai (2)" ("Visual questions in an age of popularization and magnification. 2"), *Glass & Architecture* (May 1967), pp. 12–8.

Kusanagi, Masao, tsl. *Chūshō to kanjō inyū* (Japanese translation of Worringer, *Abstraktion und Einfühlung*). Tokyo, Iwanami Shoten, 1953 (*Iwanami bunko*).

Maeno, Jun'ichirō and Sasaki, Hiroshi, tsl. *Shikichi keikaku no gihō* (Japanese translation of Lynch, *Site Planning*). Tokyo, Kajima Shuppankai, 1966.

Mishima, Yukio. *Bunshō tokuhon* ("A Reader for Writers"). Tokyo, Chūō Kōronsha, 1971 (*Chūkō bunko*, no. A-12).

Mizuno, Ichirō. "Keitai to hassei" ("Forms and origins"), *Chirigaku sōron* (*Comprehensive Treatise on Geography*), vol. 1 of *Asakura chirigaku kōza* (*Asakura Lectures on Geography*). Tokyo, Asakura Shoten, 1967.

Nakai, Masakazu. *Gendai geijutsu no kūkan* ("Space in Contemporary Art"). Nakai Masakazu zenshū, vol. 3. Tokyo, Bijutsu Shuppansha, 1964. *Origuchi Shinobu zenshū*, vol. 1, pp. 418–452. Tokyo, Chūō Kōronsha, 1956.

Nakamura, Teiichi, and Ishihara, Shūji. "Shinrin embō shikibetsu-do to shikibetsu genkai kyori no santei-hō" ("A Method for Calculating the Degree of Discernibility and the Maximum Distance for Discernibility with Respect to Forest Landscapes"), *Nihon Ringakkai-shi*, vol. 46, no. 8 (1964), pp. 274–280.

Nakamura, Yoshio, and Higuchi, Tadahiko. "Dōro keikan kōsei gihō to sono hataraki" ("A Method for Structuring Highway Landscapes and Its Function"), *Doboku Gakkai dai-nijūnikai nenji kōenkai gaiyōshū IV* (1967), p. 122.

Nakamura, Yoshio; Satō, Hironori; and Fujimoto, Takaya. "Shizen keikan keikaku no tame no jōhō shori to sono ōyō" ("On the Handling and Application of Data Related to the Planning of Natural Landscapes"), *Doboku Gakkai dai-nijūshichikai nenji gakujutsu kōenkai gaiyōshū IV* (1972), pp. 251–252.

Nijūisseiki Kenkyūkai (representative: Suzuki, Masaji). *Kokumin seikatsu to kokudo no miraizō* ("A Vision of Japan, and the Life of the Japanese People in the Future"). Tokyo, Kajima Shuppankai, 1972.

Ningen Kōgaku Handobukku Henshū Iinkai. *Ningen kōgaku handobukku* ("Handbook of Human Engineering"). Tokyo, Kanehara Shuppan, 1966.

Ōba, Iwao. *Saishi iseki* ("Relics of Ancient Religious Rites"). Tokyo, Kadokawa Shoten, 1970.

Oikawa, Kaoru, tsl. *Daichi to ishi no musō* (Japanese translation of Bachelard, *La Terre et les Rêveries de la Volonté*). Tokyo, Shichōsha, 1972.

Ōishi, Toshio, tsl. *Hiroba no zōkei* (Japanese translation of Sitte, *City Planning According to Artistic Principles*). Tokyo, Bijutsu Shuppansha, 1968.

Ōno, Susumu. *Nihongo o sakanoboru* ("Retracing the Development of the Japanese Language"). Tokyo, Iwanami Shoten, 1974 (*Iwanami shinsho*, blue series, no. 911).

Ōoka, Makoto. *Ki no Tsurayuki* ("Ki no Tsurayuki"), *Nihon shijinsen* ("Anthology of Japanese Poets"), vol. 7. Tokyo, Chikuma Shobō, 1971.

Origuchi, Shinobu. "Jokeishi no hassei" ("The Origin of Landscape Poetry").

Origuchi, Shinobu. "Haha-ga-kuni e · Tokoyo e" ("Toward the Land of the Dead Mother, Toward the Eternal Land"), *Origuchi Shinobu zenshū*, vol. 2, pp. 3–15. Tokyo, Chūō Kōronsha, 1955.

Origuchi, Shinobu. *Yoyo no utabito* ("Poets of the Ages"). Tokyo, Kadokawa Shoten, 1952 (*Kadokawa bunko*, no. to-398)

Ōta, Hirotarō. *Nihon no kenchiku* ("Japanese Architecture"). Tokyo, Chikuma Shobō, 1968 (*Chikuma sōsho*, no. 112).

Ōta, Hirotarō. *Nihon kenchikushi josetsu* ("A Preface to the History of Japanese Architecture"). Tokyo, Shōkokusha, 1969

Ōta, Minoru, tsl. *Kūkan, jikan, kenchiku* (Japanese translation of Giedion, *Space, Time and Architecture*.) Tokyo, Maruzen, 1969.

Ōtsuka, Hatsushige. "Kofun no hensen" ("Changes in the Ancient Burial Mounds"), *Nihon no kōkogaku IV—Kofun jidai, I* ("Archaeology of Japan—The Period of the ancient burial Mounds, I"), pp. 39–100. Tokyo Kawade Shobō, 1966.

Ōyama, Haruo. "Riyō kūkan to shite no ryokuchi kankyō" ("Greenbelt Environments as Utilizable Spaces"), *Randosukeepu*, no. 8 (August 1972), pp. 30–33.

Rinya-chō Keikaku-ka. *Kūchū shashin handoku kijun kaado* ("Standard Cards for Interpreting Aerial Photographs"). Tokyo, Nihon Ringyō Gijutsu Kyōkai, 1959.

Saitō, Tadashi. "Jōdai ni okeru fumbochi no sentei" ("The Selection of Grave Sites in Ancient Times"), *Rekishi chiri*, vol. 65, no. 6 (1937), pp. 13–26.

Satō, Hironori. *Shizen keikan keikaku ni kansuru kenkyū* ("Research on the planning of Natural Landscapes"). University of Tokyo Master's Thesis, 1973.

Shiga, Shigetaka. *Nihon fūkei-ron* ("Treatise on Japanese Landscapes"), 2 vols. Tokyo, Kōdansha, 1976 (*Kōdansha gakujutsu bunko*, nos. 59–60).

Shigemori, Mirei, and Shigemori, Kanto. *Kamakura jidai no niwa* ("Gardens of the Kamakura Period"). *Nihon teien-shi taikei* ("Historical Outline of Japanese Gardens), vol. 4. Tokyo, Shakai Shisōsha, 1974.

Shinohara, Osamu. *Shizen kūkan no shikaku kōzō* ("Visual Structure of Natural Spaces"). University of Tokyo, Faculty of Engineering, Master's Thesis, 1971.

Shinohara, Osamu, and Higuchi, Tadahiko. "Shizen chikei to keikan" ("Natural Terrain and Landscapes"), *Doboku Gakkai dai-nijūrokkai nenji gakujutsu kōenkai gaiyōshū IV* (1971), pp. 193–196.

Suzuki, Mitsuru. "Heiankyō no hensen" ("Development of the Capital at Heian"), *Nihon no kōkogaku VII—Rekishi jidai II* ("Archaeology of Japan VII—The Historical Period, II"), pp. 83–97. Tokyo, Kawade Shobō, 1967.

Suzuki, Tadayoshi, et al. *Kankōchi no hyōka shuhō* ("Method for Assessing the Value of Prospective Tourist Sites"). Tokyo, Japan Travel Bureau, 1970.

Takahashi, Masayoshi. *Kūchū shashin no mikata to tsukaikata* ("How to Read and Use Aerial Photographs"). Tokyo, Shinkōdō, 1965.

Takahashi, Takashi, et al. "Shikibetsu shakudo ni kansuru kenkyū" ("Study on the Measuring of Discernibility"), *Nihon Kenchiku Gakkai rombun hōkokushū,* special issue (1966), pp. 500–501.

Tanaka, Seidai. *Nihon no kōen* ("Japanese Parks"). Tokyo, Kajima Shuppankai, 1974 (*SD sensho*, no. 87).

Tange, Kenzō, and Tomita, Reiko, tsl. *Toshi no imēji*. (Japanese translation of Lynch, *The Image of the City*). Tokyo, Iwanami Shoten, 1968.

Tayama, Katai. "Sansui shōki" ("Brief Comments on Landscapes"), *Tayama Katai zenshū,* vol. 16, pp. 535–736. Tokyo, Bunsendō Shoten, 1974.

Toshi Dezain Kenkyūtai. *Nihon no toshi kūkan* ("Urban Space in Japan"). Tokyo, Shōkokusha, 1968.

Tsuchihashi, Yutaka. *Kodai kayō to girei no kenkyū* ("A Study of Ancient Songs and Ceremonies"). Tokyo, Iwanami Shoten, 1965.

Udano Town Office. *Udano-chō-shi* ("History of the Township of Udano"). Udano, Udano Town Office, 1968.

Uehara, Keiji. *Nihon fūkeibi-ron* ("Treatise on Japanese Landscape Beauty"). Tokyo, Dai-Nippon Shuppan, 1943.

Ueyama, Shumpei. *Shōyō jurin bunka* ("The Laurisylvan Culture"). Tokyo, Chūō Kōronsha, 1969 (*Chūkō shinsho*, no. 201).

Wada, Yōhei, et al. *Kankaku + chikaku shinrigaku handobukku* ("Handbook on the Psychology of Sensual and Intellectual Perception"). Tokyo Seishin Shobō, 1969.

Yamaoka, Yoshinori. "Reiki no useta tochi no ue de hito wa katariaeru no ka" ("Can People Talk Together on Land That Has Lost Its Spirit?"), *Kenchiku bunka* (October 1971), pp. 168–9.

Yamazaki, Yōichirō and Awazu, Norio, tsl. *Jōsai* (Japanese translation of Saint-Exupery, *Citadelle*). Tokyo, Misuzu Shobō, 1971.

Yanagita, Kunio. "Yamamiya-kō" ("On Mountain Shrines"), *Teihon Yanagita Kunio zenshū,* vol. 11, pp. 295–358. Tokyo, Chikuma Shobō, 1969.

Yanagita, Kunio. "Densha-kō taiyō" ("Outline Study of Shrines in Fields"), *Teihon Yanagita Kunio zenshū,* vol. 11, pp. 525–543. Tokyo, Chikuma Shobō, 1969.

Yanagita, Kunio. *Kaijō no michi* ("Sea Routes"). *Teihon Yanagita Kunio zenshū,* vol. 1. Tokyo, Chikuma Shobō, 1968.

Yanagita, Kunio. *Chimei no kenkyū* ("Study of Place Names"). *Teihon Yanagita Kunio zenshū,* vol. 11, 1970.

Yasuda, Yojūrō. *Yamato Hase-dera* ("The Hase-dera in Yamato"). Kyoto, Tankō Shinsha, 1965.

WORKS IN WESTERN LANGUAGES

Appleton, Jay. *The Experience of Landscape.* New York, Wiley, 1975.

Ashihara, Yoshinobu. *Exterior Design in Architecture.* New York, Van Nostrand Reinhold, 1970.

Aston, W. G., tsl. *Nihongi: Chronicles of Japan from the Earliest Times to A.D. 697.* Rutland and Tokyo, Charles E. Tuttle, 1972.

Bachelard, Gaston. *La Terre et les Rêveries de la Volonté.* Paris, Librarie José Conti, 1948.

Blumenfeld, Hans. "Scale in Civic Design," *The Town Planning Review,* vol. 24 (1953–4), pp. 35–46.

Bollnow, Otto Friedrich. *Neue Geborgenheit,* 2 vols. Stuttgart, W. Kohlhammer, 1955.

Crowe, Sylvia. *The Landscape of Power.* London, The Architectural Press, 1958.

Cullen, Gordon, *Townscape.* London, The Architectural Press, 1961.

Doxiades, Konstantinos A. *Raumordnung im Griechischen Städtebau.* Heidelberg and Berlin, Kurt Vowinckel, 1937.

Dreyfuss, Henry. *The Measure of Man: Human Factors in Design.* New York, Whitney Publication, 1959.

Faye, Paul, and Tournaire, Michel. "Théorie sur l'Amenagement et la Protection des Sites," *Urbanisme,* no. 125 (April 1971), pp. 26–33.

Gibson, J. J. *The Perception of the Visual World.* New York, Riverside Press, 1960.

Giedion, Siegfried. *Space, Time, and Architecture* (5th ed.). Cambridge, Harvard University Press, 1967.

Goldfinger, Ernö. "The Sensation of Space," *Architectural Review* (November 1941).

Hall, Edward T. *The Hidden Dimension*. New York, Doubleday, 1966.

Hayakawa, Masao. *The Garden Art of Japan*. New York, Weatherhill, 1973.

Hegemann, Werner, and Peets, Elbert. *The American Vitruvius: An Architect's Handbook of Civic Art*. New York, Architectural Book Publishing Company, 1922.

Honda, H. H., tsl. *The Kokin Waka-shu*. Tokyo, Hokuseido-Eirinsha, 1970.

Itō, Teiji. *The Japanese Garden—An Approach to Nature*. New Haven, Yale University Press, 1972.

Jacobs, Peter, and Way, Douglas. "How Much Development Can Landscape Absorb?" *Landscape Architecture* (July 1969), pp. 296–298.

Keene, Donald, ed. *Anthology of Japanese Literature*. Rutland and Tokyo, Charles E. Tuttle, 1956.

Litton, R. Burton, Jr. *Forest Landscape Description and Inventories*. USDA Forest Service Research Paper PSW-49, 1968.

Lynch, Kevin. *Site Planning* (2nd ed.). Cambridge, The MIT Press, 1971.

Lynch, Kevin. *The Image of the City*. Cambridge, The MIT Press, 1960.

Märtens, H. *Optisches Mass für den Städtebau*. Bonn, Max Cohen & Sohn, 1890.

Miner, Earl. *An Introduction to Japanese Court Poetry*. Stanford, Stanford University Press, 1968.

Morris, Ivan, tsl. *The Pillow Book of Sei Shōnagon*. Penguin Books, 1967.

Nippon Gakujutsu Shinkōkai, tsl. *The Manyōshū*. New York, Columbia University Press, 1965.

Norberg-Schulz, Christian. *Existence, Space, and Architecture*. New York, Praeger, 1971.

Philippi, Donald L., tsl. *Kojiki*. Tokyo, University of Tokyo Press, 1968.

Sitte, Camillo (tsl. by Collins, George R., and Collins, Christiane Crasemenn). *City Planning According to Artistic Principles*. New York, Random House, 1965.

Snellen, J. B., tsl. *Shoku Nihongi: Chronicles of Japan, Continued, from A.D. 697 to 791. Transactions of the Asiatic Society of Japan*, 2nd series, vol. 11 (December 1934), pp. 151–239; vol. 14 (June 1937), pp. 209–278. (This covers only the first six volumes of the original. The remainder has not been translated into English.)

Wolfe, Ivor de. *The Italian Townscape*. London, The Architectural Press, 1963.

Worringer, Wilhelm, *Abstraktion and Einfühlung* (10th ed). Munich, 1921.

Worskett, Roy. *The Character of Towns*. London, The Architectural Press, 1969.

Index